A Philosophy of
Free Expression
and Its Constitutional Applications

PHILOSOPHY AND SOCIETY
General Editor: Marshall Cohen

Also in this series:
RIGHTS
Theodore M. Benditt

ETHICS IN THE WORLD OF BUSINESS
David Braybrooke

MARX AND JUSTICE
THE RADICAL CRITIQUE OF LIBERALISM
Allen E. Buchanan

LUKÁCS, MARX AND THE SOURCES OF CRITICAL THEORY
Andrew Feenberg

THE REVERSE DISCRIMINATION CONTROVERSY
A MORAL AND LEGAL ANALYSIS
Robert Fullinwider

THE MORAL FOUNDATIONS OF PROFESSIONAL ETHICS
Alan H. Goldman

THE LIBERTARIAN READER
Tibor R. Machan (ed.)

MORAL PROBLEMS IN NURSING
A PHILOSOPHICAL INVESTIGATION
James L. Muyskens

READING NOZICK
Jeffrey Paul (ed.)

AND JUSTICE FOR ALL
NEW INTRODUCTORY ESSAYS IN ETHICS AND PUBLIC POLICY
Tom Regan and Donald VanDeVeer (eds.)

SEX, DRUGS, DEATH, AND THE LAW
AN ESSAY ON HUMAN RIGHTS AND OVERCRIMINALIZATION
David A. J. Richards

KANT'S POLITICAL PHILOSOPHY
Patrick Riley

EVOLUTIONARY EXPLANATION IN THE SOCIAL SCIENCES
AN EMERGING PARADIGM
Philippe Van Parijs

WELFARE RIGHTS
Carl Wellman

A Philosophy of
Free Expression
and Its
Constitutional Applications

Robert F. Ladenson

ROWMAN AND LITTLEFIELD
Totowa, New Jersey

I gratefully acknowledge the following journals and publishers for permission to use material from my previously published articles.

Chapter Two and Appendix II contain material from "Mill's Conception of Individuality " (*Social Theory and Practice*, vol. 4, no. 2 [1977]). Chapters One and Three include portions of "Freedom of the Press: A Jurisprudential Inquiry " (*Social Theory and Practice*, vol. 6, no. 2 [1980]). Chapter Four contains material from my article "Freedom of Expression in the Corporate Workplace: A Philosophical Inquiry," which will appear in *Business and Professional Ethics*, ed. J. Ellin, W. Robison, and M. Pritchard (Crescent Manor, N.J.: The Humana Press). Appendix III is material from my article "A Theory of Personal Autonomy," *Ethics* 86 (October 1975), © the University of Chicago, all rights reserved, and reprinted by permission of the University of Chicago Press.

First published in the United States in 1983 by Rowman and Littlefield,
81 Adams Drive, Totowa, New Jersey 07512.

Library of Congress Cataloging in Publication Data

Ladenson, Robert F.
   A philosophy of free expression and its
constitutional applications.

   (Philosophy and society)
   Bibliography: p.
   Includes index.
   1. Freedom of speech—United States. I. Title.
II. Series.
KF4770.L3 1982   342.73′0853   82-18106
ISBN 0-8476-6761-8   347.302853

342.73′0853
347.302853

Published in the United States of America

213440

FOR MY PARENTS

Contents

Preface and Acknowledgments

The subject of free expression has interested me in one way or another since my undergraduate years, yet I began developing the systematic ideas set out in this book only seven or eight years ago. The book reflects the influence of advice, assistance, and encouragement provided by many persons. In the spring of 1979 I conducted a seminar on the philosophy of free expression at the Illinois Institute of Technology–Chicago Kent College of Law. The seminar papers and comments of my students substantially contributed to shaping my views. When I began writing this book in the fall of 1980, the Center for the Study of Ethics in the Professions at the Illinois Institute of Technology awarded me a grant that made possible a release from teaching one course during the fall semester. Throughout the period of 1980–82, my philosophical colleagues at I.I.T.—Roger Gilman, Fay Sawyier, Jack Snapper, Warren Schmaus, and Vivian Weil—provided, both collectively and individually, a forum in which to try out ideas at various stages of development. I spent the fall semester of 1981 as Visiting Associate Professor at the University of Colorado, Boulder. My colleagues in the Philosophy Department there not only were most hospitable, but also supplied valuable comments and criticism at a colloquium where I presented a draft of my chapter on free expression in the private sector workplace. An invitation from the Institute of Society, Ethics, and the Life Sciences (The Hastings Center) to speak at a seminar on occupational health and safety in April of 1982 also provided the occasion for writing some of the material appearing in that chapter.

I am grateful to the following people for commenting on draft versions of various chapters: Leonard Boonin, Richard Eldridge, Mary Gibson, F. Patrick Hubbard, Kenneth Kipnis, Stephen Nathanson, Martin Pimsler, Frederick Schauer, Jack Snapper, Sheldon Nahmod, and Vivian Weil. I received instruction on various points from Martin Malin, Marcus G. Singer, and Aaron Snyder. Bob Goepel helped in my research of First Amendment case law. In addition, he generously allowed me to expound my views about freedom of expression to him, sometimes at excessive length, and he made valuable suggestions about how to develop certain points. Martin Pimsler and Les Rosen also listened patiently to my discourses on free expression and made valuable suggestions. Marshall Cohen, the editor of the series in which this book appears, gave appreciated advice and encouragement. Kay Kane did a magnificent job of typing both first- and second-draft manuscripts of this book.

I owe enormous debts of gratitude to three outstanding philosophers whom I am privileged to number among my friends: Bernard Gert, Irving Thalberg, and Gerald MacCallum. Bernard Gert's influence runs so deeply in my thinking about moral and political philosophy as to make acknowledgement of specific debts to him very difficult. Anyone familiar with his book, *The Moral Rules*, will undoubtedly recognize its mark upon my approach. Irving Thalberg and Gerald MacCallum provided me with much-needed encouragement and support during some difficult periods. Finally, this book is dedicated to my parents, Inez and Alex Ladenson, who taught me by their example to appreciate the virtues that foster and are fostered by the right to free expression—tolerance, open-mindedness, and respect for truth.

Introduction

In this book I present a philosophical theory of the right to free expression. The book is an attempt to overcome a pervasive difficulty that surrounds this subject. On the one hand, writings about specific issues concerning free expression seldom pay much attention to basic philosophical considerations. For this reason, one frequently finds oneself at a loss to decide between diametrically opposed positions on particular controversies. On the other hand, basic theoretical issues of free expression tend to be addressed in discussions that omit analysis of specific cases. These discussions, in turn, may seem reasonable when considered from a high level of abstraction, but one has no clear idea of their implications in practice.

My account of free expression then is intended as a mean between these two extremes. I present a philosophical analysis of free expression that incorporates the insights of major moral and political philosophers. I have also attempted, however, to illustrate an approach for applying this analysis to concrete cases. Such an approach seems to me both systematic and unified. That is, I think it yields reasonable positions by appeal to a small number of related principles on a wide variety of issues that many writers tend to regard as irreducibly disparate.

Chapter One begins by explaining why one cannot think about the First Amendment to the United States Constitution without first making clear the justification for judicial review under the Bill of Rights. Without clarity on this matter, one cannot distinguish genuine constitutional questions from policy issues appropriately resolved through the legislative process. I conceive of judicial review as a means of protecting fundamental rights grounded in basic principles of political morality. The greater part of Chapter One thus involves the development of a philosophical conception of fundamental rights. My proposal in this regard draws heavily on the ideas of John Rawls. Specifically, I suggest that establishing a right as fundamental has the following two aspects: first, one must demonstrate by way of a distinctive kind of philosophical argument, derived from Rawls's theory of justice, that certain modes of conduct constitute duties of governments. Second, such duties must be specified with enough precision that one can tell over a wide range of cases whether a violation has occurred. The latter part of Chapter One contains a comparison of the above conception of constitutionally fundamental rights with other prevailing approaches.

In Chapter Two I set out an account of the right to free expression that satisfies the foregoing two conditions for the right to qualify as constitutionally fundamental. In addressing the first condition I draw heavily on the ideas in John Stuart Mill's classic essay *On Liberty*. To deal with the second condition—the reasonable precision requirement—I introduce the concept of per se violations of the right to free expression. In this regard I contend that statutes or governmental acts violate the right to free expression if and only if they fall into one or more of seven categories. I describe these categories in detail, analyzing their theoretical bases and demonstrating their application to a substantial number of cases dealing with free expression.

Chapter Three applies the analysis of the right to freedom of expression in terms of the notion of per se violations to the topic of freedom of the press. The chapter explores a number of First Amendment questions involving the mass media. What are the implications of the First Amendment in defamation lawsuits with media organizations as defendants? Are media representatives constitutionally entitled to a testamentary privilege not to divulge information obtained through pledges of confidentiality? Should individuals be thought of as having a constitutional right of access to the media? Or, to the contrary, is the idea of such a right ruled out by the First Amendment? Does the First Amendment, in some instances, require governments to make certain information public either as a matter of course or in regard to specific requests?

Chapter Four concerns freedom of expression in the private

sector workplace. Under standard interpretations, the First Amendment only rules out *governmental* interference with the expression of beliefs and attitudes. Are there good reasons for extending a right of freedom of expression to the workplace in private enterprise? That is, should employees have the same freedom to express themselves without coercion from employers that citizens enjoy with respect to the government? Chapter Four discusses these issues from the theoretical perspective developed in Chapter Two. Chapter Four also includes some remarks about the constitutional concept of state action and about the general notion of a right to personal liberty.

This book thus is in large measure an essay on interpretation of the First Amendment. I intend it for three audiences: the legal community, consisting of judges, legal scholars, and practicing attorneys; professional philosophers; and the general literate public without specialized background in law and philosophy. Several serious problems, however, attend the task of writing this kind of book. Given the unified treatment of its subject matter, one cannot read the book profitably on a piecemeal basis, the way one might approach a general treatise on First Amendment case law. An adequate understanding of my views about most issues requires familiarity with almost the entire analysis. In addition, writing a text which adequately addresses the specialized concerns of both philosophers and constitutional scholars, while remaining at least moderately attractive for the general interest reader, presents enormous difficulties. Accordingly, I deal with this problem through the expedient of relegating details in regard to various philosophical or constitutional points to long footnotes, as well as to several appendices. I try, however, to present reasonably complete arguments for my most important theses in the main body of the text. Thus, while the nonspecialist reader is encouraged to examine the footnotes and appendices, he or she can grasp the essentials of my approach without doing so.

I

Freedom of Expression, Judicial Review, and Fundamental Rights

---

Must we allow groups who avowedly intend to abolish our rights of freedom of speech and press to exploit those rights for their own ends? Does the protection of the First Amendment, properly understood, extend to all words, no matter how offensive or obscene? Do the same standards of First Amendment protection apply to speech with a primarily commercial purpose as to speech with a political purpose? How should we establish the contours of permissable limitations upon speech based on time, place, or manner of expression? And what is "speech" for purposes of the First Amendment? Should one define it to include such actions as the wearing of insignia or armbands or the burning of draftcards? Is freedom of the press an independent, constitutionally protected liberty? Or does the word "press" merely mean "printed speech" for constitutional purposes? Should courts apply the First Amendment to the relationship between employees and managers in large private bureaucratic organizations?

The above issues all call for the interpretation of the familiar phrases "freedom of speech" and "freedom of the press" as they figure in the First Amendment to the United States Constitution.[1] None of them, however, can be resolved straightforwardly by appeal to the text of that amendment alone, which simply states of freedom of speech and press that "Congress shall make no law abridging [them]."[2]

This point becomes clearer when we note a general feature of the way we understand assertions that ascribe freedom to persons. Whether one talks of free speech, freedom of the press, free beer, free throws (in basketball), freestyle swimming, or even free will, such notions derive their intelligibility from explication in terms of three items: the class of persons having the freedom in question, the restrictions from which they are free, and the actions they are free to do or forebear. That is to say, the word freedom, as it applies to persons, denotes what logicians refer to as a triadic relationship exemplified by the schema, "freedom of . . . from . . . to do or forebear . . . ."[3] We differentiate one kind of freedom from another by filling in the blanks in different ways or, as logicians would say, by providing different interpretations of the schema.

Accordingly, the phrases "freedom of speech" and "freedom of the press" in the First Amendment merely name, but do not specify the nature of, two different kinds of complex relationships between persons, restrictions, and actions. Such specification first requires interpreting the above schema. Moreover, one cannot initially rule out an approach that explicates freedom of speech and freedom of the press in terms of several sets of interpretations rather than a single one. In other words these phrases may well best be thought of as each referring to a variety of freedoms pertinent to different kinds of situations rather than to a single wide-ranging basic freedom. On the other hand, one cannot dismiss the opposite hypothesis outright.

Where then does one look for guidance on how to render more determinate the phrases freedom of speech and freedom of the press as they appear in the text of the First Amendment? The most obvious source of guidance, First Amendment case law as decided by the United States Supreme Court, provides only moderate aid. A fact often unknown to people not deeply familiar with constitutional matters is that the voluminous body of First Amendment case law has surprisingly recent origins. The Supreme Court first interpreted the First Amendment in the 1919 case of *Schenk* v. *U.S.*[4] This case involved prosecution of an individual who expressed opposition to the involvement of the United States in World War I. Thus Supreme Court First Amendment case law concerning this now-familiar kind of circumstance spans the relatively short historical period of sixty years. Along the same lines, until 1931 the Court did not consider the question of whether imposition of prior restraint upon publications violates the First Amendment.[5] In 1957 the Court decided for the first time whether obscenity statutes violate the First Amendment, and in 1964 it first addressed the implications of the First Amendment for the law of defamation.[6] The Court began to treat extensively the rights of newspersons under the First Amendment only in the early 1970s.[7]

To be sure, a large body of First Amendment case law exists. Historically speaking, however, it would be more accurate to conceive of it as the results to date of a relatively sudden and ongoing burst of judicial activity, rather than as the outcome of a steady, long-term developmental process whereby the meanings of freedom of speech and freedom of the press have become reasonably well fixed.[8] This, of course, is not to say that consideration of First Amendment case law has little or no relevance to our problem. But it is to say that its relevance seldom lies in establishing a firm basis for interpretation of the First Amendment so as to provide guidance in applying it to new cases.

The decisions of the Supreme Court in regard to the First Amendment thus raise at least as many questions as they answer. One may inquire into the soundness or unsoundness of particular decisions. One may ponder how the Court should rule on matters it has not yet considered. These kinds of questions, in turn, raise issues about the degree of systematic coherence one finds in First Amendment case law. That is, do coherent views with regard to some questions before the Court *logically entail* certain conclusions about others? And there is the basic issue of the criteria by which we should evaluate the Court's decisions pertaining to the First Amendment.

The Problem of Judicial Review under the Bill of Rights

The last question above has an overriding importance that can be brought out by the following example. In the 1972 case of *Branzburg*

v. *Hayes,* the Supreme Court ruled that newspaper reporters have no right under the First Amendment to decline to respond to a grand jury subpoena in a criminal investigation if the testimony sought pertains to information obtained by a pledge of confidentiality.[9] Shortly after announcement of the *Branzburg* decision, congressional hearings took place before the House Judiciary Committee on proposed federal shield legislation, which would give reporters the same privilege that had been unsuccessfully urged before the Supreme Court as their due under the First Amendment.[10]

Was there any significant difference between the relevant factors with respect to the issue before the Court in the *Branzburg* case on the one hand, and the question pondered by the House Judiciary Committee on the other? That is to say, can one mark a genuine distinction between the First Amendment issue treated by the Court and the policy issue treated by Congress, both of which pertained to whether newspaper reporters should be accorded a testamentary privilege? If there is such a distinction, wherein lies the difference? If there is no distinction, then must we not therefore view the Supreme Court when it reviews legislation under the First Amendment as a superlegislature of nine unelected gurus who engage in precisely the same kind of policy deliberations as the House of Representatives and the Senate? But how can such an acknowledgment be squared with a commitment to democratic government according to which the will of the majority should prevail?

This last question constitutes the basic issue of constitutional adjudication under the First Amendment in particular and the Bill of Rights generally.[11] The issue is basic in the literal sense that all other constitutional questions involving the Bill of Rights presuppose an answer to it. Unless one can articulate a principled basis for distinguishing such questions from issues of policy appropriate for resolution in a legislative forum, then one has no grounds for ascertaining in particular cases whether a court has overstepped the proper bounds of its authority when rendering a constitutional judgment under the Bill of Rights.

The question of whether one can reconcile judicial review with the principles of democratic government is not merely basic in a theoretical sense. In case after case the Supreme Court has advanced highly questionable analyses with respect to specific First Amendment issues precisely because of uncertainty about this matter. For example, in *Buckley* v. *Valeo* the Court invalidated under the First

Amendment two provisions of the Federal Campaign Financing Act of 1974.[12] The first of these provisions placed limitations upon the amount that candidates for federal office may spend out of personal funds in support of their candidacies. The second provision placed similar limitations upon the amount individuals or groups may spend "relative to a clearly identified candidate," that is, in support of a candidate, albeit independently of the candidate's own campaign. Overturning the above two provisions, the Court noted that in justifying them the government represented as its purpose the prevention of political corruption in both reality and appearance. The Court then went on to cite a variety of reasons for believing that if implemented, the provisions would not serve this purpose, or at least not add anything to other measures in the act which appear to have the same objective.[13]

Such an approach, however, raises serious questions. By considering at all whether the Federal Campaign Financing Act's expenditure limitations serve to stem political corruption, the Court implied that such a purpose has significant constitutional relevance. That is, the Court implied that although it found that the expenditure limitations serve no such purpose, if it had found otherwise then, other things equal, it would have upheld the provisions.[14] In short, the Court appears to have considered exactly the same issue in *Buckley* v. *Valeo* as Congress did before passing the Federal Campaign Financing Act and reached a contrary opinion. But from the standpoint of democratic theory, how can one justify giving greater weight to the policy conclusions of nine unelected judges than to the determination of Congress with respect to exactly the same issue?

Clarity about adjudication under the First Amendment thus requires that one first explore the more general topic of the nature of judicial review under the First Amendment. The text of the Constitution by itself provides no guidance in this matter. Indeed, no provisions whatsoever of the Constitution explicitly confer upon the Supreme Court any power of judicial review, whether in connection with the Bill of Rights or anything else. Article III, section 1 vests the judicial power in a Supreme Court as well as in other inferior courts that Congress may establish, and Article III, section 2 specifies the kinds of cases in which such power is to be exercised. The constitutional legitimacy of judicial review cannot be inferred from these sections alone, however, because the Constitution does not define the cryptic phrase "judicial power."

That is, the principal issue for one who wishes to demonstrate an explicit textual basis in the Constitution for judicial review is precisely to establish that "judicial power," as it appears in sections 1 and 2 of Article III, refers, among other things, to a power on the part of federal courts to overturn legislation on grounds of unconstitutionality. Uncertainty with respect to this issue also makes it impossible to infer the constitutionality of judicial review from the Supremacy Clause of Article VI, which declares the Constitution to be the supreme law of the land. Such a declaration, by itself, carries no implications about whose interpretation of the supreme law of the land binds when disagreements arise.[15]

When one looks to historical source material to ascertain whether the framers of the Constitution meant to imply a power of judicial review on the part of federal courts, the evidence is equivocal.[16] In *Federalist 78*, Hamilton argued in favor of such a grant of power but, significantly, he prefaced his argument with a denial that it could be inferred directly from the Constitution itself. Instead he chose to rest his case upon a contention that the necessity of granting a power of judicial review to federal courts is entailed, with the aid of a few modest supporting assumptions, by the very idea of a federal republic. Hamilton first contended that, given the constitutionally dictated separation of powers between Congress, the President, the states, and the federal judiciary, there had to be some procedure for adjudicating conflicts that were bound to arise about the respective proper spheres of authority of these major branches of government. He felt that in the absence of such a procedure, Congress, with its power of the purse, would tend to engulf the others. Vesting a power of judicial review in the federal courts, Hamilton maintained, would be the best means of dealing with this problem in virtue of the relative independence of the federal judiciary from politics. That is, Hamilton assumed that in the vast majority of cases, only the other three major branches of government would be direct parties to conflicts with regard to the separation of powers. Accordingly, he concluded that since the Constitution provided for the relative independence of federal judges *via* lifetime tenure, the federal courts were the logical forum for adjudicating such conflicts.

In the historic case of *Marbury* v. *Madison*, commonly cited as precedent for the power of the Supreme Court to overturn acts of Congress on constitutional grounds, John Marshall's majority opinion closely followed Hamilton's line of reasoning.[17] Underscoring, as it were, Hamilton's argument, Marshall declared:

> Those, then, who controvert the principle that the constitution is to be considered, in court, as a paramount law, are reduced to the necessity of maintaining that courts must close their eyes on the constitution, and see only the law. This doctrine would subvert the very foundation of all written constitutions . . . . It would be giving to the legislature a practical and real omnipotence, with the same breath which professes to restrict their powers within narrow limits. It is prescribing limits, and declaring that those limits may be passed at pleasure. That it thus reduces to nothing, what we have deemed the greatest improvement on political institutions, a written constitution, would, of itself, be sufficient in America, where written constitutions have been viewed with so much reverence, for rejecting the construction.[18]

The crucial point to note about this argument for our purposes is that it applies only to situations where the constitutional question before a court involves the separation of governmental powers. The argument fails to address the issue of justifying judicial review with regard to cases where courts decide whether an enactment violates provisions of the Bill of Rights, which includes not only the First Amendment guarantees of freedom of speech and of the press, but others as well, such as the Fifth and Fourteenth Amendment guarantees of due process, and the Fourteenth Amendment guarantee of equal protection of the law.[19]

That Hamilton himself did not intend his argument to apply with regard to this latter kind of constitutional case is dramatically illustrated by the fact that after strenuously advocating judicial review in *Federalist 78*, he then argued with equal strenuousness in *Federalist 84* against the propriety of including a Bill of Rights in the Constitution. In this regard, Hamilton maintained that a constitutional enumeration of fundamental rights would be both unnecessary and dangerous. It would be unnecessary, he thought, because the scheme of government set out in the Constitution by its very nature tends to protect the interests that fall under a legally binding Bill of Rights. It would be dangerous because fundamental rights such as freedom of the press—this was Hamilton's example—despite their great importance defy precise definition. Accordingly, judges with the power to delineate the contours of this and other fundamental rights could draw them far too narrowly. The better course would be both to leave the fundamental rights legally undefined and to rely for their protection upon the successful operation of the constitutional scheme of government taken as a whole. It would be a mistake, Hamilton argued, to place the function of protecting fundamental rights uniquely within the province of the judiciary.

Judicial Review and a Rawlsian Conception of Fundamental Rights

Hamilton's counsel, of course, went unheeded, and the practice of judicial review in cases involving the Bill of Rights is now deeply entrenched within the American scheme of government. Nonetheless, this practice has been looked upon with considerable misgiving by an impressive array of legal thinkers. For example, Learned Hand said of it, "it certainly does not accord with the underlying presuppositions of popular government to vest in a chamber unaccountable to anyone but itself the power to suppress social experiments of which it does not approve."[20] In the same vein, Felix Frankfurter wrote, "In his First Inaugural Address Jefferson spoke of the 'sacred principle' that the will of the majority in all cases is to prevail. . . . One need not give full adherence to his view to be deeply mindful of the fact that judicial review is a deliberate check upon democracy through an organ of government not subject to popular control."[21] These views expressed by Hand and Frankfurter constitute a restatement of the basic issue concerning judicial review of legislation or other governmental acts under the Bill of Rights: why should we regard such review as a good thing despite the objection that its operation runs counter to the principle that the will of the majority should prevail? If we believed in the possibility of rule by Platonic guardians possessing an infallible knowledge of the good, there would be no problem, for in that case we would simply adopt the view that our leaders always know what is best. Since, however, virtually all of us reject such an outlook, the countermajoritarian thrust of judicial review in cases involving the Bill of Rights should seem far more troublesome.

The foregoing points simply cannot be dealt with unless one assumes the existence of fundamental rights grounded in basic principles of morality that pertain to the structure of political institutions. A closer look at Hand's and Frankfurter's common critique of judicial review in cases involving the Bill of Rights indicates why this is so. When one makes the basic propositions of this critique explicit, the following argument emerges:

1. Judicial review in cases involving the Bill of Rights is countermajoritarian.
2. Any countermajoritarian aspect of governmental institutions is incompatible with democracy unless it serves to protect fundamental rights that impose normative limitations upon the political process.
3. But there are no such rights because the assumption of their existence presupposes the validity of philosophical or religious viewpoints about which no rational agreement is possible.[22]
4. Therefore, judicial review in cases involving the Bill of Rights is incompatible with democracy.

Premises 1 and 2 of the above argument appear unassailable. Hence, a defender of judicial review in cases involving the Bill of Rights has no choice but to join the issue at premise 3. That is to say, one cannot accept as justified an institutional design whereby a small appointed body has the authority to overturn duly enacted acts of a democratically elected legislature unless one is also prepared to defend the idea that such acts conceivably could violate fundamental rights whose content and scope simply are not subject to determination through the legislative process. For, according to this latter idea, it would make no more sense to say that a society can decide collectively through legislative action about such matters than it would to say than an individual can decree—that is, make it the case simply by saying so—that a basic moral rule such as "Do not cheat" or "Keep your promises" has a special meaning in his or her case. Fundamental rights conceived of in this way would have an overwhelmingly presumptive character. To use Ronald Dworkin's apt phrase, they would "trump" all other considerations, even those that would otherwise be considered decisive.[23]

Is such a conception of fundamental rights defensible? Learned Hand emphatically denied it. Referring to the Bill of Rights, he once wrote,

That these were rights arising out of "natural laws" inherent in the structure of any society, or at least any civilized society, were notions widely accepted at the end of the eighteenth century . . . The easiest support for this attitude was that the source of "Natural Law" was the Will of God; so Saint Thomas Aquinas conceived it; so does the Church still assert it; so did the Deists of the eighteenth century . . . It is not my purpose either to assail or to defend this position . . . I shall, however, ask you *arguendo* to assume with me that the Constitution and the "Bill of Rights" neither proceed from nor have any warrant in the Divine Will either as Saint Thomas or Jefferson believed; but on the contrary that they are the altogether human expression of the will of the state conventions that ratified them.[24]

This passage suggests that, because of his skepticism with regard to the concept of fundamental rights, Hand almost certainly would have objected to the view that questions about the nature, extent, and application of the provisions of the Bill of Rights ought not to be subject to political determination. More specifically, he believed that such a view ultimately depends for its justification upon philosophical views or theological dogma about which no consensus is possible.

Rational people can differ, however, about whether Hand's views on this matter were entirely justified. While initial skepticism about the possibility of enunciating a philosophically defensible conception of fundamental rights may be warranted, neither Learned Hand nor anyone else has demonstrated the necessary failure of the attempt. Hand noted that Thomistic theology and deism have been offered as bases for such a conception. Undoubtedly neither of these views will secure widespread assent in the foreseeable future. Other philosophical bases for a conception of fundamental rights, however, may well fare much better—for example, the updated social contract theory as developed by John Rawls in *A Theory of Justice*.[25] Unlike Thomism and deism, this theory is wholly nonsectarian in that it involves no theological presuppositions whatsoever and has very weak metaphysical presuppositions. As such, one can accept it consistently with whatever views one has about the relation between human beings and a deity. Similarly, the value judgments presupposed by Rawls's theory appear to be so uncontroversial as to be compatible with any scheme of values for an individual.[26] Indeed, if this theory fails to gain universal acceptance over the long run, its failure will not stem from ultimate divergences among people in their values or spiritual beliefs.

According to Rawls's theory, valid principles of social justice are exclusively those that rational people would unanimously advocate under equal conditions and while trying to reach agreement among themselves about the foundational principles governing the structure of social institutions. In other words, the content of principles of social justice pertains to the basic institutional background against which members of society claim enforceable rights and, as Rawls would say, attempt to settle the terms of social cooperation.[27] Rawls maintains that principles with regard to this fundamental matter are valid from the standpoint of morality if, and only if, they would be unanimously advocated by all rational human beings were they to be placed in a situation where they had to decide collectively about the principles of social justice under which they were to live.

But how can we determine which rules would be so advocated by all rational human beings under equal conditions? To state the obvious, one cannot assemble them all for the purpose of deliberating upon the matter, and even if one could, how would one effect a canceling out of the various advantages that some people have over others, whether resulting from socioeconomic status or natural endowments? Rawls's theory deals with this problem by proposing the following thought experiment. Let us imagine a group of rational people, each of whom is concerned, although not solely concerned, for his or her own well-being, and who have assembled to deliberate about the supreme rules governing the structure of social institutions.[28] Let us imagine further that while deliberating about this matter, they are placed by some means or other under a "veil of ignorance" that prevents them from knowing facts that could tempt them to base their respective choices of rules on the desire to promote their own respective interests to the disadvantage of others.[29] They will, however, regard the rules selected while under the veil of ignorance as binding once the veil is removed.

Thus, as Rawls puts it, under the veil of ignorance,

no one knows his place in society, his class position or social status; nor does he know his fortune in the distribution of natural assets and liabilities, his intelligence and strength, and the like. Nor again does anyone know his conception of the good, the particulars of his rational plan of life, or even the special features of his psychology such as his aversion to risk or liability to optimism or pessimism. More than this . . . the parties do not know the particular circumstances of their own society. That is, they do not know its economic or political situation, or the level of civilization it has been able to achieve.[30]

Nor do the people under the veil of ignorance even know to which generation in the total history of their society they belong. They do, however, possess knowledge of general facts about human society. "They understand political affairs and the principles of economic theory; they know the basis of social organization and the laws of human society. Indeed [they] are presumed to know whatever general facts affect the choice of principles of justice."[31] The point of the veil of ignorance, barring knowledge of various kinds, is to "nullify the effects of special contingencies which put men at odds and tempt them to exploit circumstances to their own advantage."[32] If the people under the veil of ignorance do not know whether they are rich or poor, male or female, old or young, and so forth, then they cannot lobby for particular class interests, but rather must choose the principles of social justice (under which they will live once the veil of ignorance is removed) from a more disinterested standpoint. One may appropriately term such imaginary individuals the *rational contractors.*

Rawls's theory then suggests a way for *us* to determine valid principles of social justice. The crucial question in this regard is that of which rules rational people would unanimously advocate to serve as the supreme rules establishing the basic structure of social institutions, if they had to deliberate about the matter under a veil of ignorance. When one ponders this question certain definite conclusions emerge. First, as mentioned above, while under severe constraints on information about themselves, the individuals under the veil of ignorance possess knowledge of general facts about human society. We can thus assume that they would find the central argument of Thomas Hobbes as set forth in *Leviathan* persuasive.[33] Very briefly, according to Hobbes, human beings tend to have certain characteristics, such as pride, fear, and ambition, that continually draw them into mutually destructive conflict with one another, and as far as we can tell, the only way to cope with such a situation is through the institution of government. By the term *government* I understand here an institution in whose name some person (or persons) is commonly regarded by a distinct group of people as having the authority to make rules that determine the content of their rights and duties and to attach penalties to certain actions. The individuals under the veil of ignorance would agree that any feasible principles of social justice upon which they might decide would require the existence of a government for their implementation. They also would agree that a government cannot exist unless the people who act in its name have sufficient power to compel obedience to the rules they decree.

The substantive principles of justice unanimously acceptable to the rational contractors, however, can be thought of as moral rules that condition the exercise of government power. In other words, while governments by right have coercive powers not possessed by mere individuals, they also have special duties as well. For example, the powers of law enforcement necessary for maintaining peace in society are attended by a duty not to deprive individuals of their lives, liberties, or properties unfairly. In addition to the duties requiring governments to forebear exercising their powers in objectionable ways, others require them to pursue certain socially important ends. In this regard, according to Rawls, one central principle of social justice pertains to inequalities in the distribution of wealth and income. This principle holds that such inequalities must be deemed unjustifiable unless, with all things considered, the institutional scheme allowing them works to the long-run advantage of the least fortunate groups in society more so than any other scheme. Accordingly, governments have a duty to work for the reduction of inequalities that are unjustified from the standpoint of this principle.[34]

Rawls's approach to theorizing about the principles of social justice directly bears upon explication of the concept of fundamental rights. To illustrate its precise bearing, however, one must concentrate upon a distinction between two kinds of duties of governments. Some governmental duties are relatively clear-cut in the sense that over a rather broad range of cases, widespread agreement exists about whether a violation has occurred. For this reason, governmental institutions can be designed in such a way as to provide workable means of preventing or remedying violations of these duties. The rule that governments should not deprive individuals of life, liberty, or property in an unfair manner is an example of this first kind of governmental duty.[35]

Other duties of governments, however, do not have the above characteristic. That is, the issue of whether violations have occurred tends to be so much less clear that no proposal for systematically preventing or remedying them seems workable. Rawls's principle pertaining to inequalities of wealth and income exemplifies this second kind of duty. Extreme inequalities violate the principle, but as the interminable controversies over fairness in relative wage levels for different jobs illustrates, once the wide extremes narrow slightly, consensus of judgment virtually evaporates. Thus, while legislators who cynically oppose, or fail to support, measures for reducing unjustified inequality should be condemned, it seems impossible that any effective institutional means exist for preventing or remedying the effects of such behavior.[36]

We have then two kinds of governmental duties. With the first, violations tend to be clearly identifiable, at least relatively speaking, and thus workable means of preventing or remedying such violations are possible. With the second, neither of these characteristics applies. The contrast between these two kinds of duties corresponds roughly to a distinction of Hobbes's between circumstances in which the rules of morality (or as he terms them, the laws of nature) bind *in foro externo* and those in which they bind *in foro interno*.[37] In the former case the moral rules bind as a matter of explicit legal requirement, while in the latter they bind merely in the realm of conscience. Somewhat analogously, one may think of the first kind of governmental duty as one which at least conceivably could bind a governmental body as a matter of law.[38] By contrast, the second kind binds only those who act under color of governmental authority, such as legislators, or other elected officials, as a matter of conscience.

The concept of fundamental rights may be thought of as coinciding with the notion of the first kind of governmental duty. Establishing a right as fundamental, according to this approach, involves demonstrating from the viewpoint of rational contractors under the veil of ignorance that certain modes of behavior constitute a governmental duty. It also involves showing that the nature of this duty can be specified with sufficient precision so as to secure widespread agreement over a broad range of cases about whether a violation has occurred.

The foregoing two requirements for establishing a right as fundamental correlate with a deeply entrenched intuitive belief which most people would associate with the notion of fundamental rights prior to philosophical reflection about it.[39] The first requirement, that one demonstrate from the standpoint of rational contractors under the veil of ignorance that a certain mode of behavior constitutes a governmental duty, correlates with the intuitive idea that if a right is fundamental then its scope and content are not subject to determination through the legislative process.[40] Only basic principles of social morality take precedence over the rule that the will of the majority should prevail. Such basic moral principles, however, can be thought of precisely as those that would be chosen by the rational contractors under a veil of ignorance. It follows that only principles satisfying this latter description override the principle of majority rule.

The second requirement, which holds that one must characterize the governmental duty in question with sufficient precision so as to secure widespread agreement over a broad range of cases about whether a violation has occurred, also correlates with the above intuitive idea about fundamental rights. Even if one can establish the status of a certain mode of behavior as a governmental duty from the standpoint of rational contractors under a veil of ignorance, if disagreement frequently exists over whether a violation has occurred then it would only seem fair that the majority should decide the matter. Accordingly, unless the nature of a duty deemed governmental can be established with reasonable precision, then any requirements it imposes upon governments do not take precedence, morally speaking, over the will of the majority.

The foregoing remarks, while broadly outlining a philosophical account of fundamental rights, do not constitute an argument in its behalf. How can one be formulated? Some philosophers have believed that such an argument necessarily involves deducing the central propositions of a moral theory from self-evident principles. An account of fundamental rights that draws heavily upon Rawls's ideas admittedly cannot be so defended. The importance of this point recedes dramatically, however, when one realizes that neither can virtually anything else. Demonstrability in terms of self-evident principles is simply not a reasonable criterion of evaluation in any domain except elementary symbolic logic. As certain well-known results in mathematical research indicate, even mathematics, including geometry, cannot be thought of as based upon self-evident propositions.[41]

The standard of evaluation for moral theories is better thought of along a completely different line, a line that suggests itself when one notes the following two basic purposes that theories of morality serve. First, they facilitate theoretical understanding of the important moral concepts we employ in diverse contexts by illuminating their systematic interrelationships. Second, moral theories provide a measure of practical guidance, although in this respect they cannot supply procedures for automatically determining the correct answer to any moral question. Precisely in virtue of illustrating the systematic interrelationships between important moral concepts, however, theories of morality make it possible to keep the essential moral considerations before one's view when dealing with complex cases where such considerations are likely to be obscured. In this way they can prevent serious confusion and misunderstanding. Thomas Hobbes expressed the point cogently when he said, "The utility of moral and civil philosophy is not to be measured so much by the commodities we receive by knowing them as by the calamities we receive from not knowing them."[42]

The above two purposes of moral theories, theoretical illumination and practical guidance, suggest an approach to how one should understand the standard of evaluation for theories of morality. The strongest point one can make in favor of such a theory is that, as a consequence of holding it, one's theoretical understanding of morality coheres with his or her firm moral convictions. Under such circumstances a condition exists which Rawls calls *reflective equilibrium*.[43]

To forestall a possible misunderstanding of this approach, let us say that reflective equilibrium, as Rawls conceives it, is not just a matter of compatibility between philosophical analysis and the moral judgments one accepts prior to systematic reflection. If this were so, then moral theory could never affect one's moral judgments about specific matters. By contrast, reflective equilibrium involves a harmony that emerges from successive mutual accommodations between one's theoretical orientation to morality and one's specific moral judgments so as to bring them into alignment. As Nelson Goodman has said in connection with the justification of logical rules of inference, "The process of justification is the delicate one of making mutual adjustments between rules and accepted inferences; and in the agreement achieved lies the only justification needed for either."[44]

Does the Rawlsian account of fundamental rights then effect such an adjustment between theoretical orientation and specific moral judgments? Although I would answer this question in the affirmative, the grounds for this judgment cannot be set out in a compact, perspicuous form. The foregoing remarks provide enough basis, I think, to contend that the Rawlsian account effectively serves the first purpose of a moral theory, namely, illuminating the systematic interrelation between important moral concepts. It provides us with deeper theoretical insight into the conceptual linkage between the notions of fundamental rights and of genuine claims against the political institutions of one's society that override the principle of majority rule.[45]

That the Rawlsian account of fundamental rights serves the second purpose, providing practical guidance, can only be established by way of a detailed examination of the diverse ways in which the account bears upon major issues of social morality. Such, of course, constitutes an enormous undertaking well beyond the scope of any single study. One may think of this book as attempting to establish the value of a Rawlsian approach with respect to just one major area, freedom of expression. Accordingly, even if one found everything that follows to be persuasive, one still could not regard this book as providing *complete* grounds for the claim that a Rawlsian analysis of fundamental rights accounts for our firmest judgments of social morality in reflective equilibrium. Surely, however, if one found such an analysis genuinely helpful with respect to so problematic an area as First Amendment case law, then this would count strongly in its favor. An evaluation of the Rawlsian account of fundamental rights employed in this book thus is inseparable from an assessment of the book as a whole.

Problematic Aspects of Some Recent Accounts of Judicial Review

Some readers may feel more than a bit impatient with the admittedly dense philosophical analysis of the previous section. Such feelings are indeed understandable; even preeminent philosophers have experienced them in connection with systematic philosophizing.[46] As a sustaining thought, however, I contend that substantial rewards accrue from coming to understand the Rawlsian account of fundamental rights, rewards far beyond the possibly meager intrinsic satisfactions attending the effort itself. Rawls's account is crucial for a coherent intellectual orientation to the First Amendment and the Bill of Rights generally. Unless we can elucidate the concept of fundamental rights with at least moderate precision, the very subject matter of constitutional law, insofar as it involves the Bill of Rights, remains undefined. That is to say, without such an account of fundamental rights one simply cannot distinguish between genuine constitutional questions to be resolved by the courts and policy issues appropriately regarded as falling within the legislative province.

The justification for judicial review in cases involving the Bill of Rights is that it constitutes a major mechanism within the American scheme of government for protecting fundamental rights.[47] Fundamental rights, in turn, can be identified with principles to the effect that governments have certain precisely specifiable basic duties. Such duties are moral requirements for governmental bodies. The Rawlsian account explains why they have this status.

The foregoing justification for judicial review in Bill of Rights cases strongly suggests major difficulties with a number of recent influential writings on this subject. Consider, for example, the following passage that appeared in a collection of essays by Alexander Bickel entitled *The Morality of Consent:*

the rights which the First Amendment creates cannot be established by any theoretical definition, as Burke said of the rights of man, but are in "balance between differences of good, in compromise sometimes between good and evil, and sometimes between evil and evil". . . . The First Amendment is not a coherent theory that points our way to unambiguous decisions but a series of compromises and accommodations confronting us again and again with hard questions to which there is no certain answer.[48]

Bickel appears in the above quotation to strike a note of judicious and worldly wise skepticism. Nonetheless, his outlook reflects a fundamentally mistaken approach to constitutional adjudication under the First Amendment. If the "series of compromises and accommodations" that characterizes First Amendment case law according to Bickel differs in no essential respect from the making of policy by a legislature, then the practice of judicial review under the First Amendment stands condemned as irreconcilable with the spirit of democracy. Now one might take the quotation from Bickel, considered by itself, as a prelude to such condemnation. But a cursory glance at Bickel's other writings, not to mention his engagement in important First Amendment litigation—for example, as attorney for the *New York Times* in the Pentagon Papers case— indicates that he believed the courts have a crucial role to play in the protection of First Amendment rights.[49] An irreconcilable tension exists, however, between such a belief and the viewpoint expressed in the above quotation.

In an earlier work entitled *The Least Dangerous Branch,* Bickel appears to have held that while the Supreme Court has a legitimate role to play in resolving Bill of Rights cases, the principles it applies in doing so are too indefinite to provide meaningful guidance in demarcating the province of the Court from that of the legislature.[50] He thus argued that only through adroit use of the various devices at its disposal for declining to adjudicate an issue—such as declaring it moot or unripe—could the Court avoid encroaching upon the legislative province.[51]

Such a view, however, involves a major contradiction. On the one hand, Bickel saw the appropriate role of courts in constitutional adjudication under the Bill of Rights as that of applying basic principles of social morality to specific cases.[52] On the other hand, if the principles they apply are inherently vague to the degree Bickel suposed, then how can one seriously regard their application as a *legitimate* function of courts? Should not all essentially contestable political issues be resolved in the legislative arena? Bickel provided no answer to these questions. His suggestion—that by invoking the various procedural devices at its disposal to avoid deciding cases the Supreme Court can stay within its legitimate bounds—does not help. Without a reasonably clear account of the principles appropriate for constitutional adjudication the Court has no guidance in the exercise of its discretion not to decide.

It would seem then that an approach to justifying judicial review in Bill of Rights cases that does not analyze the philosphical underpinnings of the concept of fundamental rights will encounter serious problems. Nonetheless, most writers addressing the issue do not provide such an analysis. As an illustration, John Hart Ely has recently advanced what he terms a "participation oriented, representation reinforcing" account of the justification for judicial review in cases involving the Bill of Rights.[53] Ely insists that his approach entirely undercuts the need for philosophical elucidation of the concept of fundamental rights. In developing this view he specifically criticizes the idea that a Rawlsian framework can contribute very much to constitutional adjudication. Commenting upon Ronald Dworkin's call for a fusion of constitutional law and moral theory, he writes

The invitation to judges seems clear; seek constitutional values in—that is, over-rule political officials—on the basis of the writings of good contemporary moral philosophers, in particular the writings of Rawls. Rawls's book is fine. But how are judges to react to Dworkin's invitation when almost all commentators on Rawls's book have expressed reservations about his conclusions? The Constitution may follow the flag, but is it really supposed to keep up with the *New York Review of Books*?[54]

The above passage reflects some important confusions, Ely's rhetorical deftness notwithstanding. The fact that commentators do not accept everything Rawls says counts only against those who hold that philosophers may be consulted on constitutional matters in much the same way as oracles. As mentioned earlier, however, the claim for a Rawlsian approach to fundamental rights is that it provides a conceptual framework that genuinely aids deliberation about difficult cases. It is not claimed that it constitutes an automatic procedure for reaching determinate answers about every possible issue.

A more important criticism of Ely is that his own "participation oriented, representation reinforcing" approach to judicial review has serious problems. The approach is vague in crucial respects. Moreover, the most obvious line of thought to pursue for the purpose of eliminating that vagueness involves precisely the kind of systematic philosophizing he eschews in the above quotation. Ely describes his approach in outline as follows:

The approach to constitutional adjudication recommended here is akin to what might be called an "antitrust" as opposed to a "regulatory" orientation to economic affairs—rather than dictate substantive results it intervenes only when the "market," in our case the political market, is systemically malfunctioning. (A referee analogy is also not far off: the referee is to intervene only when one team is gaining unfair advantage, not because the "wrong" team has scored.) Our government cannot fairly be said to be "malfunctioning" simply because it sometimes generates outcomes with which we disagree, however strongly (and claims that it is reaching results with which "the people" really disagree—would "if they understood"— are likely to be little more than self-deluding projections). In a representative democracy value determinations are to be made by our elected representatives, and if in fact most of us disapprove we can vote them out of office. Malfunction occurs when the process is undeserving of trust, when (1) the ins are choking off the channels of political change to ensure that they will stay in and the outs will stay out, or (2) though no one is actually denied a voice or a vote, representatives beholden to an effective majority are systematically disadvantaging some minority out of simple hostility or a prejudiced refusal to recognize commonalities of interest, and thereby denying that minority the protection afforded other groups by a representative system.[55]

The foregoing account seems clear enough at first, but how does one identify "malfunctions" of the representative system of government, which courts justifiably can step in to set right?

Suppose someone maintains that the system malfunctions owing to the vast disparities in wealth and education in American society. May not such a person thus hold that according to the representation-reinforcing model favored by Ely, judicial intervention to rectify these disparities would be wholly justified? One might respond by distinguishing judicial decisions that endeavor to set right malfunctions of a system of representative government from decisions that aim to make an already reasonably good system even better. The idea here would be that whereas only decisions in the former category can be deemed appropriate according to Ely's conception of judicial review, constitutional rulings aimed at elimination of educational and income inequality fall into the latter one. That is, such rulings are not intended to correct basic malfunctions of a system, but rather aim to improve the operation of a system that functions in essentials as it should.

But how does one draw this distinction? It would seem that in order to do so one must first have in place an account of how representative government should work. That is to say, one needs a model of a *properly functioning* representative government in order to explain what counts as a malfunction in such a system. Ely, however, gives us no indication of how he would construct such a model. In the above quotation he cites two kinds of malfunctions. This does not help a great deal. For one thing, the malfunctions are characterized in vague terms. What kinds of circumstances count as *unconstitutional* "choking off" by the ins of processes that should be available to the outs? How do we identify *constitutionally prohibited* "refusals to recognize commonalities of interest"? For another thing, Ely gives no indication of why other kinds of circumstances should not also be considered malfunctions. Nor do the antitrust law and referee analogies he invokes in the above quotation clarify matters. To be sure, as Ely notes, both antitrust law and referees in athletic contests can be thought of as intervening only to prevent distortions, so to speak, of a process. In the former case the process is the economic system, and in the latter case, it is the playing of a particular game. But this observation sheds no light on the essential question of what kinds of things count as distortions of the representative process of government.

How might one develop a model of a properly functioning representative government in order to address this question? A natural approach would be to articulate first with some precision an account of the basic duties of government from a moral standpoint. Then, one would attempt to show that the particular institutional arrangements constitutive of representative democracy ensure, more than any other form of government, that such duties will not be violated. But one cannot argue in this way without philosophizing about the basic moral standards applicable to governments. Accordingly, Ely's representation-reinforcing approach does not eliminate the need for systematic philosophical reflection. Indeed, in all likelihood such an approach cannot be developed satisfactorily without presupposing a philosophical conception such as the Rawlsian account of fundamental rights.

Perhaps the position most overtly at odds with the view that judges should rely in large part upon a background systematic philosophical theory in constitutional adjudication under the Bill of Rights is found in Raoul Berger's book *Government by Judiciary*.[56] This book contains two parts. In the first, Berger adduces historical evidence, drawn from the legislative history of the Fourteenth Amendment, that its framers intended for the key phrases "due process" and "equal protection" to be understood in extremely narrow senses, senses which if given effect today would preclude all of the most important applications of the Fourteenth Amendment.[57] The second part contains a discussion of diverse topics having to do with constitutional history and theory wherein Berger emphatically asserts that the original intention of the framers must be regarded as binding upon all subsequent generations. Accordingly, he advocates a sweeping voluntary rollback on the part of the Supreme Court to remedy the effects of having gone, over many generations, beyond the intent of the framers in interpreting the Fourteenth Amendment.

Most historical writers who have examined the matter disagree with Berger.[59] Let us assume, however, the correctness of his views. That is, suppose we really knew that the members of the Thirty-Ninth Congress specifically intended that the due process clause bear only upon certain clearly confined procedural matters, and that the equal protection clause not apply to such matters as segregated schools, voting rights, and malapportioned legislative districts.[60]

What follows from such an assumption? Because he holds that the intention of the original framers must be treated as binding in perpetuity, Berger asserts the necessity of sweeping revisions in constitutional doctrine. *Government by Judiciary*, however, contains almost no explicit argument for the view that constitutional adjudication must proceed upon a basic premise to the effect that the original intent of the framers always controls.[61] For all practical purposes, Berger simply assumes this far from self-evident viewpoint.

It cannot be maintained that generally, regardless of domain, one interprets the words of a speaker by ascertaining his or her intent. Sometimes we settle questions of interpretation in this way. For example, if one's superior issues an unclear command one determines what he meant by asking him for further clarification. But in other instances, what the speaker meant in uttering his words bears only slightly upon the question of how best to interpret them. Poetry constitutes a paradigm of such a circumstance.

Questions of interpretation thus form a continuum with commands at one end and poetry at the other. On the extreme left-hand side of the continuum, we can locate contexts where the speaker's intent tends to control absolutely in questions of interpretation, while at the extreme right-hand side the speaker's intent counts for relatively little. Where in between should one locate constitutional interpretation by courts under the Bill of Rights? This question can only be answered by looking to the basic purposes such interpretation serves, namely, protection of fundamental rights. Beliefs about the role of ascertaining the original intent of the framers necessarily depend upon one's views about how best to secure enjoyment of the rights one deems fundamental. Figure 1 helps to illustrate this point.

The gray area in the circle represents intuitive judgments with regard to questions concerning fundamental rights. The dark core at the center represents the area of substantial agreement, while the increasingly lighter shading as one moves to the periphery indicates the realm of decreasing consensus. The ellipse C represents an approach to constitutional adjudication so far off base that it fails even to encompass the area of core agreement. The circle B represents an approach only slightly better than C. Circle B captures our core area of agreement about fundamental rights, but is so vague that it allows constitutional judgments far in excess of anything that would follow from a reasonable conception of fundamental rights. The circle A represents an approach which captures only a small portion of the core and nothing else.

Now argument for any approach to constitutional interpretation

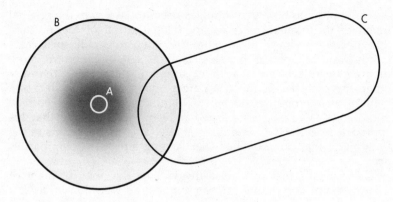

Figure 1

under the Bill of Rights necessarily involves establishing that it satisfies the following two conditions:

1. The approach makes it possible to ascertain the nature of those rights deemed fundamental, with sufficient precision that attempts to apply that the approach will not result in the situations depicted by B. or C.
2. The approach provides sufficient guidance that its application will not result in the situation depicted by A.

Satisfaction of these two conditions constrains any proposal for interpreting the Bill of Rights, including the view that the original intent of the framers always should control. Indeed, this view must satisfy yet another condition, namely, that the rule, always look to the original intent, *alone* satisfies conditions 1 and 2 above.

As far as I can see, however, none of the discussion and analysis in *Government by Judiciary* bears upon any of these matters. Berger comes closest to addressing them in the following remark:

Why is the "original intention" so important? The answer was long since given by Madison: if "the sense in which the Constitution was accepted and ratified by the Nation . . . be not the guide in expounding it, there can be no security for a consistent and stable government, more than for a faithful exercise of its powers." A judicial power to revise the Constitution transforms the bulwark of our liberties into a parchment barrier.[62]

Berger appears to hold that if judges need not ascertain the original intent of the framers in cases involving the Bill of Rights, then they necessarily have an absolute discretion to decide such cases in any way they please. But this claim, as stated, is nothing more than a categorical denial, without supporting argument, that any other approach beside the one Berger endorses is acceptable as a method of interpreting the Bill of Rights. Berger may be correct, but if so, this can be established only by first showing that his approach satisfies the conditions above, and then demonstrating in addition that none of the other leading alternative approaches does so.

The principle that one must always take the original intent of the framers as controlling in constitutional adjudication under the Bill of Rights does not have a privileged position, as Berger supposes.[63] It is just one possible approach among others, and can only be evaluated alongside them in terms of criteria such as outlined above. Accordingly, if the analysis of freedom of expression in succeeding chapters is persuasive, then Berger's general views have little significance for constitutional adjudication under the First Amendment.

Summary

First Amendment cases present such an array of issues that in order to approach them coherently one needs an organizing perspective. This cannot be achieved, however, without first clarifying the justification for judicial review in constitutional adjudication under the First Amendment and the Bill of Rights generally. In the absence of clarity on this matter, one cannot distinguish genuine constitutional questions in these domains from policy issues appropriately resolved through the legislative process.

According to one important line of thought about American political institutions, a legally binding Bill of Rights protects fundamental rights and thereby imposes definite conditions upon the exercise of authority by the state with respect to individual citizens. According to this idea, questions about the nature, extent, and application of fundamental rights are not subject to determination by a legislature. Despite the deep entrenchment of this strain of thought about American democratic government, a number of leading jurisprudential figures have voiced skepticism about it, most prominently Learned Hand and Felix Frankfurter.[65] Hand, in particular, maintained that belief in the existence of fundamental rights not subject to political determination depends for its justification upon philosophical views or theological dogma about which no consensus is possible.

Against Hand's skeptical view I contend that one *can* articulate a convincing philosophical account of fundamental rights. This account, which draws heavily upon the ideas of John Rawls, treats fundamental rights as principles to the effect that governments have certain basic duties that admit of reasonably precise specification. Such duties are moral requirements for governmental bodies. Basic ideas from Rawls's theory of social justice can be employed to explain why they have this status.

A philosophical account of fundamental rights can be established only by showing that it effects satisfactory mutual adjustment between the theoretical orientation toward morality that people find attractive and the moral judgments they make about specific matters.[66] In essence, this entire book constitutes an attempt to show that an account of fundamental rights strongly influenced by Rawls and other major philosophers accomplishes this end with regard to views about freedom of expression.

Even if one should not regard this attempt as successful, however, it seems that a comparable account—that is, one that places primary reliance upon systematic philosophy—is needed to justify judicial review under the Bill of Rights. At least, our survey of recent writings on this subject indicates that serious problems attend any approach that does not aim for philosophical clarity about the concept of fundamental rights. It would seem that either such clarity can be achieved or the practice of judicial review under the Bill of Rights has no justification.

II

The Right to Freedom of Expression: Philosophical Bases and Primary Applications

The previous chapter opened with pointed questions about how the First Amendment applies in diverse circumstances. Although these questions remain unanswered, the foregoing treatments of fundamental rights and the justification of judicial review constitute a substantial first step in addressing them. The next step, with which this chapter concerns itself, involves an account of the right to freedom of expression that satisfies the conditions laid down in Chapter One for regarding a right as fundamental. Answers to most of the aforementioned First Amendment problems will emerge in this chapter. The subsequent two chapters will deal with those problems that remain.

Freedom of Expression:
Basic Philosophical Considerations

According to the approach set out in Chapter One, establishing that a right is fundamental for constitutional purposes has two aspects. First, one must demonstrate by way of an argument, from the standpoint of rational contractors under the veil of ignorance, that certain modes of behavior constitute a governmental duty. Second, one must go on to show that the nature of this duty can be specified with sufficient precision so as to secure widespread agreement over a broad range of cases about whether a violation has occurred. An analysis of the right to freedom of expression, conceived of as constitutionally fundamental, thus involves showing that this right satisfies the above two conditions. The second and third sections of this chapter will take up condition two. The first condition is our immediate concern.

The philosophical basis of any fundamental right lies in an argument, from the standpoint of rational contractors under the veil of ignorance, that a certain mode of conduct constitutes a governmental duty. How then should we specify the content of the duty of government as it relates to freedom of expression? The basic idea is that if a government undertakes to shape the attitudes and beliefs of its citizens, it must confine itself to rather narrow means of accomplishing this end and forebear to use the wide range of coercive devices at its disposal. To describe this in more detail, the expression of attitudes and beliefs at times can lead to very undesirable consequences, consequences that when caused in any other way would be regarded as so grave that behavior causing them ought to be legally prevented. Nonetheless, for those who regard the right to freedom of expression as fundamental, these possible consequences do not constitute a valid justification for placing limitations upon the content of what may be expressed. Along the same line, a government generally may use its coercive powers in order to effect conditions that it judges would be beneficial for its citizens. In some instances we can even say with great confidence that everyone would be better off holding certain attitudes and beliefs, rather than others. Nonetheless, advocates of the right to freedom of expression regard as deeply objectionable certain kinds of governmental prohibitions or requirements aimed at effecting changes in the consciousness of citizens, even if such changes might be for the better.

That governments have a duty of the foregoing kind in regard to freedom of expression is not self-evidently reasonable, but rather requires substantial argument in its behalf. Indeed, from one vantage point the notion of such a duty has an air of irrationality about it, brought out nicely by the following quotation from Justice Holmes's dissenting opinion in *Abrams* v. *U.S.*:[1]

Persecution for the expression of opinions seems to me perfectly logical. If you have no doubt of your premises or your power and want a certain result with all your heart you naturally express your wishes in law and sweep away all opposition. To allow opposition by speech seems to indicate that you think the speech impotent, as when a man says that he has squared the circle, or that you do not care wholeheartedly for the result, or that you doubt either your power or your premises. But . . .[2]

In essence, we can describe the philosophical problem of freedom of expression as that of determining what comes after the word "But" in the foregoing quotation.[3] That is, why should the opportunity to express attitudes and beliefs be thought of as so valuable that even if governmental authorities possess nearly absolute confidence in the correctness of their views, they nonetheless should feel bound not to interfere with the expression of different views by others?

Consideration of this problem inevitably leads to the second and third chapters of John Stuart Mill's classic essay *On Liberty*.[4] These chapters respectively contain two answers to the above question that are enormously important for our purposes. Both answers provide a kind of support for belief in the fundamentality of the right to freedom of expression that would secure the unanimous acceptance of rational contractors under a veil of ignorance. As such, by plugging them in, so to speak, to an analysis of freedom of expression as a constitutionally fundamental right, one meets the first condition which any such analysis must satisfy. At any rate, I will now try to make this contention plausible.

Boiled down to essentials, Mill's argument in chapter two of *On Liberty* can be stated thus. As just noted, the expression of attitudes and beliefs can precipitate substantial harm. For this reason, one might regard endeavoring to control the thought of its citizens as a legitimate governmental function. To illustrate this view, Hobbes wrote in *Leviathan*, "It is annexed to sovereignty [the right] to be judge of what opinions are averse, and what conducing to peace; and consequently, on what occasions, how far, and what men are to be trusted withal, in speaking to multitudes of people; and who shall examine the doctrines of all books before they be published."[5]

Consider, however, the consequences of this approach. Since

no one is infallible, such a far-flung scheme of coercive regulation would result inevitably in widespread acceptance of seriously mistaken viewpoints with respect to important matters. Even worse, this benighted condition of society would persist in all likelihood for many generations because of the absence of the most obvious means for overcoming it, free expression. In addition, even false views may contain a substantial element of truth or have the capacity to stimulate creative thought. Hence, these considerable benefits to society would also go by the board were we to deal with the problems posed by free expression in the above manner. In effect, then, Mill argues that whatever advantages might accrue from an effective method of thought control, the evils associated with it account for much more in the balance.

Moreover, according to Mill's argument as he states it in chapter two, very little ground exists between the full control of expression and a virtual hands-off policy. This is because any proposed basis for controlling expression, though it ostensibly does not go all the way, necessarily runs an unacceptable risk of reintroducing the very kinds of features that make full control objectionable. Such a result obtains whether one specifies a special subject matter, mode of presentation, or motivation as the ground for limiting expression.[6] No reason exists for believing that any of the above kinds of grounds can be articulated in a way that does not open the door in principle to the evils that attend full-scale thought control. At least every such attempt at proposing these kinds of grounds has been woefully inadequate.[7] Accordingly, once restrictions upon expression go into effect, society has no choice but to rely upon the humanity and sound judgment of governmental authorities to avoid abusing them. But given the enormity of the social interest at stake—namely, avoiding thought control—such a choice is patently unacceptable.

The argument in chapter two of *On Liberty* is clear, extremely detailed, and well known. My summary of it adds nothing and breaks no new interpretive ground. I only wish to point out that Mill's argument has direct philosophical relevance for purposes of constitutional analysis. That is to say, rational contractors under a veil of ignorance would unanimously accept it. Its premises appear compelling, presuppose no special knowledge, and logically support the conclusion of the argument. Accordingly, it would seem that one can say that the notion of a right to freedom of expression satisfies the first condition for regarding a right as constitutionally fundamental.

One might object that the above conclusion was drawn too rapidly. Mill's argument, after all, involves a balancing of the respective costs and benefits associated with regulating expression in order to control thought. Can we say categorically that *all* rational people under a veil of ignorance would assess the costs and benefits as did Mill? Indeed, what if we had a Hobbesian rational contractor? Might not someone take such a dim view of human nature that when confronted with the stark choice between freedom of expression and thought control posed by Mill, he or she would opt for the latter without flinching?

I think not. Unregulated expression of attitudes and beliefs occasionally leads to serious trouble. Total regulation, by contrast, virtually guarantees it. This conclusion follows simply from the incontestable proposition that no omniscient human being exists. Interestingly enough, although the passage from Hobbes cited earlier expressed a distinctly hard line against free expression, closer reading of his philosophical works reveals a far more indecisive stance highly uncharacteristic of Hobbes.[8] In the passage immediately following the lines quoted above Hobbes writes:

> though in matters of doctrine nothing ought to be regarded but the truth; yet this is not repugnant to regulating the same by peace. For doctrine repugnant to peace can no more be true than peace and concord can be against the law of nature. It is true that in a commonwealth, where by the negligence or unskillfulness of governors, and teachers, false doctrines are by time generally received, the contrary truths may be generally offensive. Yet the most sudden and rough busling [sic] in of a new truth that can be does never break the peace, but only sometimes awakes the war. For those men that are so remissly governed, that they dare take up arms to defend, or introduce an opinion are still in war; and their condition not peace, but only a cessation of arms for fear of one another; and they live, as it were, in the precincts of battle continually.[9]

Hobbes first suggests that full-scale regulation of expression really need not be thought of as odious, for a rational sovereign will only concern himself or herself with suppressing falsity. That is, "doctrine repugnant to peace can no more be true than peace and concord can be against the law of nature." Of course, this line of argument is hardly reassuring because it presupposes that the sovereign can unerringly distinguish truth from falsity. Hobbes seems to recognize tacitly the problems with taking this line, for he then goes on to concede that in some circumstances (namely, "where by the negligence or unskillfulness of governors, and teachers, false doctrines are by time generally received") expressing true beliefs may well create some commotion. His effort to explain this away, however, is rather extraordinary. If the expression of a belief creates social turmoil, then ipso facto this indicates the existence of latent universal warfare wherein everything is permitted. Hence, under such circumstances, stating the truth does not ". . . break the peace but only sometimes awakes the war."

The striking upshot of all this seems to be that, the sovereign's absolute right to control the expression of attitudes and beliefs notwithstanding, one may with right say whatever one wishes *just in case* it has a tendency to create social disruption. That is, if one's words have such a tendency, that fact by itself indicates that, appearances to the contrary, a situation of latent total warfare exists in which the constraints of morality do not apply.[10] Hence, since in such circumstances one can do whatever one wishes blamelessly, it follows that one can also say anything without thereby being at fault. In all candor, I doubt that Hobbes wished to hold this position, despite the fact that his exact words in *Leviathan* commit him to it. Nonetheless, the peculiar turn of his remarks seems to indicate that not even Hobbes could wholeheartedly endorse the idea of full-scale governmental control of expression.[11]

Although the argument in chapter two of *On Liberty* is both widely known in its essentials and well understood, the same cannot be said of Mill's argument in chapter three, entitled "Of Individuality as One of the Elements of Well-Being." Nonetheless, this argument, when properly interpreted, constitutes an essential component of the analysis of freedom of expression as a constitutionally fundamental right.

To understand Mill's conception of individuality and the argument he based upon it, one must examine closely his remarks about the evils of conforming to custom "merely as custom." In particular, the following passage is of the utmost importance:

to conform to custom merely as custom does not educate or develop . . . any of the qualities which are the distinctive endowment of a human being. The human faculties of perception, judgment, discriminative feeling, mental activity, and even moral preference are exercised only in making a choice. He who does anything because it is the custom makes no choice. He gains no practice in discerning or in desiring what is best. The mental and moral powers are improved only by being used. The faculties are called into no exercise by doing a thing merely only because others do it, no more than by believing a thing only because others believe it. If the grounds of an opinion are not conclusive to a person's own reason, his reason cannot be strengthened but is likely to be weakened by his adopting it.[12]

This passage occurs in the context of a criticism of people who do not place a high value on individuality. Mill tacitly suggests that such people are committed to holding that custom ought to be followed merely as custom. For Mill, then, to refuse to conform to custom merely as custom is to express one's individuality. Accordingly, since Mill insists that only those who refuse to follow custom slavishly have a chance to develop the qualities that are "the distinctive endowment of a human being," it seems to follow that to cultivate individuality is in "large part" to develop these qualities, among which he lists subsequently "observation to see," "reasoning and judgement to foresee," "activity to gather materials for decision," "discrimination to decide," and "firmness and self-control to hold to [one's] deliberate decision."[13] All of these, Mill asserts, can be gained only through exercise, and such exercise can be gained only through choosing one's own "plan of life."

Given that Mill refers to the aforementioned qualities as "the distinctive endowment of a human being," one might take him as arguing that they should be fostered because they are essential human characteristics, that is, characteristics that differentiate fully developed human beings from other animals. There is, however, another interpretation of why Mill attaches so much importance to these qualities that is more congruent with his general philosophical outlook.

According to Mill, "He who does anything because it is the custom makes no choice. He gains no practice either in discerning or in desiring what is best. The mental and moral powers like the muscular powers are improved only by being used." Since the mental and moral powers that Mill here considers instrumental in discerning or desiring what is best are precisely the same as those he refers to as being the distinctive endowment of a human being, it follows that these qualities too are instrumental in discerning or in desiring what is best. We would thus expect Mill to hold that the cultivation of individuality is the development of qualities that are instrumental in discerning or in desiring what is best, and indeed this is his express view. As mentioned before, Mill explicitly states that the more one's individuality is developed the more valuable one becomes oneself, and therefore the more potentially valuable one becomes to others.[14]

Mill underscores his commitment to utilitarianism twice in *On Liberty:* once in the introduction and again at the beginning of chapter three. Consequently, if we assume that the standard of value underlying these judgments is none other than the greatest happiness principle, which plays so crucial a role in Mill's utilitarian philosophy, we have a sophisticated yet unmistakably utilitarian argument for the desirability of cultivating individuality. To assemble all the premises:

1. To cultivate individuality is to develop certain qualities— for example, observation, judgment, discrimination, firmness of will, and so on—that are the distinctive endowment of a human being.
2. Such qualities are instrumental in discerning or desiring what is best. Thus, in the proportion to which an individual has them, he becomes more valuable to himself and is therefore capable of being more valuable to others.
3. For a utilitarian, (a) "what is best" is what is most productive of happiness and (b) something is valuable to the extent that it is productive of happiness.
4. Accordingly, such qualities are abilities and capacities the possession of which, more than any other qualities, enables an individual to promote both his own happiness and the happiness of others. Therefore,
5. the cultivation of individuality is desirable and the hindering of its development undesirable.

In light of the foregoing, the connection between individuality on the one hand and liberty of thought and action on the other becomes evident. The latter should exist in view of its status as a basic necessary condition of the former.

Two additional points must be made concerning these arguments. First, Mill explicitly identifies the abilities and capacities whose development constitutes the cultivation of individuality with reason.[15] Immediately after pointing out that these abilities and capacities can only be developed through exercise, Mill adds that "if the grounds of an opinion are not conclusive to the person's own *reason* his *reason* cannot be strengthened, but is likely to be weakened by his adopting it" (emphasis added). Thus Mill's utilitarian account of the value of cultivating individuality contains a pronounced strain of pragmatism. The cultivation of individuality amounts to the development of reason, and reason, in turn, is thought of as a set of abilities and capacities which, more than any other aspect of human individuals, enables one to obtain goods and avoid evils.[16] The second point to note in connection with Mill's arguments is that he does not rest his case for individuality upon a claim that everyone who develops it inevitably will be happier than otherwise. Such a result may obtain, but not necessarily. Mill's primary contention is that the human race collectively and over the long run benefits from the cultivation of individuality. This is the point of his claim to appeal to utility only in the largest sense.[17]

For Mill, then, the cultivation of individuality can be identified with the development of reason. Such an identification is apt because an important connection exists between the development of the abilities and capacities constituting reason and one crucial aspect of the concept of individuality, namely, self-direction. To begin with, people possess a wide range of dispositions, among them impulses, emotions, habits, attitudes, beliefs, and various kinds of abilities and capacities such as to make deductions and inferences, to formulate hypotheses, to empathize, to keep one's temper, to see the humor in a situation, and so on. These dispositions may be referred to as aspects of a person. Second, for any human action or motivation the list of antecedent conditions constituting its complete explanation would have to include reference to a wide variety of different factors, most prominent among them the natural environment, the person's physiological state, cultural conditions broadly construed, and aspects of the person. The more developed the abilities and capacities that constitute reason, the more it is that aspects of the person function as the differentiating factors in explanations of human action and motivation. The question, Why did X do (feel, believe that) Y? is roughly elliptical for the question, 'Why did X do (feel, believe that) Y when other people did not? Accordingly, an answer to this question consists in citing the factors that make the difference between X and others.[18] When reason is developed to a high degree, aspects of the person rather than features of the environment tend to make the difference in explanations of human action and motivation. On the other hand, for those people who can only conform to custom because their abilities and capacities constituting reason were never developed, the differentiating factors in the explanation of their actions and motivation tend to be primarily features of the background environment. So in an important sense, the greater the development in human beings of the abilities and capacities that comprise reason, the more human beings can be thought of as self-directed individuals.

The argument in chapter three of *On Liberty* thus points out another grave evil that stems from regulating the expression of attitudes and beliefs besides those identified in chapter two. Such regulation hinders the development of individuality; and for the reasons Mill adduces, individuality, like truth, would be acknowledged by the rational contractors as one of the greatest goods. Accordingly, chapter three provides another independent philosophical basis for the right to freedom of expression. Rational contractors under a veil of ignorance would regard both truth and individuality as so important that they would reject any governmental scheme that undermined the effort at realizing them, no matter how attractive it otherwise seemed. Because of its connection with these two values, then, the right to freedom of expression stands vindicated of the charge of irrationality expressed in the quotation from Holmes at the outset of this section. People who regard their views as absolutely certain may feel they have no use for this right. But one need only reflect upon the enormous social value of truth, the comparable value of individuality, and the nonexistence of infallible human beings to recognize that the right to freedom of expression serves precisely to protect us from such people.

Primary Applications

HOW TO USE *ON LIBERTY*
WHEN THINKING ABOUT THE FIRST AMENDMENT

The foregoing account admittedly lacks precision concerning the duties of governments with respect to freedom of expression. For purely philosophical purposes, however, this does not matter a great deal. One only needs to know what would constitute gross violation of these duties to appreciate the force of Mill's arguments in chapters two and three of *On Liberty*. Constitutional adjudication, however, requires much more precision.

How can this be achieved? A natural approach would be to attempt to distill Mill's ideas to a clear, succinct principle for application in specific cases. Unfortunately, such efforts would be futile. No one has ever yet enunciated a clear, brief proposal that also captured the diverse ways Mill's ideas work out in practice. Consider, for example, the following carefully constructed suggestion of Thomas Scanlon, which he terms the Millian Principle.

There are certain harms which, although they would not occur but for certain acts of expression, nonetheless cannot be taken as part of a justification for legal restrictions on these acts. These harms are: (a) harms to certain individuals which consist in their coming to have false beliefs as a result of those acts of expression; (b) harmful consequences of acts performed as a result of those acts of expression, where the connection between the acts of expression and the subsequent harmful acts consists merely in the fact that the act of expression led the agents to believe (or increased their tendency to believe) these acts to be worth performing.[19]

Scanlon's Millian Principle seems not only clear and concise, but also definitely in the spirit of Mill's arguments. Nonetheless, problems arise immediately when one assesses its practical implications. To begin, the Millian Principle, while clear in the abstract, would not be easy to apply. The principle specifies considerations that may not be taken into account as justifications for legally restricting expression. But how does one identify justifications for a given restriction? In virtually every case hypotheses about the justification for a statute are underdetermined by the statutory language.[20] In addition to this problem, the Millian Principle appears at once far too narrow and far too wide in the scope it allows for free expression. As an example of its excessive narrowness, a decree that forbade publication of specific information concerning a purely public matter that happened to embarrass a highly placed public official would not clearly violate either condition (a) or condition (b) of the principle. As for its excessive width, the Millian Principle appears to imply that the law of defamation cannot be reconciled with the right to freedom of expression. When A sues B for defamation he alleges, among other things, that B made statements of a kind that tend to harm his reputation.[21] Accordingly, in effect A alleges that B's words increased the tendency of other individuals to believe certain harmful acts worth performing, namely, those appropriate when one comes to believe ill of a person. The law of defamation then appears to violate condition (b) of Scanlon's Millian Principle.

As will be illustrated in Chapter Three, defamation law indeed raises problems for an analysis of the right to freedom of expression. A view that depicts the two as inherently at odds, however, seems clearly mistaken. The foregoing account of Mill's arguments indicates that the right to freedom of expression should be thought of essentially as ruling out governmental activities involving a substantial danger of thought control. But such a danger cannot be said to exist in a legal system simply because the possibility exists within it for private parties to bring defamation actions against one another.

Consider an even more striking example of the unacceptably wide scope for expression allowed by the Millian Principle. Suppose the owner of a pond places this sign prominently alongside it.

POND FROZEN SOLID

GREAT SKATING

ENJOY!

A CHRISTMAS PRESENT FOR ALL
THE KIDS IN THE NEIGHBORHOOD
FROM THE OWNER OF THIS POND

Let us assume the owner, a malicious fiend, knows the ice to be dangerously thin.[22] The Millian Principle implies that taking the sign down would violate his right to freedom of expression. In light of counter-examples such as this, it scarcely surprises one to find that even Scanlon himself concedes that the Millian Principle, when considered without explication, directly contradicts Justice Holmes's famous dictum that "the most stringent protection of free speech would not protect a man in falsely shouting 'fire' in a crowded theatre and causing a panic."[23] Scanlon of course goes on to present a reasonably plausible treatment of this stock Holmesian counter-example.[24] He treats it, however, directly in terms of the philosophy he believes to underlie the Millian Principle. The principle itself really does not figure in his explanation.

Scanlon's attempt to capture the spirit of Mill's philosophical outlook in chapters two and three of *On Liberty* probably constitutes the best of its kind. I have criticized it not to chide Scanlon for carelessness, but to indicate the impossibility of any concise statement of the principles of freedom of expression. But how should one proceed if not by endeavoring to formulate a single rule as precisely as possible? I think a brief look at antitrust law, of all things, provides enormous assistance in suggesting another approach. Section one of the Sherman Act forbids "every contract, combination in the form of trust or otherwise, or conspiracy in restraint of trade or commerce among the several States or with foreign nations." No court could possibly apply this broad proscription to specific controversies with literal exactitude. All contracts restrict trade in some way. To decide cases under section one of the Sherman Act, the Supreme Court has therefore developed a special form of analysis termed the per se approach.[25]

According to this approach, certain kinds of contracts and combinations, such as price-fixing agreements, division of markets, and group boycotts, have been singled out as inherently in opposition to the basic purpose of the Sherman Act as the Supreme Court conceives it, namely, the maintenance of price competition among business enterprises.[26] If a court classifies a specific business arrangement as falling under one of these categories, it deems that arrangement to violate section one of the Sherman Act simply in virtue of this fact. In other words, when faced with antitrust litigation courts do not ask such questions as "Does this price-fixing agreement violate the Sherman Act?" but rather, "Is the particular business arrangement at issue in this case a price-fixing agreement?" If so, it violates the Sherman Act regardless of what else might be said for it. Hence, the designation of per se violation applies to price-fixing agreements, as well as to other business arrangements considered inherently inimical to the maintenance of price competition.

Ideally, a judicial mode of analysis for interpreting statutes should satisfy the demands of both precision and intellectual coherence. In the case of the Sherman Act, with its highly general wording, these two demands conflict. The per se approach thus may be thought of as an attempt to reach the most satisfactory accommodation between them.[27] Precision enters into the analysis through articulation of relatively determinate categories of proscribed business arrangements, that is, the per se violations. Such an approach, if carried through with success, makes intellectual sense because the courts do not define the per se violations arbitrarily, but rather in light of a background conception of the basic objectives of the Sherman Act.

More generally, it seems that a per se approach in any domain is advisable under the following three conditions: first, the basic rationale for a law admits of relatively clear characterization; second, despite such clarity no succinct formula exists for use in applying the law to specific cases; third, the absence of such a formula notwithstanding, substantial agreement is obtainable about what kinds of activities constitute clear violations of the law. Under these three circumstances, following a per se approach constitutes the better part of jurisprudential wisdom. The only alternatives are precise standards purchased at an excessively high cost in arbitrariness, or intellectually coherent principles that fail to provide sufficient guidance for resolving actual controversies.

The general outline of my proposal for achieving the degree of precision necessary for constitutional adjudication under the First Amendment may now be apparent. Any reasonable approach to First Amendment adjudication must occupy a satisfactory middle ground between those who seek vainly to boil down the principles of free expression to a one- or two-sentence formula, and those who categorically reject any attempt at intellectual systematization. Toward this end, I propose utilizing a per se approach that involves identification of certain kinds of statutes and governmental acts as inherently violative of the right to freedom of expression. I will contend that seven different kinds of governmental restrictions upon expression constitute per se violations of this right. Each of these per se violations will be derived from my exposition of the basic philosophy of free expression.

A per se approach to First Amendment adjudication not only has analogues in the law, but in moral philosophy as well. For example, Mill and Kant, however divergent their theoretical perspectives, both advocate something very much like it. In chapter two of *Utilitarianism,* Mill states emphatically that the principle of utility, though central to moral thought, cannot be applied directly to specific situations. He holds instead that one must employ it as a guide to formulating more determinate moral rules which can then serve to resolve concrete moral issues.[28] Similarly, Kant regards as purely formal the supreme principle of morality that he enunciates in *The Groundwork of the Metaphysic of Morals,*

"Act only on those maxims which thou can will as a universal law."[29] That is to say, he believes one cannot employ this principle directly to reach moral judgments about specific matters. In part two of *The Metaphysic of Morals*, however, he deduces more determinate moral principles from the formal principle in conjunction with general propositions about human nature.[30] Mill and Kant, then, each maintain that the moral principles that their respective theories posit as supreme must be applied, so to speak, wholesale rather than retail. Among contemporary philosophers, Rawls also envisages his basic principles of justice as not directly applicable to specific problems of social morality. Rather, their application proceeds by way of a substantial number of mediating principles.[31]

The discussion that follows thus aims to satisfy the second condition that an account of freedom of expression as a constitutionally fundamental right must satisfy—namely, serviceability for the resolution of actual controversies. I do not, however, wish to depict my specific account of the per se violations as engraved on stone tablets. There may be others besides those I shall enumerate.[32] If so, however, this presents no serious problem, for two reasons. First, the ensuing remarks should make clear the kind of reasoning that goes into identifying categories of per se violations. Hence, this approach not only specifies the categories that courts should employ in First Amendment adjudication, but also indicates the pertinent considerations for introducing new ones. Second, given the nature of these considerations it seems unlikely to me that there could be many more than seven per se violations. Accordingly, the approach generates a set of workable standards for constitutional adjudication.

THE *PER SE* VIOLATIONS

1. Sedition laws. Sedition laws may be defined as those that make acts of expression punishable specifically because of their tendency to undermine duly constituted authority.[33] Section 2 of the Alien Registration Act of 1940 exemplifies a typical form such laws assume. This law, commonly known as The Smith Act, sets severe criminal penalties for anyone who

1. Knowingly or willfully advocates, abets, advises, or teaches the duty, necessity, desirability, or propriety of overthrowing or destroying the

government of the United States . . . or . . . any political subdivision therein by force, violence, or by the assassination of any officer of any such government.
2. Organizes or helps or attempts to organize any society, group, or assembly of persons who teach, advocate, or encourage the overthrow or destruction of any such government by force or violence; or becomes or is a member of, or affiliates with, any such society, group, or assembly of persons knowing the purpose thereof.[34]

The Smith Act has the two characteristic marks of sedition laws. First, it applies to certain acts of expression, namely, advocating, advising, teaching, or encouraging. Second, it forbids such acts of expression because of their seditious tendencies—that is, because their natural consequence, should they substantially influence public opinion, would be to undermine the government of the United States. Sedition laws confer upon governmental authorities the exclusive right to decide whether or not the benefits outweigh the costs with respect to permitting public discussion on various issues. But as Mill forcefully pointed out, such an arrangement makes no sense unless we make the manifestly unreasonable assumption that there exist infallible, perfectly benevolent human beings whom we can accurately identify as such in order to place them in positions of political power. The case against sedition laws derives from a straightforward application of Mill's arguments in chapter two of *On Liberty*.

Sedition laws admit of variation in certain respects. They may differ substantially in degree of precision. They may or may not include as an element of the offense the specific intent to undermine duly constituted legal authority. Some may be more restricted than others with respect to time, place, or manner of expression. The Millian objection to sedition laws, however, applies regardless of these variations. A law defining sedition precisely and including specific intent as an element of that definition is less objectionable, from the standpoint of due process, than a sedition law without these characteristics. Mill's arguments in chapter two of *On Liberty*, however, apply alike to both kinds of laws. Governments can employ precisely framed laws no less than vague ones to control thought. In the same way, while sedition laws of restricted scope may do less damage than do the unrestricted variety, this hardly justifies them. A justification exists only if one can precisely enunciate special circumstances under which the general objections to sedition laws do not apply, but this no one has ever succeeded in doing. Perhaps the most plausible possibility is that under wartime conditions a government may restrict expression in otherwise impermisable ways. Upon reflection, however, such a view must be rejected.[35] Public issues during war tend to be no more clear-cut than during peacetime. Accordingly, sedition laws applied in time of war retain their predictably repressive character. Writing of the voluminous prosecutions under federal and state sedition legislation during World War I, Zechariah Chafee noted:

It became criminal to advocate heavier taxation instead of bond issues, to state that conscription was unconstitutional though the Supreme Court had not yet held it valid, to say the sinking of merchant ships was legal, to urge that a referendum should have preceded our declaration of war, to say that war was contrary to the teachings of Christ. Men [were] punished for criticizing the Red Cross and the Y.M.C.A., while under the Minnesota Espionage Act it [was] held a crime to discourage women from knitting by the remark, "No soldier ever sees those socks."[36]

It would appear then that not even war can justify sedition laws.

The foregoing remarks appear consistent with the approach taken by the U.S. Supreme Court in its most recent treatment of sedition laws. In *Brandenburg* v. *Ohio*, a unanimous Court declared unconstitutional Ohio's criminal syndicalism statute, a typical sedition law, which indeed was virtually identical in text to a California statute whose constitutionality the Court had upheld in *Whitney* v. *California* some forty-two years earlier.[37] The decision in *Brandenburg* thus explicitly overruled *Whitney*. In this regard the Court said,

[N]either the indictment nor the trial judge's instructions to the jury in any way refined the Ohio statute's bald definition of crime in terms of mere advocacy not distinguished from incitement to imminent lawless action. The statute thus falls within the condemnation of the First Amendment: . . . [t]he contrary teaching of *Whitney* v. *California* . . . cannot be supported and that decision is therefore overruled. . . . later decisions have fashioned the principle that the constitutional guarantees of free speech and free press do not permit a State to forbid or proscribe advocacy of the use of force or violation of law except where such advocacy is directed to inciting or producing imminent lawless action and is likely to incite or produce such action.[38]

The Court's unanimous acceptance of the above-quoted principle would seem to indicate that, for all practical purposes, the unconstitutionality of sedition laws has become a fixed point in First

Amendment jurisprudence. *Brandenburg* v. *Ohio*, however, must be viewed in historical perspective. The earliest First Amendment cases involved prosecutions during World War I under the Federal Espionage Act of 1917. In every instance the Court upheld the prosecutions at issue.[39] In the first of these cases, *Schenk* v. *U.S.*, Justice Holmes enunciated the "clear and present danger" test as a basis for deciding First Amendment cases. Shortly thereafter, however, in the wake of hysteria caused by the Bolshevik Revolution, the Court made it clear that the word "present" in the clear and present danger test need not be equated with "imminent." The following passage from the majority opinion in *Gitlow* v. *New York* graphically illustrates this point:

[B]y enacting the present statute the State has determined through its legislative body, that utterances advocating the overthrow of organized government by force, violence, and unlawful means, are so inimical to the general welfare and involve such danger of substantive evil that they may be penalized in the exercise of its police power. That determination must be given great weight. . . . . That utterances inciting to the overthrow of organized government by unlawful means, present a sufficient danger of substantive evil to bring their punishment within the range of legislative discretion is clear. Such utterances, by their very nature, involve danger to the public peace and to the security of the State. They threaten breaches of the peace and ultimate revolution. And the immediate danger is none the less real and substantial because the effect of a given utterance cannot be accurately foreseen. The State cannot reasonably be required to measure the danger from every such utterance in the nice balance of a jeweler's scale. A single revolutionary spark may kindle a fire that, smouldering, for a time, may burst into a sweeping and destructive conflagration. It cannot be said that the State is acting arbitrarily or unreasonably when in the exercise of its judgment as to the measures necessary to protect the public peace and safety it seeks to extinguish the spark without waiting until it has enkindled the flame or blazed into conflagration.[40]

The various opinions of the Supreme Court in the 1920s provided the occasion for Holmes's and Brandeis's eloquent dissents now widely regarded as among the classic statements of the philosophy of free expression in the twentieth century.[41]

The 1930s and 1940s saw the emergence of a somewhat less restricted view of the First Amendment, although the basic principles enunciated in the 'twenties concerning sedition laws remained intact.[42] Any doubts about this were laid to rest in the early 'fifties when the Court upheld the constitutionality of the Smith Act in

Dennis v. *U.S.*[43] With the gradual easing of cold war tensions, however, the Court again expanded the range of constitutionally protected expression, albeit frequently through indirect methods that thwarted prosecutions and legislative investigations under various sedition laws without directly raising First Amendment issues.[44] This process had its stops and starts, but by the late 'sixties matters had evolved to a point where the Court could stand unanimously behind the opinion in *Brandenburg* v. *Ohio.*

In view of this historical background, confident statements that *Brandenburg* has laid sedition laws to rest seem somewhat overly optimistic. Moreover, the impact upon the Court of drastic shifts in the national mood raises a basic problem for the protection of fundamental rights. The stops and starts just alluded to in the evolution of First Amendment case law, from *Dennis* v. *U.S.* in 1952 to *Brandenburg* v. *Ohio* in 1969, appear in one major instance to have been a direct response to overt pressure by Congress. Outraged by the spate of cases limiting the subversive-hunting activities of both federal and state officials, in 1957 Senator Jenner introduced legislation to withdraw the jurisdiction of the Supreme Court from cases dealing with loyalty programs and state sedition laws. Jenner's proposal was defeated in the Senate by a narrow 49–41 vote.[45] Thereafter for a time, the Court was substantially more circumspect about placing restrictions upon Congress and the states with respect to their various attempts at rooting out heresy.[46]

Sedition laws thus present a problem for an account of constitutional adjudication under the First Amendment. On the one hand, they clearly contravene the First Amendment; on the other hand, the climate of political opinion might be such that by striking down a given sedition law on First Amendment grounds, the Court would provoke a disastrous backlash. Hamilton's characterization of the Court as the least dangerous branch cuts two ways.[47] The Court's limited power not only prevents it from overstepping its bounds, but also in some instances from carrying out one of its basic functions, the protection of fundamental rights. How then should conscientious Supreme Court justices proceed when they genuinely believe that striking down sedition legislation in a particular instance would result in certain political retribution?[48]

There appear to be only three possible responses to this question. First, one might regard the general judicial duty to give effect to the rights of the parties as literally absolute—that is, even as binding upon Supreme Court justices in politically explosive constitutional cases. Such a view seems extraordinary, however, insofar as it implies that judicial duty may require the justices of the Supreme Court to provoke the Court's very destruction. Second, one might frame the duty of the justices more broadly as requiring them to protect fundamental rights through the most effective means available. According to this view, giving effect to the rights of the parties in constitutional cases constitutes the primary, but not necessarily the only, way the justices may do their duty. Taken without qualification, however, this suggestion would force a major revision in our conception of the Supreme Court. Characterizing the judicial duty of Supreme Court justices as simply the protection of fundamental rights through the most effective available means brings to mind the broad grants of authority under which federal agencies, such as the Federal Trade Commission, Federal Communications Commission, and Environmental Protection Agency, function. Do we really wish to conceive of the Supreme Court on rough analogy with these agencies; for example, as the Federal Super Commission for the Protection of Fundamental Rights?

Now in virtue of its *certiorari* jurisdiction, the Court has considerable discretion with respect to the cases it considers.[49] Nonetheless, it seems to me that, unlike commissioners of a regulatory agency, the justices would abuse this discretion if they used it for any purpose other than screening out cases that do not present important constitutional questions. They are not free, morally speaking, to formulate personal agendas for the protection of fundamental rights and then to vote whether or not to grant *certiorari* on the basis of how deciding a given case at a particular time fits in with the agenda.

A third view, which seems to me the correct one, conceives of the justices as neither absolutely bound nor absolutely unfettered with respect to the means at their disposal for protecting fundamental rights. According to this approach they have a general duty to decide each case in terms of the most salient principles concerning fundamental rights. Such a duty, however, does not apply in extraordinary situations where a particular decision on the basic constitutional merits could reasonably be expected to precipitate a response, such as Senator Jenner's in the 1950s, that would significantly undermine the capability of the Court to protect fundamental rights.[50] In such a circumstance this approach would countenance, to speak a bit paradoxically, the conscientious choice not to decide a case on principle. Where deciding a case on straightforward First Amendment grounds runs the risk of political disaster, a Supreme Court justice thus may conscientiously opt for the next best course.

Unhappily, this conclusion introduces substantial vagueness into our conception of responsible judicial behavior in constitutional cases under the Bill of Rights. The idea of the next best course clearly has a high degree of context-dependence. In some instances a judge may conclude the next best course involves disposing of the case at hand by appeal to procedural considerations or statutory interpretation, in a way that reaches the same practical outcome for the immediately affected party as would obtain were the case to be decided on grounds of basic constitutional principle.[51] In other instances, however, such a relatively cheerful compromise may not be possible. Here a conscientious justice might reluctantly choose to avoid the issue by voting not to grant *certiorari.* Thus, a wide room for disagreement will almost always exist about what would constitute the next best course. By the same token, assessments of the political risks involved in taking a stand on principle will vary from justice to justice, in some cases primarily because of purely subjective factors, such as degree of personal courage. Nonetheless, no alternative other than this third approach seems consistent with the moral and practical complexities of constitutional adjudication under the Bill of Rights.

By the same token, while I regard my account of how to interpret the First Amendment as serviceable for deciding the overwhelming majority of cases, I also acknowledge extraordinary situations where using it would not be desirable. Yet even in the extraordinary situations it figures indirectly. One cannot identify the latter independent of a theory of constitutional interpretation under the Bill of Rights. That is, before one can characterize a decision as both necessitated by basic constitutional principles and politically impossible, one needs a systematic account of those basic principles.[52]

2. Obscenity Laws. Obscenity laws can be readily identified as those forbidding acts of expression on general grounds of their offensiveness. The federal obscenity statute (18 U.S.C. sec. 1461) whose pertinent language reads in part as follows, is typical.

Every obscene, lewd, lascivious, or filthy book, pamphlet picture, paper, letter, writing, print, or other publication of an indecent character . . . is declared to be nonmailable and shall not be conveyed in the mails or delivered from any post office or by any letter carrier.

Whoever knowingly deposits for mailing or delivery anything declared by this section to be nonmailable, or knowingly takes the same from the mails for the purpose of circulating or disposing thereof, or of aiding in the circulation or disposition thereof shall be fined not more than $5,000 or imprisoned not more than five years or both.

Obscenity laws have two predominant rationales. Traditionally their supporters have viewed them as attempts to protect the moral fabric of society by forbidding acts of expression that tend to corrupt morals.[53] More recently, however, one finds the strong suggestion that obscenity laws serve another entirely separate function, that of giving effect to predominant community attitudes.[54] According to this suggestion, the mere fact that most people in a community find certain acts of expression offensive constitutes a strong, and in most cases sufficient, reason, in and of itself, for suppressing them.[55]

Both of these purported justifications directly violate the spirit of Mill's arguments in chapters two and three of *On Liberty*. The case against sedition laws carries over directly to obscenity legislation conceived of primarily as a device for stemming the tide of moral corruption. Judgments in this regard are no less difficult than those about what acts of expression run the risk of undermining respect for legitimate government. Given inherent human fallibility, authorizing public officials carte blanche to protect the moral fabric of society through enforcement of obscenity legislation would in all likelihood have deeply undesirable long-range consequences. Alternatively, when viewed as a way of giving effect to a community's standards of propriety, obscenity laws contravene Mill's basic argument in chapter three. Imposing one's standards of taste on others necessitates regarding the value of a world conforming to those standards as greater than that of a world in which others have the opportunity to develop their own standards. That is to say, it involves a deliberate policy decision to foster regimentation rather than individuality. But Mill's argument in chapter three indicates that individuality, properly understood, ought not be subordinated to any other consideration, save that of securing adherence to basic moral rules.[56]

One common response to the foregoing Millian critique of obscenity laws posits a hierarchy among various subject matters in terms of relative social significance. According to this approach, acts of expression should be accorded a degree of judicial support commensurate with their places in such a hierarchy.[57] This proposal founders, however, as soon as one demands precision in framing the boundaries of various subject matter areas for purposes of differentiating them with respect to levels of protection under the First Amendment. Alexander Meiklejohn, perhaps the best thinker ever to follow the above approach, drew a distinction between "public" and "private" spheres of discussion.[58] Cognizant, however, of the obvious pitfalls attending such a contrast when drawn without qualification, he explicated his category of public speech as encompassing not only everything said pertaining to matters of public interest, but also bearing upon such matters, or *conceivably* bearing upon them.[59] One is at a loss to imagine what this would exclude. More recently, proposals have been put forward which identify the class of unprotected acts of expression in terms of such properties as "glorifying violence" or "treating women like animals." That these properties can be defined in a way that eliminates their obviously high degree of subjectivity, and its attendant potential for grave abuse, however, has never been made credible.

The overwhelming case against obscenity laws notwithstanding, it appears unlikely that they will be declared unconstitutional in the near future. The Supreme Court first dealt with the topic of obscenity from a First Amendment standpoint in *Roth* v. *U.S.*, a 1957 case wherein the Court emphatically rejected a First Amendment challenge to 18 U.S.C., section 1461, the federal obscenity statute quoted earlier.[60] Since that time the Court's treatment of obscenity cases has taken unpredictable twists and turns that appear to defy coherent interpretation.[61] To cite just one illustration, in *Jacobelis* v. *Ohio*, decided some seven years after *Roth* in 1964, the Court split *six* ways with respect to both the definition of obscenity and the rationale, or lack thereof, for not protecting obscene expression.[62] In this case Justice Stewart expressed the view that obscenity laws must be limited to forbidding hard-core pornography. As to the definition of this latter term, however, he could only observe, "I know it when I see it."[63]

This comment of Justice Stewart illustrates in a nutshell the fundamental problem with obscenity laws. Obscenity and pornography defy general characterization. That is to say, any attempt to define these terms for the purpose of classifying actual books, films, theatrical performances, and so forth, inevitably results in a scheme in which the gray area vastly exceeds the domain of clear-cut cases. Accordingly, any serious attempt to determine whether materials are obscene will necessarily involve a case-by-case review either before or after dissemination. But no fallible human being can rationally presume himself or herself capable of deciding such issues for the entire society. Writers on obscenity laws, both pro and con, often focus upon the possible effects of pornography upon readers. But the argument against obscenity laws involves no premises whatsoever about either the nature or effects of pornography. By contrast, it rests expressly upon recognizing the grave evils a society invites by regulating expression upon the basis of its possible effects. This point deserves emphasis not only for its intrinsic importance, but also because one finds it so persistently ignored.[64]

The most recent statement of Supreme Court standards with respect to obscenity appears in *Miller* v. *California*.[65] The Miller test stipulates three conditions for holding material obscene. First, an average person applying contemporary community standards would find that, taken as a whole, it appeals to prurient interest. Second, the material must depict or describe sexual conduct in a patently offensive way as defined by appropriate state law. Third, the material, taken as a whole, must lack serious literary, artistic, political, or scientific value.[66] Given the patent incongruity of the Miller test with Mill's basic philosophy of free expression, a detailed critique seems unnecessary. Referring to the Miller test, Lawrence Tribe has said, "the Supreme Court's bare majority in 1973 for yet another definition of the obscene and yet another set of rationales for its suppression has produced a formula likely to be as unstable as it is unintelligible."[67] This apt statement summarizes matters in a way that requires no further comment.

3. *Censorship.* In common parlance the term "censorship" has both a broad and a narrow sense. Only the latter need concern us, however, for in the broad sense censorship applies to any restriction upon expression of which the listener happens to disapprove. This is not so much a use as an abuse of the term.[68] Censorship in the narrow sense refers to making illegal certain precisely identified acts of expression.[69] So defined, censorship

differs from both sedition and obscenity laws in the following respect. At times a genuine issue may arise as to whether a defendant's acts of expression really were seditious or obscene in terms of relevant statutory definitions of these terms. By contrast, such a question generally does not arise when one violates censorship laws. The matter tends to be much more clear-cut. Either one published a censored book, said a censored word on the air, exposed a forbidden region of human epidermal surface in a film, or one did not.

Censorship so obviously contravenes basic Millian arguments for freedom of expression as to make a demonstration of this point superfluous. As with sedition and obscenity laws, the bases commonly enunciated for distinguishing legitimate from illegitimate exercises of the power to censor invariably are arbitrary and capricious. Primarily for this reason, citation of literature censored at one time or another seldom fails to astound. Consider the following *very* partial list: *The Bible, Alice in Wonderland, The Adventures of Sherlock Holmes, Don Quixote, The Sun Also Rises, The Origin of Species, All Quiet on the Western Front, King Lear,* Mickey Mouse cartoons, *The Grapes of Wrath, The Merchant of Venice, Studs Lonigan, Lysistrata, The Koran, The Talmud, Paradise Lost, Robinson Crusoe, H.M.S. Pinafore, The Critique of Pure Reason, The Sorrows of Young Werther,* and *Tom Sawyer.*[70] One exaggerates only slightly in saying that every literary work of unusual merit has been censored at least once.

Do any circumstances justify censorship? The only credible one pertains to acts of expression in the course of entertainment programs or educational materials specifically intended for an audience of young children. In such a circumstance the Millian arguments do not apply with full force. One need not assume infallibility on the part of regulators to justify content regulations of television programs for young children. In the same way, such regulations do not undermine the development of individuality by depriving children of the opportunity to make their own choices. This is because one presumes that young children have not yet crossed the threshold beyond which development of the abilities and capacities comprising reason depends primarily upon their unrestricted exercise.

The foregoing condition of justifiable censorship is quite narrow. It applies only in circumstances where exercise of parental authority may be difficult. Thus, one cannot justify general censorship of children's books for with books, unlike television programs, parents can exert their control effectively through purchasing decisions. It also applies only to entertainment programs and educational programs expressly intended for young children as an audience. One cannot then, as did the majority in a recent Supreme Court decision, reasonably regard the mere possibility that young children may listen or view a program not specifically intended for them as a justifiable basis for censoring it.[71] Acknowledging that censorship may be justified where young children are involved, then, does not compromise its characterization as a per se violation. Children need adult guidance. The problem with censorship is that it presumes we all bear the same relationship to governmental authorities that young children bear to adults.

4. *Prior Restraints.* For purposes of defining per se violations of the First Amendment, prior restraints may be identified with direct governmental action that makes it literally impossible for one to communicate with others effectively.[72] Governments exercise prior restraint, among other ways, by seizing books from library shelves, films from projection rooms, and printing plates from print shops. In this sense prior restraint is a primary means, but not the only one, whereby governments seek to enforce sedition, obscenity, or censorship laws. Theoretically, such laws could exist without prior restraint if they provided only for fine or imprisonment in case of violation. Conversely, prior restraints could be imposed without these kinds of laws. This would be the case if governmental authorities prevented one from publishing an item without any prior notification that doing so was forbidden.[73]

Such unfettered power of prior restraint constitutes the most sweeping device for repressing expression. Everything that counts against the other devices counts against it as well. Moreover, use of prior restraint only as a means of enforcing statutorily defined restrictions upon expression, by and large, would be equally unacceptable. Such restrictions in most instances take the form of other per se violations of the First Amendment, namely, sedition, obscenity, or censorship laws, and the like. If an end cannot be justified, then neither can the means to it.

Like censorship, however, prior restraints appear justifiable in one highly restricted circumstance. Where the performance of certain acts of expression will beyond a reasonable doubt create substantial risk of serious imminent harm to persons or property, then a government may justifiably impose prior restraints. For example, suppose someone plans to write an article disclosing the names of the dozen most reliable underworld informers. Governmental authorities would be justified in preventing its publication. To cite another example proposed by Archibald Cox, no newspaper during World War II would have had a right under the First Amendment to publish, for Nazi eyes, that because of the cryptographic work at Bletchley, British authorities were reading the orders of the Nazi high command.[74]

In the above kind of circumstance the connection between expression and universally acknowledged serious harm is so close that one can delegate authority to impose prior restraints without fear that doing so opens the door to all-out measures for thought control. The requirement that governmental authorities satisfy a stringent standard of proof beyond a reasonable doubt before securing authorization for prior restraints assures their infrequent application.[75] Moreover, substantial risk of imminent serious harm to person or property constitutes a stable terrain on which to draw the dividing line between acceptable and unacceptable grounds for imposing them. That is to say, the analogy, for legal purposes, between these and other kinds of harms generally tends to be uncompelling.[76] Characterization of prior restraint as a per se violation of the First Amendment thus involves conceiving of its unjustifiablity as almost, but not quite, absolute.

5. *Penalization.* Governmental authorities at times seek to control thought not only by attaching criminal sanctions to acts of expression, but also by penalizing individuals who adhere to certain beliefs, whether they express them or not. I use the term "penalization" to refer to such endeavors. In the recent past penalization most frequently has taken the form of declaring adherents of unpopular beliefs ineligible for benefits that accrue to everyone else as a matter of course. For example, section 9(h) of the Taft-Hartley Act provided that no labor organization could obtain the benefits of the National Labor Relations Act unless it filed with the National Labor Relations Board an annual affidavit, in which each officer of the organization swore that he or she was not a Communist and did not believe in, support, or belong to any organization that advocates overthrow of the United States government by force or other illegal methods.[77]

Other federal laws or actions of federal officials have made

belief in the desirability of overthrowing the United States government by force a ground for not granting a radio operator's
license, not granting a passport, and taking away accumulated
social security benefits.[78] On the state level, adherence to such
beliefs has been grounds for denying admission to the bar and
for exclusion from eligibility for a veteran's property tax exemption.[79]
Penalization also may proceed by imposing burdens upon adherents
of disfavored viewpoints from which others are normally immune.
Most often this takes the form of harassment by law enforcement
officials or administrative agencies.[80]

The case against penalization, like that against the other per se
violations so far considered, follows directly from Mill's argument
in chapter two of *On Liberty*. Penalization only makes sense as a
deterrent against widespread acceptance of beliefs deemed undesirable. But who should be authorized to make this determination?
Again, given the inherent fallibility of human beings, vesting such
authority in public officials would be a grave mistake. The consequences of doing so almost certainly would be far worse than
those of not doing so.

In most instances one can determine with relatively little difficulty
whether people have been penalized for adherence to certain
beliefs. Any law or administrative decree that explicitly makes
such adherence a basis for the denial of generally available benefits
clearly constitutes penalization. So also does the imposition of
burdens normally not placed upon others. Legislators and admin-
istrators, however, sometimes employ penalization surreptitiously.
That is to say, they institute measures intended to penalize those
who adhere to certain beliefs without making such adherence
explicit grounds for imposing burdens or denying benefits. These
cases often present very difficult problems of proof. It would seem,
however, that one may say that penalization obtains wherever
belief that a measure will have the effect of penalizing adherents
of certain beliefs can be imputed constructively to a legal rulemaker.
That is, if any reasonable lawmaker would have known that certain
legislation imposes a special burden upon those who accept a
particular viewpoint, or deprives such individuals of a generally
available benefit, then the legislation constitutes an instance of
penalization. In deciding whether to impute the above belief
constructively to a lawmaker, it is entirely appropriate for courts
to examine the totality of circumstances surrounding adoption of
the measure at issue.

Problems of a substantially more difficult nature arise, however, in cases where the benefit denied to an adherent of some unpopular belief is not one to which he or she would otherwise be entitled, for example, an academic position. Such cases present the general problems of proof common to all cases of alleged discrimination. I have no new insight on this vexing matter. Clearly some middle ground must be found between categorically denying or categorically accepting an allegation of discrimination on its face. Some refinement of current procedures under federal and state civil rights legislation or under nongovernmental guidelines, such as those developed by the American Association of University Professors, is probably the best one can hope for in this regard.[81]

6. *Regimentation.* The sixth per se category, regimentation, differs from the others considered thus far in pertaining not to legal prohibitions, but rather to legal requirements. Regimentation is the coercive exercise of governmental power to secure outward expression of support for certain attitudes and beliefs. It involves creating an appearance as a necessary first step in transforming that appearance to reality. Regimentation thus proceeds on the theory that compelling outward expression of governmentally favored doctrines will create the best climate for them genuinely to take root. As such, it clearly contravenes Mill's basic ideas in chapter three of *On Liberty.* Enacting statutes whose enforcement would constitute regimentation involves a deliberate choice to stifle individuality.

In the United States regimentation primarily has taken two forms; compulsory professions of support, such as saluting the flag, and loyalty oaths. Under extremely totalitarian regimes, regimentation at times has involved compulsory attendance at political rallies and indoctrination lectures. In *West Virginia State Board of Education* v. *Barnette* the Supreme Court held compulsory flag salute laws to violate the First Amendment. Justice Jackson concluded the majority opinion in this case with the following unequivocal statement that strongly suggests the present analysis of regimentation:

If there is any fixed star in our constitutional constellation, it is that no official, high or petty, can prescribe what shall be orthodox in politics, nationalism, religion, or other matters of opinion or force citizens to confess by word or act to their faith therein. If there are any circumstances which permit an exception they do not now occur to us.[82]

The Court has not taken as forthright a position in connection with loyalty oaths. Nonetheless, as a cumulative result of its various decisions with regard to them, the imposition of meaningful loyalty oaths on both federal and state levels has become virtually impossible.[83] The Court thus appears especially hostile to regimentation.

7. *Vagueness and Overbreadth.* The seventh type of per se violation, vagueness and overbreadth, differs from the previous six in not being independently definable. That is to say, a general characterization of vagueness and overbreadth must refer to the other per se violations. Regarding a law as impermissibly vague involves judging it too vague. Likewise, an impermissibly overly broad law is one deemed too broad. But too vague or too broad by what standard? The other six kinds of per se violations supply an answer to these questions. A statute regulating expression is impermissibly vague when its range of application has such uncertainty that, under a reasonable interpretation, the statute tacitly confers powers upon governmental officials that they would have explicitly under statutes falling into one or more of the categories of per se violations. Analogously, an impermissibly overbroad statute regulating expression has such a broad sweep as to vest in public officials the same powers they would have directly under sedition, obscenity, censorship laws and the like.

The case against vague and overbroad laws is thus evident. They make possible precisely the same kinds of repression associated with the other six kinds of per se violations. Justice Stewart stated the point well in *Cramp* v. *Board of Public Instruction*, a case in which the Court held unconstitutionally vague a Florida statute requiring state employees to take an oath that included the language, "I have not and will not lend aid, support, advice, counsel, or influence to the Communist Party."[84]

While it is perhaps fanciful to suppose that a perjury prosecution would ever be instituted for past conduct of the kind suggested, it requires no strain of the imagination to envision the possibility of prosecution for other types of equally guiltless knowing behavior. It would be blinking reality not to acknowledge that there are some among us always ready to affix a Communist label upon those whose ideas they violently oppose. And experience teaches that prosecutors too are human.[85]

The Court has frequently employed reasoning similar to that

of Justice Stewart's in other cases besides those involving loyalty oaths. One often finds it asserted that when dealing with breach of the peace statutes, crowd control laws, and permit requirements for demonstrations and parades, the Court employs a principle to the effect that reasonable limitations upon time, place, and manner of expression do not violate the First Amendment.[86] As stated, however, this principle is too indefinite for clear understanding as long as the criteria of reasonableness remain unexplicated. A close look at time, place, and manner cases strongly suggests that considerations of vagueness and overbreadth constitute such criteria. That is, the Court looks primarily to vagueness or overbreadth in order to determine whether or not a statute unreasonably limits expression with respect to time, place, and manner.[87] Indeed, such an approach has become so deeply entrenched that one might well restate Justice Holmes's famous dictum thusly: "the most stringent protection of free speech would not protect a man in falsely shouting fire in a crowded theatre and causing a panic," but, it would prevent the state from doing so by way of vague or overbroad laws.

Some Hard Cases

The preceding discussion should suffice both to identify the seven categories of per se violations and to establish that any governmental act classifiable as one or more of them infringes upon the First Amendment. No argument has yet been offered, however, to show that infringement of rights under the First Amendment obtains only if one or more of the per se violations has taken place. In other words, the analysis thus far establishes the occurrence of a per se violation as sufficient but not as necessary for identifying transgressions of the First Amendment.

Unfortunately, this latter point is much more difficult to demonstrate. Indeed, one cannot do so by way of a relatively compact argument, but only through inductive means. That is, an analysis that takes the occurrence of one or more of the seven per se violations as necessary for transgressing the First Amendment will appear plausible only if it seems convincing when applied over a broad range of specific cases. If the analysis accounts for one's most firmly settled convictions about freedom of expression and seems genuinely helpful in resolving troublesome cases, then to that extent the criteria it posits for First Amendment adjudication stand vindicated. At least they so stand until one comes to regard them as inadequate to deal with new difficult circumstances. Accordingly, claims of comprehensiveness for the foregoing account can be made credible only by applying it to diverse cases in a way that leads one to determinate and plausible conclusions about them. With such an end in view this section treats a number of recent controversies involving freedom of expression that for one reason or another have been widely regarded as problematic.

TOLERATING THE INTOLERANT

Must groups who explicitly advocate the violation of basic liberties be allowed the right to express their opinions? Such a question, I think, poses an emotional rather than an analytical dilemma. The dilemma is emotional because it pits justifiable hatred of the ideas such groups represent—not to mention horror at the prospect of their realization—against respect for free speech. It does not, however, pose an analytical dilemma, for the basic principles of free expression apply to this circumstance straightforwardly. A government could forbid such groups from expressing their views only by way of sedition laws, censorship laws, prior restraints, or statutes that are unacceptably vague or overbroad. In short, any conceivable basis in law for silencing them would appear to constitute a per se violation of the First Amendment.

The controversy in late 1976 over a threatened demonstration by a group of Nazis in the predominately Jewish Chicago suburb of Skokie illustrates this point. A Nazi group, which calls itself the National Socialist Party, planned a series of demonstrations in Jewish communities, including Skokie. The Nazis were denied permission to demonstrate in a Skokie park because of a local park district ordinance requiring them to obtain $350,000 in liability and property damage insurance. They then planned a demonstration in the village for May 1, 1977, to protest the park district ordinance. On March 20 the Nazis notified the Skokie police chief of their plans and assured him that the demonstration would be brief, peaceful, and orderly. News of the planned demonstration predictably caused considerable agitation in Skokie as well as in the general Chicago area. Because of this sentiment the village attempted to prevent the demonstration. It first obtained a preliminary injunction in state court and then on May 2, 1977, enacted three separate ordinances.

The first of these, #994, was a comprehensive permit system for all parades or public assemblies of more than fifty persons anywhere within Skokie. It required all permit applicants to obtain $300,000 in liability insurance and $50,000 in property damage insurance. The other two ordinances, #995 and #996, were both criminal measures: #995 prohibited the dissemination of material that incites racial or religious hatred, with intent to incite such hatred; #996 prohibited public demonstrations by members of political parties while wearing military-style uniforms. These ordinances were also enforced through the permit mechanism of #994, which also required that a permit be denied to public assemblies that engage in activity prohibited by #995 or #996.[88]

All three of the above ordinances clearly constitute per se violations of the First Amendment. Ordinances #995 and #996 are both unacceptably vague. They in effect grant the village precisely the same powers it would have explicitly under sedition or censorship laws. Insofar as #994 authorizes denial of permits based upon #995 or #996, it too has the same defects. Had any of these statutes been enacted under ordinary conditions their incompatibility with the First Amendment in all likelihood would not have been contested by any responsible person. Skokie's response to the Nazis was not unusually clumsy. That is to say, the Nazi demonstration simply could not have been prevented in any way consistent with the First Amendment. All other efforts in this regard would have had essentially the same objectionable character as the Skokie ordinances.

At times one finds it suggested that under circumstances such as those in Skokie, standing upon principle constitutes a form of misguided self-righteousness.[89] According to this view, when faced with a group like the Nazis a governmental body should simply silence them and worry later about the justification for doing so. It seems extraordinary, however, that anyone paying serious attention to the consequences of this proposal could genuinely endorse it. How does one tell which groups are "like the Nazis?" Everyone from vendors of "hardcore pornography" to the government of the state of Israel has been so denounced.[90] One cannot respond by dismissing such denunciations as frivolous, for this simply compounds the problem. How can situations be prevented where governmental officials might give effect to them, their frivolousness notwithstanding? Obviously it will not do to answer this latter question by suggesting that positions of governmental power should be occupied only by people who happen to agree with oneself. In his dissent from a decision by the New York Court of Appeals upholding the conviction of Benjamin Gitlow under the state's Criminal Anarchy Act, Justice Pound made the following remark, which, perhaps more than any other single statement, illustrates the reason for acknowledging a right of the Nazis to demonstrate in Skokie: "Although the defendant may be the worst of men . . . the rights of the best of men are secure only as the rights of the vilest and most abhorent are protected."[91]

DANGEROUS INFORMATION

In 1979 *The Progressive*, a small-circulation, monthly periodical dealing with political and social issues, entered into final preparation for publishing an article by freelance journalist Howard Morland about the design and manufacture of hydrogen bombs. Morland's article contained no officially classified information whatsoever, but rather was based upon what he had been able to surmise from interviews and general reading. Morland himself was not a trained scientist, having had only a few college physics courses. Before publishing his article, the editors of *The Progressive* sent it to a number of reviewers for prepublication editorial comments. One of the reviewers, unbeknownst to the editors of *The Progressive*, passed it on to an M.I.T. physics professor, who in turn sent it to the U.S. Department of Energy. Shortly thereafter government attorneys filed a motion in federal court to enjoin publication of the article as a breach of national security, citing as the legal basis for such an injunction the Atomic Energy Act, which states in part that

the term "restricted data" means all data concerning (1) design, manufacture, or utilization of atomic weapons; (2) the production of special nuclear material; or (3) the use of special nuclear material in the production of energy, but shall not include data declassified or removed from the restricted data category.[92]

A federal district court judge granted a preliminary injunction barring publication of the article. Eventually, however, the government lost interest in prosecuting the case because it was shown that most of the data Morland relied upon not only had been declassified by officials at the Los Alamos Research Laboratory many years earlier, but also was easily obtainable in declassified government reports, some of which could be borrowed from the Los Alamos Public Library.[93]

This case, like that of the Nazi march in Skokie, seems to raise emotional rather than analytical problems. Obviously one shudders at the prospect of a terrorist organization some day constructing a thermonuclear device. The thought that such an organization could succeed in doing so partly because of information obtained from a particular magazine article prompts an almost instinctive emotional response to concur in its suppression. But can one rationally defend this response? The definition of restricted data cited above, which served as legal authority for the injunction, is so manifestly overbroad one wonders what writings or utterances on the subject of nuclear energy lie outside its reach. Notice that the definition covers *all* data whether classified or not.[94] When a governmental body classifies information it limits the disclosure of information already in its possession. The phrase "restricted data" in the Atomic Energy Act applies not only to such data but also to information in private hands, which the government does not yet posssess. This means that restricted data includes virtually any statement anyone might ever happen to make on the subject of nuclear energy.

Could a narrower definition be drafted which avoids overbreadth problems? Such a definition would have to distinguish dangerous, or potentially dangerous, information from innocuous facts. It seems doubtful, however, that this could be accomplished without using statutory language that explicitly defines "restricted data" to comprise "dangerous" or "potentially dangerous" information relating to nuclear energy. Such a definition would be no less objectionable than the current one in the Atomic Energy Act. It would be as vague as the other is overbroad. Again, as in the case of the Nazi march, the above kind of reasoning at times is impatiently dismissed as excessively legalistic. But the maxim "suppress now and justify later" has no more to commend itself here than elsewhere.

Commentators on the government's case against *The Progressive* have concentrated almost exclusively upon the social risks associated with publishing Morland's article. Legislative provisions, such as the definition of restricted data in the Atomic Energy Act, also pose grave dangers, which tend to be overlooked. To remove as broad a subject as nuclear energy from the realm of public debate creates the very substantial risk that momentous decisions about such matters as whether to develop a major new weapons system or nuclear reactor will be made by a relatively small group of government officials whose members concur in their fundamental assumptions. Under such circumstances it becomes highly likely that the group will disregard or not give adequate weight to points of view and concerns at odds with its own basic orientation. Indeed, something very much like this appears to have occurred during the 1950s and 1960s with respect to the development of nuclear power plants.[95] To prevent important technical information from falling into the wrong hands a government can classify information rather than utilize sweeping provisions, such as the definition of restricted data in the Atomic Energy Act.[96] No comparable protection exists, however, to ensure that government officials who cut off free debate on policy issues concerning nuclear energy will take all the relevant factors into account. Stating the problem in its starkest terms, we run the risk of being immolated in a nuclear holocaust either through the actions of terrorists or as an ultimate consequence of major errors in judgment by our own government. The probability of the latter is at least as great as, and probably greater than, that of the former. This unsettling truth strongly suggests that we should retain our commitment to the principles of free expression even in cases involving potentially dangerous information, such as Howard Morland's description of hydrogen bomb technology in *The Progressive*.

SYMBOLIC SPEECH

As noted at the outset of this book, interpreting the First Amendment involves for the most part analyzing the word "freedom" in the phrases freedom of speech and freedom of the press.[97] But what does "speech" mean for purposes of First Amendment adjudication? One can express attitudes and beliefs through countless other means besides speech in the sense of vocalization or writing. People can, for example, express their feelings of patriotism by displaying the flag, parading on the Fourth of July, and buying war bonds. But they can do so as well by pummeling individuals they regard as unpatriotic. Which modes of expression are protected by the First Amendment and which are not?

The Supreme Court's answer to this question has little systematic basis. The primary rule appears to be that acts of expression employing means other than vocalization or writing may be regulated for the sake of "substantial governmental interests."[98] Unfortunately, however, case law has done little to resolve the inherent vagueness of this latter phrase.

In *U.S.* v. *O'Brien* the Court held that a 1965 amendment to the Universal Military Service and Training Act, which made it a felony to knowingly mutilate, destroy, or burn a draft card, satisfied the substantial governmental interest standard.[99] Other than making some general remarks about how draft cards facilitate a selective service system, however, the Court said little about why the 1965 amendment served purposes of such importance as to override concern for freedom of expression.[100] Indeed, the evidence appears to be that no serious effort had ever been made to enforce the rule requiring a person to carry his draft card with him at all times. Not only that, Congress passed the 1965 amendment in great haste and on its own initiative; there was no testimony whatsoever from representatives of the Selective Service Commission indicating a need for such legislation.[101]

A year after the *O'Brien* decision, the Court struck down as unconstitutional in *Tinker* v. *Des Moines* a rule imposed by principals of the Des Moines public schools that forbade wearing black armbands in class indicating opposition to the Vietnam War.[102] In so ruling the Court refused to take at face value the proffered justification for the rule as a reasonable means of maintaining school discipline. In this case then the Supreme Court appeared willing to place the regulation at issue under substantially more vigorous scrutiny than in the *O'Brien* case. In all likelihood the Court was correct in asserting that school authorities could maintain effective discipline without the ban on armbands. Hence, the ban hardly seems to have served any compelling needs. But the reasons cited in *O'Brien* for the rule against burning draft cards do not appear much stronger.

How then does one compare the interests served respectively by the regulations at issue in *O'Brien* and *Tinker* for degree of "substantiality"? It would seem that from the standpoint of our theory of First Amendment adjudication this is the wrong question altogether. Enunciating two separate standards of review for acts of expression as did the Court, depending upon whether they involved vocalization or writing on the one hand, or conduct on the other, creates major analytical problems. Such an approach inevitably leads to the use of notions like "substantial governmental interest" with their probably ineliminable vagueness. One deals with the problem more cogently by making no distinctions whatsoever between acts of expression on the basis of how they convey expressive content, and by asking of any regulations upon such acts whether they constitute per se violations. If so, then an infringement of the First Amendment has occurred. Otherwise it has not.

How would the *Tinker* and *O'Brien* cases come out if analyzed in this way? The restriction in *Tinker* clearly amounted to censorship. As part of the case record, evidently the principals of the Des Moines public schools admitted that their rule against wearing armbands was not a general dress code regulation, but rather it specifically endeavored to prevent protest against the Vietnam War.[103] The rule thus made a precisely identified act of expression illegal and thereby constituted a per se violation of the First Amendment. That the forbidden act involved neither vocalization nor writing is irrelevant.

The *O'Brien* case, however, presents a more difficult problem for analysis. On the one hand, common sense indicates (at least to me) that the 1965 amendment to the Universal Military Service and Training Act, which made intentional destruction of one's draft card a felony, was motivated by vindictiveness toward those who opposed the Vietnam War or by a desire to suppress their opposition to it. The amendment thus sprung from attitudes that clearly run counter to the principles of free expression enunciated in Mill's *On Liberty*. Despite this fact, however, the amendment is not readily classifiable as either a sedition law, censorship law, penalization measure, unacceptably overbroad measure, or the like. That is, it does not appear to fall into any of the seven proscribed categories of per se violations.

But why should one regard this as troublesome? Such a question relates back to the basic problem about constitutional adjudication under the Bill of Rights discussed in Chapter One, namely, what distinguishes constitutional Bill of Rights cases, appropriately re-solvable by courts, from policy issues within the legislative province? The answer to this question is that the former, unlike the latter, concern application to particular circumstances of fundamental rights whose nature and scope are not subject to determination by the majority will through the legislative process. This answer, however, inevitably raises the further question of whether one can enunciate a notion of such rights that at one and the same time is philosophically plausible and sufficiently precise for use in constitutional adjudication. If not, then judicial decisions with respect to fundamental rights amount to nothing more than policy decisions of precisely the same type as those resolved by legislatures, albeit in different terminology.

It would seem that the problem with the statutory provision in O'Brien pertains to the motivation behind it which raises the question of whether the Court could evaluate congressional motives in a case such as this without usurping the primary legislative role. As mentioned earlier, in some situations one may constructively impute a legislative motive to penalize. Such may be done where, in light of the surrounding circumstances, reasonable legislators would have known that a given measures has the effect of imposing special burdens upon or takes away generally available benefits from the adherents to certain viewpoints.[104] But the statutory provision at issue in O'Brien cannot clearly be thought of in this way.

Could judicial inquiry into legislative motivation go beyond a constructive imputation without encroachng upon legitimate legislative authority? Unfortunately, in all likelihood this is not possible. As noted earlier, hypotheses about the purposes behind a statute tend to be grossly underdetermined by statutory language. In other words, notorious uncertainty attends judgments about legislative motivation. According courts the general authority to review statutes under the First Amendment on the basis of the underlying motivation for enacting them would result in blurring the line of demarcation between courts and legislatures to such an extent as to raise questions about the legitimacy of judicial review under the Bill of Rights.

When brought to bear upon the O'Brien case, these systemic considerations would appear to suggest that the Supreme Court decided correctly in upholding the 1965 amendment, although for the wrong reasons. Predictably, such a conclusion leaves one not entirely happy. It entails the constitutionality of a clearly punitive law and the concomitant absence of a valid constitutional claim on the part of individuals punished under it. As Melville's novel Billy Budd dramatically illustrates, however, this is not the only jurisprudential matter where emotions must give way to the cold demands of intellect. Just as Captain Vere could not have pardoned Billy Budd consistently with a conception of his role as an officer that the reader must deem legitimate, so also it would seem that the justices of the Supreme Court could not have responsibly voided O'Brien's conviction on First Amendment grounds. Such a conclusion seems unavoidable.

COMMERCIAL SPEECH

In *Valentine* v. *Chrestenson*, a 1942 case, the Supreme Court held that speech with a primarily commercial purpose has no protection whatsoever under the First Amendment.[105] The rule in *Valentine* remained reasonably firm as First Amendment doctrine until the mid-1970s.[106] During the period of 1974–76, however, in successive judgments the Court intimated the *Valentine* rule may not be absolute, then authoritatively declared it not to be so, and finally overruled *Valentine* altogether in the case of *Virginia Board of Pharmacists* v. *Virginia Consumer Council*.[107] The issue in this case was whether a Virginia statute declaring it unprofessional conduct for a licensed pharmacist to advertise the price of prescription drugs violated the First Amendment.[108] In striking down the statute with only one dissenting vote, the Court noted several respects in which a rule withholding protection of the First Amendment from acts of expression motivated by economic interest is over-broad.[109] Such a rule applies, for example, to the parties in labor disputes, and even worse, gives a government blanket authority to censor myriad information relating to commercial matters of general public interest.[110]

The Court, however, declined to state explicitly that commercial speech must be accorded exactly the same degree of protection under the First Amendment as the expression of attitudes and beliefs in other contexts, such as literary endeavor or political debate. In this regard Justice Blackmun, writing for the majority, said,

In concluding that commercial speech, like other varieties, is protected, we of course do not hold that it can never be regulated in any way. Some forms of commercial speech regulation are surely permissable. We mention a few only to make clear that they are not before us and therefore not foreclosed by this case.[111]

Justice Blackmun then went on to cite, as examples of justifiable limitations upon commercial speech, time, place, and manner restrictions, rules against false or deceptive advertising, and rules that forbid advertisements proposing illegal transactions.[112] The passages cited from the majority opinion thus leave open the question of how much commercial speech is protected by the First Amendment. Consistent with these passages the Court could either accord it exactly similar treatment to other kinds of speech or deal with it somewhat differently. The issue depends upon precisely what specific kinds of restrictions the Court would countenance under Justice Blackmun's three broad categories.

The unresolved issue in the *Virginia Pharmacy Board* decision has engendered a voluminous commentary, which was initiated in the decision itself by way of concurring opinions on the part of Chief Justice Burger and Justice Stewart. The theory of First Amendment adjudication outlined in this chapter, however, suggests a straightforwardly affirmative answer to the question of whether an identical standard should apply in cases involving commercial speech as in those that involve literature or politics. According to this approach, regardless of context, one deals with First Amendment issues by asking whether or not a per se violation has occurred. If not, then the law or other governmental action in controversy withstands scrutiny under the First Amendment. If there was such a violation, then it does not.

The only possible basis for criticising this approach would be belief that it fails to account for firm intuitions one might have about important kinds of circumstances involving the regulation of commercial speech. Such a belief, however, appears unwarranted. That is, treating commercial speech on an exact par, from the standpoint of the First Amendment, with speech concerning other subjects does not necessitate an absurdly latitudinarian view at odds with current practice. The belief that it does tends to involve substantial mistakes with respect to the theory of First Amendment adjudication. The following passage from Justice Stewart's concurring opinion in *Virginia Pharmacy Board* illustrates this point.

Today the Court ends the anomalous situation created by Chrestensen and holds that a communication which does no more than propose a commercial transaction is not "wholly outside the protection of the First Amendment" . . . . But since it is a cardinal principle of the First Amendment that "government has no power to restrict expression because of its message, its ideas, its subject matter, or its content," the Court's decision calls into immediate question the constitutional legitimacy of every state and federal law regulating false or deceptive advertising. I write separately to explain why I think today's decision does not preclude such governmental regulation.[113]

Justice Stewart takes as a "cardinal principle" of the First

Amendment that "government has no power to restrict expression because of its message, its ideas, its subject matter, or its content." Having stated so broad a principle he then sees a need to show how the decision in *Virginia Pharmacy Board* does not rule out regulation of false and deceptive advertising. Justice Stewart then makes some curious remarks in this regard. He draws an analogy between the pertinent issues of free expression posed by regulation of advertising and related problems that arise when dealing with both libel law and cases under the National Labor Relations Act, which involve possibly coercive statements by employers in the context of representation elections.[114] Justice Stewart thus maintains that regulation of false and deceptive advertising resembles regulation of speech in other circumstances that constitute exceptions to the sweeping principle *he laid down as absolute* at the outset of his opinion. In short, he contradicts himself.

The problem here stems from a common mistake, which, as noted earlier, pervades theories of First Amendment adjudication, namely, that the basic principles of free expression can be boiled down to a succinct formula for direct application in specific cases. Justice Stewart enunciated a principle of such breadth that it rules out regulation of false and deceptive advertising as violative of the First Amendment. His principle, however, also rules out libel law and regulation pertaining to remarks by employers in NLRB representation elections, not to mention restrictions upon shouting fire in a crowded theatre.[115]

A more sensible view would have it that while most regulation of false and deceptive advertising does not violate the First Amendment, some such regulation does. The standard for distinguishing permissable from impermisable restrictions in this domain should be the per se violations. That is, restrictions upon advertising which amount to censorship or which employ vague language, or which are couched in overbroad terms, and so forth, violate the First Amendment. Those which cannot be so categorized withstand constitutional review. Such an approach appears to achieve a reasonably happy reconciliation of theoretical views and deeply entrenched intuitions about justifiable restrictions upon advertising.

"EQUAL TIME FOR CREATIONISM"

In the 1968 case of *Epperson* v. *Arkansas* the Supreme Court overturned an Arkansas statute that forbade presentation of the theory of evolution in primary and secondary public schools.[116]

Thirteen years later, in 1981, the Arkansas legislature passed another law on the subject, this time requiring that public school teachers who discuss evolution in the classroom must also devote "equal time" to discussing the idea of divine creation.[117] Fundamentalist religious groups are now pressing vigorously for similar laws throughout the United States and in some instances have succeeded on the local level. On January 5, 1982, however, U.S. District Court Judge William R. Overton declared the Arkansas equal time for creationism law unconstitutional.[118] Judge Overton based his decision upon a relatively straightforward application of the Supreme Court's approach in *Epperson v. Arkansas.*

The law that forbade teaching the theory of evolution and that was struck down by the Court in *Epperson* was a paradigm case of censorship. The Supreme Court, however, did not cite this consideration as the basis for its decision. Rather, it held that the law violated the Establishment Clause of the First Amendment, which requires separation of church and state. The law declared unconstitutional in *Epperson* made no mention whatsoever of any religion, but simply forbade teaching a scientific theory that offended some influential religious groups. Judge Overton reasoned, in effect, that if such a law violates the Establishment Clause, then it would appear that so also must "equal time for creationism" statutes, which *explicitly require* teaching a religious doctrine, or more precisely, require that it be taught as a condition of the right to do other teaching. Judge Overton thus overturned the Arkansas statute without even mentioning any of the issues it raises with respect to freedom of expression.

In virtue, then, of their clearly religious character, "equal time for creationism" statutes do not appear to raise deeply vexing problems for constitutional analysis. Nonetheless, consideration of such statutes suggests another issue about freedom of expression that, while not pertaining to them directly, is still genuinely difficult. Laws that explicitly forbid the teaching of particular viewpoints in public schools smack of censorship. By the same token, laws expressly requiring the inclusion of certain viewpoints have an air of regimentation about them—that is, they would appear to create, so to speak, a captive audience. But how does one distinguish censorship and regimentation from the legitimate exercise of pedagogic discretion by school authorities, including teachers? Planning a curriculum or course syllabus necessarily involves a process of inclusion and exclusion.

One might quite naturally respond to this query by saying that it all depends upon motivation. That is, we have legitimate exercise of pedagogic discretion whenever school authorities engage in course planning with genuine educational concerns in mind. On the other hand, as soon as they use their discretion for the purpose of grinding doctrinal axes, then we no longer have education, but constitutionally proscribed indoctrination.

Such a response, while theoretically sound, in all likelihood cannot be articulated with sufficient precision for use in constitutional adjudication. What makes motivation genuinely educational? Mill's account of individuality in chapter three of *On Liberty* supplies guidance with respect to this question. That is, the fostering of individuality, as understood by Mill, may be considered the basic aim of primary and secondary education.[119] Unfortunately, however, few issues are more inherently controversial than that of which educational approaches best achieve this aim. Thus, it simply would not work for courts to take as their rule for adjudication that school authorities will be deemed to have engaged in censorship and regimentation whenever their decisions about curricular matters do not serve to foster the individuality of pupils. Application of such a rule would put judges squarely in the place of educators. It appears then that except for a few exceptional circumstances, judges must decline to review decisions by school authorities with regard to such matters as course planning and book selection.[120] Such an approach regrettably leaves wide latitude for abuse, but there seems to be no viable alternative.

One must sharply distinguish, however, curricular decisions by school personnel from similar decisions by state legislatures. None of the problems attending judicial scrutiny of the former attend review of the latter. Indeed, the two cases appear to require exactly reverse treatment. In other words, while curricular decisions by school authorities should be accorded a strong presumption of justifiability from the standpoint of the First Amendment, courts should apply the exact reverse presumption in evaluating such decisions when they emanate from a state legislature. State legislatures have neither direct responsibility for, concern with, nor experience in curricular matters. Accordingly, one can presume their forays into this area stem not from genuine educational concerns, but rather, from illegitimate motives, such as the desire to censor or regiment.

Judged by this standard, equal time for creationism statutes clearly violate the First Amendment. Insofar as they require the teaching of one position as a condition of teaching others they constitute a form of regimentation. This tends to be obscured because the term "equal time" suggests a misleading parallel with the equal time provision of the Communications Act of 1934, which applies to candidates for political office. No reason exists for thinking that the same standards should apply in classroom situations as in a form of regulated rivalry such as democratic elections for political office. The equal time provision with respect to the latter serves primarily as a means of maintaining political stability. That is, losers in a political contest accept defeat more readily if they regard as fair the general rules under which it took place. Such a consideration hardly applies in educational contexts.

Moreover, the Communications Act equal time rule is really a misnomer insofar as it does not assure candidates equal air time, but rather only equal access to it.[121] The rule simply requires that if stations sell air time to a bonafide candidate, they may not decline to sell comparable air time to other bonafide candidates for the same office. It does not require stations to provide political candidates a forum. By contrast, the Arkansas equal time for creationism statute mandates that if a teacher lectures on the theory of evolution then he or she must provide a forum for adherents of belief in divine creation. This difference is crucial. Since broadcasters need not provide a forum for political candidates, one seldom confronts the problem of *who* should get equal time. The Arkansas statute, however, faces intractable problems in this regard. Suppose I have my own personal theory of the origin of species— they neither evolved through natural selection nor were created by God, but rather they constitute the visible manifestations of platonic eternal essences. Am I entitled to equal time? If not, why not? It will not do to dismiss my hypothesis as "unscientific." According to spokespersons for the creationist cause, it was precisely such an attitude of the scientific community toward their view that, in large part, stimulated their drive for a statutory guarantee of a place for creationism in public school science courses.[122]

Thus, since the Arkansas law only requires the teaching of creationism, and not of other theories, in the event that teachers discuss the theory of evoution, it counts as a form of regimentation. That it constitutes a slightly attenuated form, insofar as the requirement to teach creationsim is only triggered by the presentation of a specific other viewpoint, does not matter. In antitrust law one kind of per se violation is the tying arrangement. This exists under certain circumstances where the opportunity to do business with a seller is made conditional upon doing other business with that same seller.[123] One can think of equal time for creationism statutes metaphorically as a kind of unconstitutional tying arrangement that ties the right to speak about a given matter to a requirement that one express views one may not accept.

Summary

In virtue of Mill's arguments in chapters two and three of *On Liberty*, the right to freedom of expression fulfills the first condition that a right deemed fundamental must satisfy. That is, both Millian arguments would receive the unanimous assent of rational contractors under a veil of ignorance. The second condition of fundamental rights requires that they be specifiable with sufficient precision so that one can identify violations with relative clarity over a wide range of cases. Unfortunately, however, Mill's arguments resist distillation into a concise formula applicable in specific instances. For this reason, the notion of per se violations of the right to freedom of expression was introduced. Each category of per se violation acquires its status as such because the statutes or governmental acts falling under it inherently conflict with the underlying philosophy of free expression as enunciated by Mill. Since the categories admit of relatively precise characterization, they make it possible to apply the Millian philosophy in a reliable and systematic way to particular circumstances.

The preceding discussion obviously did not treat every important First Amendment issue. Nonetheless, it is hoped that it covered a sufficiently wide range to make reasonably clear how their analysis in terms of the notion of per se violations should work. I think I may claim intellectual coherence and relative precision as virtues of this analysis. Of course, whether it renders conclusions on the specific matters discussed that accord with one's considered judgments in reflection equilibrium is a question for each reader himself or herself to decide.

III

Freedom of the Press

The First Amendment explicitly guarantees not only free speech but also freedom of the press. Does the theory advanced in Chapter Two constitute a sound framework for determining what counts as a violation of the latter as well as of the former right? One would have to answer this question negatively under two circumstances. First, a person who becomes convinced that the First Amendment accords the press rights beyond those held by individuals would have to concede that the seven per se violations alone do not provide guidance in making the content of the right to freedom of expression more determinate. Second, one might conclude that the press holds no distinctive First Amendment rights, and yet still refuse to believe that all such rights can be accounted for simply in terms of the per se violations. One might think that the rights unaccounted for include several that the press deems especially significant. In this chapter I will suggest that these positions are unwarranted and that the theory of the previous chapter provides substantial guidance in thinking about a broad range of First Amendment issues concerning the press.

The Major Questions

While many Supreme Court decisions in one way or another raise questions about freedom of the press, none has ever stated cat-

76

egorically whether or not the press has as a matter of basic constitutional principle independent First Amendment rights not held by individuals. Two relatively early and important cases in the 1930s, *Near v. Minnesota* and *Grosjean v. American Press Co.*, involved media organizations. But in both of them the Court struck down statutes that constituted clear per se violations of the First Amendment.[1]

In *Near v. Minnesota* the Court invalidated a Minnesota statute that provided for the abatement, as a public nuisance, of any "malicious, scandalous, and defamatory" newspaper, magazine, or other periodical, and also of obscene periodicals. Under this statute, truth was a defense only "if published with good motives and for justifiable ends." The statute also provided for granting of temporary or permanent injunctions not only enjoining repetition of objectionable issues but also stopping the newspaper entirely.[2] In retrospect it would seem that this Minnesota statute may well have set a record for simultaneous per se violations, being at one and the same time an obscenity statute, a prior restraint law, excessively vague, and overbroad. Accordingly, *Near v. Minnesota* did not enunciate any First Amendment rights uniquely possessed by the organized communications media.

The facts of the second case, *Grosjean v. American Press Co.*, were as follows: Louisiana, while under the control of Huey Long, imposed a special 2 percent tax on the gross receipts of any newspaper in the state with a circulation of more than 20,000 per week. There were thirteen such newspapers, of which twelve were opposed to Long's regime. In contrast, most of the smaller papers supported Long. Nine of the affected newspapers brought suit in federal court to enjoin enforcement of the tax law. A permanent injunction was granted and the Supreme Court unanimously affirmed it.[3] As in *Near v. Minnesota*, however, the Court did not enunciate any special First Amendment rights of the press, but rather disposed of the *Grosjean* case by subsuming it directly under one of the per se violations, penalization. The following words from Justice Sutherland's majority opinion make this clear:

The form in which the tax is imposed is in itself suspicious. It is not measured or limited by the volume of advertisements. It is measured alone by the extent of the circulation of the publication in which the advertisements are carried, with the plain purpose of *penalizing* (my italics) the publishers and curtailing the circulation of a selected group of newspapers.[4]

Of course, the press has a strong interest in combating sedition laws, prior restraints, censorship, and the other per se violations. Many individuals have argued, however, that satisfactory resolution of a number of issues involving the press requires an expanded conception of First Amendment rights. In this regard the following four issues have been generally considered most important:

1. The law of defamation and the First Amendment: How does the First Amendment bear upon the common law of libel and slander?
2. Confidentiality privilege: Do newspersons have an immunity under the First Amendment from having to divulge their sources to law enforcement authorities?
3. Right to a media forum: Do individuals have First Amendment rights under some circumstances to present their beliefs and attitudes in specific media forums? That is, are there circumstances in which the First Amendment requires newspapers, television stations, and so forth, to allow certain individuals print space or air time? Or, to the contrary, does the First Amendment forbid any statutes that would compel media organizations at times to provide individuals a forum?
4. Right of access to information: Does the First Amendment require governments to make certain information public either as a matter of course or in response to specific requests?

This chapter will treat each of the above issues successively with the aim of showing that one can provide a plausible account of them without going beyond the notion that there are only seven per se violations of the First Amendment.

THE LAW OF DEFAMATION AND THE FIRST AMENDMENT

In the landmark case of *New York Times* v. *Sullivan,* decided in 1964, the Supreme Court came to grips for the first time with the problem of how the First Amendment bears upon the common law of defamation. *Sullivan* and the cases following in its wake have brought substantial changes in the traditional rules pertaining to this area of law. Hence, a few words by way of background about the law of defamation as it existed at the time *New York Times* v. *Sullivan* was decided are necessary.

According to the traditional common law of defamation, a plaintiff made out his or her case by establishing that the defendant intentionally communicated a statement to some third party that tended to injure the plaintiff's reputation. The defendant in turn had but two defenses, truth or privilege. That is, one could defend against a defamation suit either by convincing the trier of fact, whether judge or jury, that what one had said was true, or by establishing that one's words fell under any of a number of special circumstances included in the common law rules that exempted a person from liability for statements ordinarily considered to be defamatory.[5]

The common law of defamation differed from other comparable civil law causes of action for personal injury in two major respects. First, it did not condition liability on failure to exercise reasonable care. One was liable for a false defamatory statement regardless of how careful one may have been to establish its veracity. Second, for the most part, damages were presumed. That is, a plaintiff did not have to allege and prove injury to himself or herself as a condition of securing recovery.[6] On the other hand, these two factors, which seemingly made defamation an attractive cause of action of plaintiffs, were counterbalanced by the fact that the privileges noted above were multifarious, complicated, and tended to vary substantially from one jurisdiction to another. These countervailing factors generally ensured that lawsuits for defamation would be extremely prolonged, expensive, and uncertain as to their outcome.[7]

Writing of the common law of defamation in 1947, Chafee described it as "confused, archaic, with no relation to modern life." He complained that litigation in this area invariably degenerates into a "free-for-all [wherein] . . . the result . . . depends [solely] . . . upon whether the jury likes the plaintiff."[8] Despite its unsatisfactory character, however, or perhaps precisely because of it, the law of defamation generally was not considered a systematic threat to freedom of expression. Its absurd complexity and antiquated peculiarities tended to make the outcome of litigation so uncertain as to discourage the use or threat of defamation suits as a club with which governmental officials might bludgeon those whose opinions displeased them.[9]

Or so it seemed until the 'sixties. An advertisement placed in 1960 by supporters of Dr. Martin Luther King in the *New York Times* recounted the repressive activities of local officials in Birmingham, Alabama, with several minor inaccuracies and exaggerations. An Alabama jury awarded the Birmingham chief of police, Sullivan, who was not mentioned by name in the ad, $500,000 in damages.[10] The *Times* appealed this award, ultimately to the Supreme Court, which in 1964 overturned it in the case of *New York Times* v. *Sullivan* and in doing so introduced sweeping changes into the common law of defamation.[11] Writing for the majority, Justice Brennan declared that "Libel can claim no talismanic immunity from constitutional limitations. It must be measured by standards that satisfy the First Amendment."[12] As for these standards, the Court held that in actions for defamation brought by a public official for defamatory falsehood relating to his or her official conduct, a damage award may not be granted unless the official proves that the statement in question was made with "actual malice," that is, with knowledge of its falsity or with reckless disregard of whether it was true or false.[13] Applying this standard to the Sullivan case, the Court found that its facts did not support a finding sufficient for imposition of liability for defamation upon the *New York Times*.

The actual malice standard places a substantially heavier burden upon public officials than upon ordinary individuals as plaintiffs in actions for defamation. The Court reasoned that such was necessitated by the First Amendment because of the dangerously close parallel, illustrated emphatically by the *Sullivan* case, between a civil action for defamation by a public official arising out of comment upon his or her official conduct and a criminal prosecution for seditious libel. That is to say, the Court pointed out that in effect the traditional common law of defamation allows public officials to realize substantially the same aims through civil litigation that they might achieve through criminal prosecution if there were laws on the books that made it a crime, as in the Soviet Union, to libel or slander the state.[14] Since such laws, however, are clearly proscribed by the First Amendment, it would seem natural, so the Court reasoned, to say that any other laws that could be used for identical purposes must be placed under strict constitutional scrutiny.[15]

The Court's reasoning in *New York Times* v. *Sullivan* essentially constituted an instance of overbreadth analysis. That is to say, in effect the Court found certain aspects of the common law of defamation objectionable from a constitutional standpoint because of their overly broad sweep. These aspects would make it possible for government officials to do precisely what they would be able to accomplish under the explicit warrant of sedition laws. Accordingly, the Sullivan decision would appear consistent with the thesis that basically seven and only seven modes of governmental action constitute violations of the First Amendment.

Subsequent cases concerning the relationships between the law of defamation and the First Amendment in the wake of *New York Times* v. *Sullivan*, however, cannot be reconciled so easily with the per se analysis. In the case of *Curtis* v. *Butts*, decided in 1966, the Court extended the Sullivan actual malice standard to cover actions for defamation brought by public figures generally, that is to say, actions brought by people in the public eye, whether governmental officials or not.[16] Justice Harlan, who wrote the majority opinion, acknowledged that the analogy between civil actions for defamation and prosecutions for seditious libel does not hold when the plaintiff is a public figure other than a public official. He stated, however, that the actual malice standard should be extended nonetheless for the following two reasons: first, public interest in news stories involving nongovernmental public figures generally is no less than in stories pertaining to public officials, and second, public figures, whether governmental or not, generally have at their disposal greater means to combat the ill effects of defamation than do ordinary individuals in virtue of the greater attention paid them by the media.[17]

The above rationale marked a significant departure from the reasoning in *New York Times* v. *Sullivan*. To argue, as did Justice Harlan, that under the First Amendment the actual malice standard should be extended to nongovernmental public figures because the public generally has as much interest in such persons as it does in public officials strongly suggests a view according to which the role played by the press in keeping the public informed is so important that as a matter of basic consitutional principle the traditional common law of libel should be changed to accomodate it. That is, the reasoning that controlled in *Curtis* v. *Butts* seems to imply that the First Amendment requires certain treatment to be accorded the press that is not accorded ordinary individuals. While the rationale in *New York Times* v. *Sullivan* applies with equal cogency to cases where public officials might bring action against ordinary individuals as it does to cases where the defendant is a media concern, the *Curtis* rationale carries no such implication. Thus the *Sullivan* decision may be thought of as entirely consistent with the account of how to interpret the First Amendment set out in Chapter Two. Justice Harlan's line of reasoning in *Curtis* v. *Butts*, however, constitutes a fundamentally different approach premised upon other considerations.

It should also be noted that Justice Harlan's second reason for extending the actual malice standard to cover nongovernmental public figures is not logically independent of his first reason, but rather presupposes it. This becomes evident upon reflection as to why the comparatively favorable situation of nongovernmental public figures for minimizing damage from defamatory statements should be regarded as having any relevance at all from the standpoint of the First Amendment. One can regard it as relevant only if one first believes that the role of the press in keeping the public informed has special First Amendment significance; for given such a belief the question of how to balance the public interest in enabling the press to carry out this role against the interest of individuals in maintaining their reputations conceivably becomes constitutionally important. The point about the comparatively advantageous position of nongovernmental public figures for mitigating damages from defamatory statements becomes pertinent insofar as it suggests that when such individuals are plaintiffs in defamation suits the balance should weigh in favor of the press.

In the 1971 case of *Rosenbloom* v. *Metromedia, Inc.,* the Court in a five-to-three decision applied the actual malice standard in a situation where the plaintiff was neither a public official nor a public figure but had been prominently involved in a matter that received substantial attention from the major daily newspapers of Philadelphia as well as on local radio and television news programs.[18] The Court, however, could not agree upon a controlling rationale. Justice Brennan, in an opinion joined by Chief Justice Burger and Justice Blackmun, urged that the *Sullivan* standard be extended to cover not only public officials and public figures, but also individuals involved in matters of general public interest.[19] Justices Black and White, however, the other members of the Court in the five-person majority, concurred on respectively different grounds.[20] Likewise, among the minority, Justices Marshall and Harlan each had his own view about how the case should have been analyzed.[21]

This uncertain situation was somewhat resolved three years later in the case of *Gertz* v. *Welch*.[22] Elmer Gertz, a Chicago lawyer, had represented the family of an adolescent killed by a Chicago policeman, who was later convicted of murder. Gertz, although highly respected in Chicago as an attorney, had played only a very minor role in public affairs, and his name was not generally known to the public. *American Opinion,* the voice of the John Birch Society, published by Robert Welch, Inc., ran an article which supposedly exposed a left-wing conspiracy against the police and which hurled numerous false and defamatory charges at Gertz, such as that he was a Communist and had an extensive criminal record. Gertz brought suit for defamation in federal court and obtained a favorable verdict despite the fact that he offered no proof that Robert Welch, Inc., knowingly or recklessly disregarded the truth with respect to the charges leveled at him. The judge in district court, however, overruled the verdict of the jury and entered a judgment for the defendant. This judgment was then affirmed by the court of appeals.

In dealing with the *Gertz* case the Supreme Court had to resolve two basic questions. First, was Gertz a public figure for purposes of applying the actual malice standard? Second, if not, did the actual malice standard nonetheless apply to him in virtue of his being a principal actor in an event of general public interest? That is, should the standard advocated by Justice Brennan in *Rosenbloom* v. *Metromedia* be adopted? The Court answered both questions in the negative. Gertz was held not to be a public figure because he had achieved no "general fame or notoriety in the community" and did not seek to affect public opinion or "thrust himself into the vortex" of a controversial issue of general interest.[23] As for the second question, Justice Stewart declared in his majority opinion that extending the actual malice standard to defamation of ordinary individuals whenever an issue of general public interest is involved would abridge to an unacceptable degree the right of individuals to protect their reputations.[24] With *Gertz* the line was thus again drawn at public figures with respect to the "actual malice" standard, as it had been in *Curtis* v. *Butts.*[25]

The *Gertz* case appears to be holding firm as the considered statement of the Supreme Court on the constraints of the First Amendment with respect to the common law of libel. Subsequent cases have filled in relatively minor details.[26] What then should one think about *Gertz?* To begin, the Court's decision not to cut the path that it appeared it might in *Rosenbloom* v. *Metromedia* seems well considered. Extension of the actual malice standard to ordinary individuals who happened to be major participants in matters of public interest would have given the press virtual immunity from defamation lawsuits as a matter of constitutional principle under the First Amendment. When one considers the question of how to define "matters of major public interest" it seems difficult not to equate such matters with *newsworthy* events. And whose judgment but the media's may be reasonably regarded as authoritative with regard to newsworthiness? Now, indeed, Justice Black consistently argued from *Sullivan* through *Rosenbloom* that all actions for defamation, whether against the media or mere individuals, are proscribed by the First Amendment.[27] But as discussed in Chapter Two, this view of the matter seems clearly mistaken. The First Amendment should be thought of as applying essentially to governmental activities involving the *danger of thought control.* Such danger, however, cannot be ascribed to a given legal system simply because the possibility exists within it for private parties to bring actions for defamation against one another.

The Court's approach in *Gertz*, however, seems questionable in one important respect. According to Justice Stewart, the crucial constitutional problem in defamation cases involving media organizations as defendants is that of balancing the social interest (enabling the media to inform the public) against the interest of the individual (to maintain his or her reputation). Such a viewpoint implies that in the above kinds of cases we have a *prima facie* conflict between two fundamental rights, namely the right of the press to be unhindered by libel suits in doing its job of informing the public, and the right of individuals to protect their good names, and thus a necessity of redefining these rights to reach a mutual accomodation. That the press has this right as a matter of basic constitutional principle, however, seems dubious to me.

Had the Court not required public officials to satisfy more stringent standards for proving defamation than ordinary individuals, as it did in *New York Times* v. *Sullivan*, the possibility would have existed that such officials could systematically harass the media through libel suits as a way of controlling news stories. For example, federal attorneys could then have instituted defamation actions throughout the country in a coordinated manner. Such a danger, however, is not posed by defamation suits involving nongovernmental public figures as plaintiffs. Admittedly, such suits could grievously hamper the operation of particular media concerns in particular cases. That they could paralyze the media across the board, as it were, so that it could not carry out its function of informing the public is exceedingly remote.

By the same token, had the actual malice standard not been extended to cover nongovernmental public figures, the media admittedly might well have had to be far more circumspect in printing or broadcasting news items about such individuals, at least when a possible defamation problem might have been involved. It does not follow from this, however, that nongovernmental public figures must be treated like public officials for purposes of defamation law. Even if the media had to be more circumspect about publishing items that might adversely affect the reputations of nongovernmental public figures, in all likelihood it could still carry out effectively the two functions of providing information about public affairs and, more generally, keeping people in touch with contemporary culture. The inescapable conclusion thus appears to be that the Court should have stopped at *New York Times* v. *Sullivan* and applied the actual malice standard only to public officials.

The foregoing argument should not be taken as suggesting that individuals have a fundamental right to protect their reputations that takes precedence over problems for the press posed by defamation actions. Indeed, just as the right of the press to be unhindered by libel suits cannot be regarded as constitutionally basic, a person's admittedly great interest in maintaining his or her reputation does not establish the existence of a fundamental right in this regard. It may well be that affording the press statutory protection with substantially the same content as the Court's rulings in *Curtis* v. *Butts* and *Gertz* v. *Welch* would be desirable. One cannot argue, however, that given inaction by Congress the Court had to step in and protect the media. This could only be said if the rights claimed by the media should be thought of as fundamental. The considerations adduced here, however, suggest this view to be mistaken.

CONFIDENTIALITY PRIVILEGE

In the 1972 case of *Branzburg* v. *Hayes*, the Supreme Court dealt concurrently with three separate cases, each of which raised the issue of whether newspaper reporters are entitled under the First Amendment to decline to respond to a grand jury subpoena in a criminal investigation if the testimony sought pertains to information obtained by a pledge of confidentiality.[28] The five-to-four ruling was that reporters have no such entitlement, with Justice White writing the majority opinion and Justices Douglas and Stewart each filing dissents.

In his majority opinion Justice White first reviewed the role of the grand jury, underscoring its necessarily broad powers in virtue of its role. He then stated that no compelling reason had been advanced why such powers should be curtailed where reporters are involved.[29] As for the argument that requiring reporters to testify will both undermine their credibility with the people upon whom they depend for information and create a generally diffident attitude in newsrooms about basing stories upon confidential information, Justice White dismissed such considerations as merely speculative.[30] The dissenters, Douglas and Stewart, however, took them far more seriously, asserting that the case record bore ample evidence that requiring reporters to divulge information obtained in confidence would have precisely these consequences.[31]

In *Zurcher* v. *The Stanford Daily*, decided in 1978, the issue was whether police can obtain material from a newspaper newsroom during a criminal investigation simply through an ordinary search authorized by a search warrant, rather than having to obtain a *subpoena duces tecum* under which the newspaper turns the requested material over to them.[32] The ruling was that the police may do so, and again Justice White wrote the majority opinion with Justice Stewart filing a dissent. Justice White focused primarily upon Fourth Amendment aspects of the case, and he dismissed the claim that it posed any significant First Amendment issues with a brisk allusion to the line of reasoning he set out in *Branzburg* v. *Hayes*.[33] Justice Stewart also again stood by the position he took in the *Branzburg* case but, unlike Justice White, he took the occasion of *Zurcher* to restate that position in detail.[34] He also pointed out that the *Stanford Daily* did not claim an absolute right to withhold from the authorities material obtained in confidence, but only claimed a constitutionally mandated immunity from searches in which the authorities directly enter the newsroom. Accordingly, Justice Stewart concluded that while the factors in favor of the position of the press that obtained in *Branzburg* were also present in *Zurcher*, the considerations on the other side were less substantial. Several months following *Zurcher*, the Court refused to review the constitutional privilege claims of a *New York Times* investigative reporter, Myron Farber.[35]

It should be noted at the outset that no per se violations appear involved in the failure to grant members of the press immunity from having to provide testimony in criminal trials and investigations or to submit to searches. Accordingly, one who wishes to argue that the First Amendment protects confidential relationships between reporters and their sources may go about it in either of only two ways. First, one must set out reasons for holding that, contrary to the per se approach of Chapter Two, the First Amendment requires that everyone, press and ordinary individuals alike, have the above-mentioned legal immunities; or two, one must provide an independent constitutional analysis of freedom of the press—that is to say, an analysis according to which certain rights under the First Amendment pertain specifically to the press alone. In either case, one's account would have to satisfy the two conditions enumerated in Chapter One for any account of a right deemed constitutionally fundamental. First, it must include a plausible line of argument to the effect that rational contractors under a veil of ignorance would regard a certain mode of conduct as a governmental duty; second, the duty, in turn, must be specified with sufficient precision to determine over a wide range of cases whether violations have occurred.

It seems highly implausible to regard the right to freedom of expression as implying a general right of everyone not to have to provide testimony to law enforcement authorities in the course of criminal investigations or trials. Likewise, it seems that one stretches too far in striving to bring a general freedom from on-the-premises police searches under the ambit of the First Amendment. The second of the approaches for arguing a constitutionally required shield for journalists to protect their confidential relationship with sources thus seems the only possible course. That is, one must provide an independent constitutional analysis of freedom of the press. In this regard, then, the primary question is whether an argument can be enunciated that would convince the rational contractors that governments have a duty not to compel journalists to supply authorities with information they have obtained through pledges of confidentiality.

One might attempt to meet the burden of persuasion by arguing that the press serves functions of such enormous importance that carrying them out requires constitutional protection.[36] Shortly after the *Branzburg* decision was announced, congressional hearings took place in 1973 on the question of whether federal shield legislation for reporters ought to be enacted.[37] All of the many reporters called to testify spoke in favor of such legislation and stressed as the primary point in its favor that, in their opinions, the *Branzburg* decision would have severely adverse effects on investigative reporting, particularly the kind that aims at exposing governmental corruption.[38]

Can the exposure of corrupt public officials then be identified as a constitutionally fundamental role played by the press? It seems to me that profound objections can be raised against such a view and that such objections are best formulated in terms of the following dilemma: in particular cases either corruption in government is an inherent, systematic aspect of the socio-political fabric within a given community, or it is not. If the former, then investigative reporting by the press simply will be of no avail in putting an end to corruption; if the latter, then the efforts of the press, however praiseworthy, probably are not essential for dealing with it.

Taking the first horn of the dilemma, one might argue that when government corruption goes beyond certain limits it corrodes democracy so badly that keeping corruption within those limits can be considered a role of fundamental importance from a constitutional standpoint. In areas where corruption already exists to a high degree, however, people's expectations generally become so deeply accommodated to bribes, kickbacks, payoffs and the like, that anything short of major institutional change can bring about only a temporary abatement of these practices. Under such circumstances, throwing the old rascals out simply delays for a short time the inevitable accession to office of new ones.

On the other hand, if corruption in government has not become an integral part of the way of life within a community, then the watchdog activities of the press, though not inherently futile, cannot be considered indispensable, at least not in theory. Where political powers are separated among different organs of government, and where real competition for office among political parties exists, investigative reporting is just one among several ways that the corrosive effects of official corruption upon democratic government can be stemmed. To be sure, if these conditions did not obtain, then investigative reporting would be the only way this could be done. One cannot conclude automatically, however, that under such circumstances investigative reporting could only be carried on by relying heavily upon confidential information. Increased statutory protections of various kinds for governmental employees who expose official wrongdoing might well suffice to create a climate in which the need of investigative reporters to rely upon confidential information would diminish.[39]

The foregoing argument should not be misunderstood as dismissing investigative reporting on grounds of being either inherently ineffective or insignificant. Obviously, such reporting has great value, and its total demise would be a severe loss. Instead, the foregoing argument speaks to the issue, basic for purposes of constitutional analysis, of whether we want to conceive of our political and social institutions in such a way that investigative activities of reporters with respect to official corruption are to be thought of as playing an essential role in preserving democracy as a matter of basic institutional design. That is, should we hold that if we were designing a government *de novo*, we would predicate it upon an assumption that the primary protection against the dangers posed by official corruption will be watchdog activities on the part of the press? The preceding argument suggests that we should not, because it appears that circumstances generally will be such that either the press simply cannot do the job, or that, if it can, other effective means for doing the job will exist as well.

The proposition that newspaper reporters should be recognized as having a right under the First Amendment not to reveal their sources thus stands on a quite different footing from the principle suggested in Chapter Two as embodying the central core of First Amendment doctrine, namely, that governmental authorities should never commit any of the per se violations. That the government refrain from restricting expression in these ways is so necessary for avoiding the evils to which Mill calls our attention in chapters two and three of *On Liberty* that were we to set up a government *de novo*, we would design it explicitly to minimize such restrictions. By contrast, we can doubt whether the role of the press in bringing official corruption to light is likewise so crucial that as a theoretical matter we would want to incorporate specific provisions for facilitating performance of this role into the design of basic political institutions.

Thus, while the press undoubtedly plays a valuable role in exposing corruption in government, this role cannot be thought of as constitutionally fundamental. The question still remains, however, whether shield legislation to protect the confidential relationship between reporters and their sources is desirable even if not constitutionally required. On the one hand, such legislation obviously would facilitate investigative reporting. On the other hand, one might argue that, aside from the obvious inhibiting effect of shield laws on criminal investigations, certain other dangers may result from making investigative reporting too easy. Perhaps the most serious of these is that as the price, so to speak, of running exposé stories goes down, the press will tend to concentrate upon them to the exclusion of other kinds of journalistic endeavors with arguably greater social importance.

This latter point inevitably leads to the consideration of another function of the press that might be urged to merit special constitutional protection, namely, keeping the public informed. Such a function clearly should be regarded as having far more constitutional significance than exposing official corruption. For all practical purposes, the press exclusively supplies information about public affairs upon which to base decisions in voting. Moreover, even those who doubt the significance of voting in a mass democracy must acknowledge that other means of political participation exist for the highly motivated—for example, directly contacting public officials or working with various organizations—and that intelligent decisions about whether, and in what way, to undertake such actions must be based upon information supplied by the press.

Of equal significance to its function of providing information about political affairs, the press puts people in touch with the dominant culture. That is to say, many of the most important broad cultural developments may not touch our lives directly; even if we were to rub shoulders daily with the prevailing trends, we probably would need a great deal of collateral information to interpret and to come to terms with them personally. The press, then, is indispensable in fostering personal development insofar as it facilitates our understanding of contemporary culture so that we can adapt it to the particular circumstances of our lives.

One can question, however, whether the undeniably important role of the press in keeping the public informed absolutely requires reporters to be accorded a right not to reveal their sources. To be sure, at times highly sensitive disclosures about public officials can dramatically affect one's political stance in regard to a particular issue. For the most part, however, the possibility of informed political belief depends primarily upon the availability of news and commentary about the major public issues of the day, which it would seem the press can provide without extensive use of confidential sources whose identity would be likely to figure crucially in criminal investigations. As for the role of the press in putting individuals in touch with the prevailing cultural trends, this would seem to require even less reliance upon information obtained with pledges of confidentiality. One can say, then, that while the role of the press in informing the public may well have special importance from a constitutional standpoint, acknowledging a right of reporters to refrain from divulging their sources does not appear to be crucial for the press to perform this role.

To summarize briefly the ground covered thus far in this section, we can begin by noting that two suggestions have been consistently put forward as to the functions carried out by the press that merit special attention from the standpoint of the First Amendment—to wit, exposing corruption by government officials and keeping the public informed. Upon examination, however, it turns out that the first of these functions, though obviously important, cannot be thought of as constitutionally significant. The second function, by contrast, has constitutional significance, but it probably can be fulfilled even if the confidential relationship between reporters and their sources is not deemed to be protected under the First Amendment. It must be emphasized that none of this should be taken as belittling the importance of a free press for a democratic society. The point is rather that a correct understanding of the precise nature of that importance indicates certain constitutional positions to be questionable.

RIGHT TO A MEDIA FORUM

The seven per se violations of the First Amendment all involve governmental action that forbids or requires expression of beliefs and attitudes. Is such a conception too narrow? Should one also regard the First Amendment as imposing a duty upon governments to facilitate conditions which increase the probability that a sizeable number of people will actually receive the message one wishes to communicate? The Supreme Court appears to have answered this question negatively. In two important cases during the 1970s that dealt respectively with broadcast and print media, the Court rejected the idea of a First Amendment right to a forum in either domain.

The first case, *Columbia Broadcasting System* v. *Democratic National*

Committee, originated with complaints filed before the Federal Communication Commission in 1970 by the Democratic National Committee and an anti-Vietnam war group challenging a CBS policy of refusing all editorial advertisements.[40] The FCC upheld CBS, but the court of appeals reversed on the ground that "a flat ban on paid public issue announcements is in violation of the First Amendment, at least when other sorts of paid announcements are accepted."[41] The Supreme Court, however, disagreed and reinstated the ruling of the FCC.

In his majority opinion Chief Justice Burger first emphasized the indications in the Federal Communications Act of 1934, which set up the FCC, "that Congress intended to permit private broadcasting to develop with the widest freedom consistent with its public obligations."[42] He then posed the question of whether the various interests in free expression of the public, the broadcaster, and the individuals require broadcasters to sell commercial time to persons wishing to discuss controversial issues.[43] On this matter the Chief Justice concluded, "To agree that debate on public issues should be 'robust and wide open' does not mean that we should exchange public trustee broadcasting, with all its limitations, for a system of self-appointed editorial commentators."[44]

In the second case, *Miami Herald Publishing Co. v. Tournillo*, a unanimous Court held unconstitutional a Florida statute that granted a political candidate a right to equal space to reply to criticism and attacks on his record by a newspaper.[45] In the majority opinion, again written by Chief Justice Burger, arguments for "an enforceable right of access to the press' and the claim "that Government has an obligation to ensure that a wide variety of views reach the public" were reviewed at some length.[46] The Chief Justice responded to them as follows: "However much validity may be found in these arguments, at each point implementation of a remedy such as an enforceable right of access necessarily calls for some mechanism, either governmental or consensual. If it is governmental coercion, this at once brings about a confrontation with the express provision of the First Amendment and the judicial gloss on the Amendment. . . . [A] Government-enforced right of access inescapably 'dampens the vigor and limits the variety of public debate.' " And even if there were no such consequences to the (Florida) statute it would nevertheless be invalid "because of its intrusion into the function of editors."[47]

These two cases appear to have ended conjecture during the

early 1970s that the Supreme Court would interpret the First Amendment so as to imply the right, at least in some measure, to a mass media forum. Jerome Barron, perhaps the most vigorous adherent of this approach, made the case for it thus:

the free marketplace of ideas depicts an ideal, not a reality. There *are* enormous limitations on the "power of thought to get itself accepted in the competition of the market." In Holmes' concept of the marketplace of ideas the only limitation on the currency of ideas is an intellectual one. Ideas in a mass society are transmitted in the mass communications media of television, radio, and the press. Admission to them assures notoriety and public response. Denial assures obscurity and apparently frustration. . . . the traditional liberal position on ideas is essentially Darwinian. Ideas engage in a life of moral combat and the fittest survive. In this struggle, the continuing menace has been seen to be government. That private power might so control the struggle of ideas as to predetermine the victor has not been considered. But increasingly, private censorship serves to suppress ideas as thoroughly and as rigidly as the worst government censor.[48]

What should one make of Barron's contentions? If indeed those responsible for editorial decisions in the broadcast and print mass media have the power "to suppress ideas as thoroughly and as rigidly as the worst government censor," then it certainly would seem anomalous to regard their decisions as beyond the reach of the First Amendment. But are Barron's views, as stated above, credible? It would seem not. A strong government can effect a penetrating, far-reaching, and long-lasting suppression of ideas and attitudes through systematic actions that fall within the seven categories of per se violation. It can enact sedition, obscenity, and censorship laws, impose prior restraints, penalize people who express officially disapproved-of views in other ways, make the avowal of certain beliefs and attitudes mandatory, and control expression through vague or overbroad laws. The claim that a newspaper or television network could achieve the same results as those of a government that systematically employed the seven basic means of suppressing expression frankly seems hyperbolic. The broadcast and printed mass media exert enormous influence in shaping the public consciousness. When one has an audience or reading public in the millions, one stands a far better chance of affecting people than otherwise. So much is obvious. But neither of these observations suggests that those who allocate air time or print space have powers of suppression remotely akin to those at the disposal of even a moderately strong government.

Barron's words nevertheless may be taken in a less literal way that renders his position a bit more plausible. Given his extensive reliance in the foregoing quotation upon Holmes's famous metaphor, "the marketplace of ideas," one might take Barron as contending that acknowledgment of a First Amendment right to a mass media forum would conduce to making this marketplace function more effectively. As Holmes noted in his *Abrams* dissent, "the best test of truth is the power of [a] thought to get itself accepted in the competition of the market."[49] Thus, since the marketplace of ideas in one of its essential aspects serves as a device for obtaining the truth and avoiding falsity, any social policies that unquestionably further these ends should be thought of as required by the First Amendment. According to this line of reasoning, however, acknowledging the right to a mass media forum constitutes precisely such a policy.

The problem with this argument is that it simply errs in its assertion that acknowledging the right to a mass media forum *unquestionably* will further the essential value of truth served by freedom of expression. Rational people can differ in good faith about this matter. At first blush it seems plausible that providing the opportunity for more individuals to speak their piece on radio, television, or in the mass printed media will make for more thorough examination of items already on the public agenda and for the introduction of important new items that otherwise might have been entirely ignored. But strong grounds exist for doubting this. In a high-technology mass society the problem is not so much providing a forum as providing favorable conditions for a sizeable audience. With the advent of cable television it has become possible to expand dramatically the supply of air time. Those who choose to take their messages to the public, however, still must find ways to attract its attention.

The experience with cable television in New York City highlights the difficulties in this regard.[50] As of July 1, 1971, the two cable television companies then operating in Manhattan were required by New York City regulations to set aside two channels respectively for sporadic one-time users and individuals who wished to reserve given time periods. New York seemed like a good place to implement such an innovation. The city had a large number of cable subscribers, two healthy cable-operating companies, and a cable audience with varied tastes potentially receptive to avant garde video programming. New York's other advantages, of course, include a unique range of cultural and artistic activities and a virtually inexhaustible supply of performers and program producers.

Yet despite these seemingly favorable conditions for creating an effective right to a mass media forum, the first few years of experience in New York City were not a success. Special publicity efforts by a private foundation did not suffice to make the general public aware of the availability of the two public access channels. Moreover, those who used them confronted formidable organizational problems and expense. A 1972 analysis concluded that the public access channels did not reach a general audience:

> If a large distributed audience is desired, public access channels are ineffective. Informing the potential audience of a program can be as expensive as the production itself. Because public access channels will not reach a broad audience in the near future, they are not adequate substitutes for conventional television; they are not yet adequate as a forum for the presentation of competing views on controversial issues.[51]

In Canada, where cable television developed earlier than in the United States and has substantial penetration, two studies have found essentially the same results as in the New York experience.[52]

It cannot be said then that acknowledging the right to a mass media forum *unquestionably* will further the essential values associated with freedom of expression. For this reason the First Amendment does not imply this right. Assertion that it does conflicts with the initial requirement of a constitutionally fundamental right—that one can specify a governmental duty in regard to the matter at issue (in this case, providing members of the public with access to the mass media) that would be unanimously agreed to by the rational contractors. Rights to a mass media forum created by statute conceivably could be compatible with the First Amendment, but acknowledgment of such rights does not constitute a constitutional necessity.

The above conclusions accord with the final judgment of the Supreme Court in both *CBS* v. *DNC* and *Miami Herald* v. *Tournillo.* The first of these cases, however, raises a further issue which must be treated separately. In rejecting the notion of broad First Amendment rights to a forum in the mass broadcast media, the Court noted that Congress had chosen to deal with the problems to which advocates of such rights call attention by way of the regulatory mechanisms set up under the authority of the Federal Communications Commission. Referring to the theory upon which was based the right to a media forum urged in the *CBS* v. *DNC* case, the Court noted:

> So sweeping a concept of state action would go far in practical effect to undermine nearly half a century of unmistakable Congressional purpose to maintain—no matter how difficult the task—essentially private broadcast journalism held only broadly accountable to public interest standards . . .[53]

The problem with this contention is that the public interest standards referred to by the Court in the above passage are themselves highly suspect from a constitutional standpoint. That is to say, some conceivable approaches to the problem of effecting fairness, balance, and the airing of diverse viewpoints in the broadcast media may well satisfy the requirements of the First Amendment. But a substantial question exists as to whether those now in place do so.

An analysis of the problems in this respect requires a very brief history and overview of federal broadcast regulations.[54] As a result of the rapid emergence of commercial radio in the 1920s, a chaotic situation developed in which, owing to the fact that space on the electromagnetic spectrum could not accommodate all those who wished to use it, several radio stations often simultaneously attempted to broadcast on the same frequency.[55] A general recognition thus arose of the need for allocating broadcast frequencies. Congress responded with the Federal Radio Act of 1927.[56] This act created the Federal Radio Commission, a body that was given the power to issue broadcast licenses if "the public convenience, interest, or necessity will be served thereby," to control location, power, wavelength, and nature of services, and to make regulations to minimize interference. The Commission was also authorized to require applicants for licenses to submit information about their proposed service, as well as other information of a financial and personal nature. The Radio Act also included a specific regulation to the effect that a station that gave or sold air time to a candidate for public office must also afford equivalent access to other candidates for the same office.[57] The Act forbade the Radio Commission from censoring programs or interfering "with the right of free speech by means of radio communications."[58] The Communications

Act of 1934, which is the current statutory basis of federal regulatory authority in broadcasting, transferred the powers of the Federal Radio Commission to the Federal Communications Commission.[59] The basic allocation pattern of broadcast licenses, however, was not changed. The powers over broadcasting created by the 1927 act carried over to the Federal Communications Commission with little or no change. In addition, section 303 of the Communications Act authorized the FCC to make general regulations for broadcasting in the public interest.

The Commission thus functions under an extremely broad delegation of authority. What constitutes the public interest for purposes of broadcast regulation? The FCC gave a definitive statement on this matter in a 1949 report called *Editorializing by Broadcast Licensees*.[60] This report concluded that the public interest imposes a two-part duty on broadcasters. First, they must devote reasonable time to coverage of controversial issues of public importance, and second, they must afford reasonable opportunity for contrasting viewpoints to be heard on such issues. This two-part standard, which has come to be known as the Fairness Doctrine, constitutes the primary basis upon which the Commission evaluates broadcast licensees.

The 1949 report, however, left satisfaction of the requirements of the Fairness Doctrine to the licensee's discretion. The Commission stated that it would apply the doctrine only when reviewing the licensee's overall performance at the time of license renewal every three years. That is to say, the Commission stated that it would not apply the Fairness Doctrine on a program-by-program basis. No particular program had to be "fair" if overall programming met the requisite standard.

The 1960s, however, saw the FCC substantially change the approach it enunciated in 1949. In 1962 the Commission began to consider fairness complaints about specific programs promptly, rather than waiting until the broadcaster's license renewal date. The following year it required licensees to fulfill fairness obligations at their own expense if no forthcoming program would air other sides of controversial issues. In 1967 the commission laid down two regulations that under certain circumstances give individuals access to air time. First, a broadcaster who takes a definite position for or against a political candidate in an editorial must notify the candidates opposed, or the rivals of the candidate supported, and offer them an opportunity to respond. Second, when during the presentation of views on a controversial issue of public importance, an attack is made on the "honesty, character, integrity, or like personal qualities of an identified person or group," the person or attacked group must be notified, provided with a transcript of the attack, and given an opportunity to respond.[61]

These two 1967 rules were strongly opposed by the broadcast media as infringements of their right to freedom of expression. Two years later, however, in the case of *Red Lion Broadcasting Company* v. *FCC*, a unanimous Supreme Court upheld both rules.[62] Writing for the Court, Justice White declared:

Where there are substantially more individuals who want to broadcast than there are frequencies to allocate, it is idle to posit an unbridgeable First Amendment right to broadcast comparable to the right of every individual to speak or publish . . . [A]s far as the First Amendment is concerned, those who are licensed stand no better than those to whom licenses are refused. A license permits broadcasting, but the licensee has no constitutional right to be the only one who holds the license or to monopolize a radio frequency to the exclusion of his fellow citizens.

There is nothing in the First Amendment which prevents the Government requiring a licensee to share his frequency with others and to conduct himself as a proxy or fiduciary with obligations to present those views which are representative of his community and which would otherwise by necessity be barred from the airwaves.[63]

The *Red Lion* case thus constitutes a ringing endorsement by the Supreme Court of the Fairness Doctrine. Nonetheless, serious doubts about it remain from the standpoint of the principles of free expression. Section 303 of the 1934 Communications Act, upon which the Fairness Doctrine is based, authorizes the FCC to promulgate regulations in the public interest.[64] On its face, so sweeping a delegation of power would seem unconstitutionally overbroad, since the Commission itself determines what constitutes the public interest in this context. Nor does the Fairness Doctrine itself, as enunciated by the Commission, make things substantially more determinate. Broadcasters must devote *reasonable* time to coverage of controversial issues of *public importance* and must afford *reasonable opportunity* for contrasting viewpoints to be heard on such issues. Ultimate authority lies with the Commission to determine whether broadcasters have satisfied these highly general criteria. Under the personal attack rule laid down in 1967, the Commission has the authority to determine whether broadcasted remarks about an individual constitute an attack on his or her "honesty, character, integrity, or like personal qualities." (In reference to this last matter, it should be noted that in the *Red Lion* case the Court upheld for broadcasting precisely the same kind of rule that it unanimously struck down as a violation of the First Amendment with respect to printed media in *Miami Herald* v. *Tournillo*.)

How then can one justify such an extensive delegation of authority that has all the earmarks of the seventh per se violation of the First Amendment, namely, vagueness and overbreadth? The foregoing quotation from the majority opinion in *Red Lion* indicates that the Court answered this question exclusively by noting the unavoidability of federal regulation in order to allocate broadcast frequencies. The fact that regulation is necessary to accomplish the important but minimal task of controlling the interference problem, however, scarcely implies the justifiability of an overbroad delegation of authority to the FCC. In the CBS case Justice Burger noted that "very early the licensee's role [under the federal regulatory scheme for broadcasting] developed in terms of a 'public trustee' charged with a duty of fairly and impartially informing the listening and viewing public."[65] Such a conception, though hardly inevitable, in itself indeed seems legitimate. One might hold, quite plausibly, that the airwaves constitute a resource of such potential value that those who are granted licenses to broadcast over them should be made to pledge that they will operate their stations in ways that conduce to the public good. Conceiving of broadcasters as public trustees, however, hardly requires the adoption of regulatory arrangements that violate the First Amendment.

The problem, by and large, has not been actual abuse of power by the FCC, which, like most other federal regulatory agencies, appears to have been captured, more or less, by the interests it seeks to regulate.[66] That is to say, the overwhelming majority of FCC rules and adjudications reflect the point of view of the broadcast industry. But in light of the Commission's seemingly overbroad statutory powers a basic question of First Amendment principle remains. Can one justify the Fairness Doctrine from a constitutional standpoint? Neither Justice White's words in *Red Lion* nor Chief Justice Burger's in *CBS* v. *DNC* pertaining to this matter would appear sufficient.

To summarize then, it seems that the Supreme Court correctly decided the *CBS* v. *DNC* and *Miami Herald* v. *Tournillo* cases from the standpoint of our theory of constitutional adjudication. In *CBS* v. *DNC* the Court held that the First Amendment does not require broadcasters to provide the spokespersons of various viewpoints with a media forum by accepting their offers to pay for editorial advertisements. This appears correct because the refusal to accept such offers does not fall under any of the seven categories of per se violation. In *Miami Herald* v. *Tournillo* the Court invalidated a Florida statute requiring that newspapers provide print space to candidates for political office whom they had personally attacked. Again, this decision is sound given the inherent vagueness of the phrase "personal attack."[67] One aspect of the CBS case, however, must be criticized. A lengthy passage of the majority opinion clearly presupposed that the Fairness Doctrine employed by the Federal Communications Commission is consistent with the First Amendment, a supposition about which the preceding analysis raises serious questions.

RIGHT OF ACCESS TO INFORMATION

Per se violations of the First Amendment with respect to the press prevent or discourage it from disseminating news or opinion. But what about governmental regulations that have the effect of making it more difficult for the press to gather news? Should one also regard these as infringements upon the constitutionally protected right of freedom of the press? If so, then do we not have a significant instance of First Amendment violation which our theory cannot accommodate? The first of these two questions should be answered negatively. The reasons for this require some care and detail to elucidate.

In three separate cases during the mid-1970s in which various press organizations claimed a right under the First Amendment to enter prisons for the purpose of investigative reporting, the Supreme Court upheld the regulations in question, which barred the press from access to the penal facilities.[68] Up to recently, then, the Court has seemed almost completely unreceptive to the idea of a First Amendment right of access to information. In the 1980 case of *Richmond Newspapers* v. *Virginia*, however, the Supreme Court held the First Amendment to forbid judges from closing criminal trials, at least in the absence of extraordinary circumstances.[69] Richmond Newspapers has been heralded in some very influential quarters, including at least one Supreme Court justice, as acknowledging the right of access to information hitherto rejected by the Court. Justice Stevens wrote a concurring opinion in *Richmond Newspapers* which concluded with the following remark:

> Until today the Court has accorded virtually absolute protection to the dissemination of information or ideas, but never before has it squarely held that the acquisition of newsworthy matter is entitled to any constitutional protection whatsoever. . . . [F]or the first time, the court unequivocally holds that an arbitrary interference with access to important information is an abridgment of the freedoms of speech and of the press protected by the First Amendment.[70]

One eminent commentator, Anthony Lewis, reads *Richmond Newspapers* as Justice Stevens does.[71] He thus attaches enormous importance to the case, and sees a need for the Court to address further questions concerning the scope of the right of access to information that he believes it to proclaim. Just how important *Richmond Newspapers* will prove to be, however, remains a very open question, Justice Stevens's concurring opinion notwithstanding. A brief look at the highly unusual circumstances of this case throws considerable doubt upon whether the Court will use it as the starting point for extensive development of a right of access to information.

Exactly a year to the day before the Court rendered its decision in *Richmond Newspapers*, the Court declared in the case of *Gannett Co.* v. *DePasquale* that "members of the public have no constitutional right under the Sixth and Fourteenth Amendments to attend criminal trials."[72] The *Gannett* case arose out of a situation in which, upon the request of defense counsel and approval of the prosecution, the judge in a criminal case barred the public from a pretrial hearing on a motion to suppress evidence. The Gannett Publishing Company moved to set aside the order closing the hearing on the ground that it conflicted with the right to a public trial guaranteed by the Sixth Amendment. In a five-to-four decision the Court ruled that the Sixth Amendment's guarantee of the right to a public trial "runs to the defendant alone, not to the public."[73] That is to say, only the defendant has standing to object if the right has been violated.

Although the inclusion of three concurring opinions, which in some respects conflicted with each other, clouded the meaning of the *Gannett* decision, both the press and the judiciary widely perceived it as giving lower court judges a broad license to close courtrooms.[74] The press reacted with strong criticism which in some measure may have affected the Court. Somewhat out of the ordinary, four justices made extracurricular comments on the *Gannett* decision within a few months after it was rendered.[75] In the words of Anthony Lewis:

It all suggested that the Justices might welcome an opportunity to undo at least some of what they had done. But it would be awkward for them to reconsider the meaning of the Sixth Amendment after that question had been so thoroughly discussed in both majority and dissenting opinions [in *Gannett*]. Thus, if a factually compelling case came along, one in which the Supreme Court wanted to find a basis for setting aside the closing of a courtroom, the Court might have to use the path that *Gannett* left open: the First Amendment.[76]

Richmond Newspapers provided the Court with just the opportunity that Lewis conjectured it desired. The case had exactly the same factual pattern as in *Gannett*, except that the defendant sought and was granted closure of an actual trial rather than a pretrial hearing. The Virginia Supreme Court denied the appeal of the Richmond Newspapers to have the closure order overturned. In a seven-to-one decision the Supreme Court reversed the ruling of the Virginia Supreme Court. There was no majority opinion, but all six justices in the majority who wrote separate opinions based their grounds for reversal on the First Amendment.

Such a decision appears on its face as warmly receptive to, if not a ringing endorsement of, the idea that the First Amendment implies a right of access to information. Closer examination, however, reveals that this is not so. For one thing, although seven justices reversed the closure order in the *Richmond Newspapers* case on First Amendment grounds, they nonetheless could not agree upon a controlling rationale, as manifested by the six separate opinions in support of reversal. For another, upon reading those opinions one comes away with a curious impression. Although each opinion cites the First Amendment as the basis for reversal, none of them involves even remotely familiar First Amendment reasoning relating the matter at issue to the basic right of freedom of expression. Justice White cryptically registered his agreement with disposition of the *Richmond Newspapers* case on First Amendment grounds. He also noted, however, that had *Gannett* been decided correctly, *Richmond Newspapers* would never have reached the Court.[77] Justice Blackmun, in a somewhat lengthier opinion, expressed an identical viewpoint.[78] Justices Burger, Brennan (with Marshall's concurrence), and Stewart all emphasized that maintenance of public confidence in the integrity of the judicial process requires that trials be closed to the public only in extraordinary circumstances.[79]

Such a position indeed seems reasonable. The judiciary almost certainly would break down if people generally came to believe that as a matter of course the parties and the judge had it in their power to prearrange the outcome of a trial. But one is at a loss to discern the relationship between this observation and the First Amendment. It is not precisely clear where one should place the claim that an adequately functioning system of criminal justice requires or presupposes certain conditions, but intuitively it would seem far more related to one's basic rights in the area of criminal procedure than to freedom of expression.

It may well be that Justices White and Blackmun were correct in expressing the view that the Court decided *Gannett* wrongly. One can certainly make a case that the consideration regarded as paramount in *Richmond Newspapers* more comfortably falls under the Sixth Amendment than the First. A requirement that criminal trials be public not only protects the accused but also provides a substantial measure of insurance against corruption instigated by defendants with sufficient influence of either an economic or political nature to fix their cases. The inherent logic of the Sixth Amendment right to a public trial then does not necessitate construing that right as purely personal to the defendant and routinely waivable by him or her. It may be thought of as serving systemic purposes that go beyond personal concern for individual defendants. Reflecting upon such systemic purposes tends to dissipate whatever sense of incongruity may attend conceiving of a due process right as not purely personal to defendants. Another example in this regard is the beyond-a-reasonable-doubt standard of proof in criminal cases. Though the right of criminal defendants to be judged by such a standard would appear to count as a requirement of due process, nonetheless we need not think of it as grounded primarily in concern for individuals accused of crimes. Its rationale pertains more to fundamental aspects of the relation between governors and governed.[80]

Thus, while the Court has acknowledged a right of the public, based in the First Amendment, not to be excluded from criminal trials, one can question whether this really augurs the development of a new constitutional concept of a general right of access to information. Certainly nothing in the *Richmond Newspaper* opinions constitute an adequate theoretical basis for such a development.

The question still remains, however, whether one can enumerate other, more satisfactory, bases. Keeping in mind the two basic conditions that a right must satisfy to be constitutionally fundamental, it seems not. The first such condition, in this case, stipulates that one can make a plausible argument to the effect that rational contractors under the veil of ignorance would regard the government as having certain duties to assure the public an opportunity to acquire information concerning various matters. But what duties about what matters? Could the rational contractors reach even a general agreement about this issue? When one considers the range of activities performed and decisions made by governmental officials at all levels, it seems implausible to suppose that agreement could be achieved concerning even weak principles about the circumstances requiring them to make information available to the public.

Consider, for example, the following proposal for defining the contours of a right of access to information advanced by Anthony Lewis.

The question in each case should be whether . . . the denial of access prevents accountability . . . . One advantage of looking at the problem in terms of accountability is that it gets past generalized, unsophisticated claims of "the right to know" . . . about everything at once. In our intrusive world privacy is an increasingly important value, not least for official decision makers. Consider the example often given, the Supreme Court's own conferences. I think the Court could not function if its conferences were opened to the press and the public—televised, shall we say. An undifferentiated notion of the "right to know" sweeps Supreme Court conference within it. But it is not necessary for us as citizens to have access to those conferences in order to scrutinize the Court's work. For the Court acts only by what it does in public: its decisions published in full and with an obligation to give reasons for them. That is the basis for accountability of that institution.[81]

Lewis's proposal seems plausible enough on first reading, but the impression rapidly weakens when one considers what judgments will be necessary concerning how much information should be made available in specific cases to maintain "accountability" of a governmental entity. They will require that one decide how much information should be disclosed mandatorily to guard against abuse of power, waste, maladministration, and the like, consistent with leaving an official body sufficient control over the information it possesses to carry out its primary function. But again, when one considers the number of governmental bodies at all levels—zoning commissions, police forces, boards of education, U.S. Senate sub-committees, the various grants offices of the National Science Foundation, the National Security Council, etc., it scarcely seems credible that the courts could fashion general guidelines for dealing with all of these issues.[82] Instead, they are probably best dealt with one at a time through legislative deliberation.[83] The idea of a constitutional right of access to information thus appears un-tenable. It would seem not to satisfy the first condition required of a constitutionally fundamental right.

Summary

The most important issues of freedom of expression that affect the press can be analyzed satisfactorily in terms of the idea that there exist only seven basic categories of First Amendment violation. One need not broaden the theory outlined in Chapter Two to account for freedom of the press. With regard to the law of defamation and the First Amendment, our analysis confirms the essential soundness of the Supreme Court's landmark decision in *New York Times* v. *Sullivan*. It also suggests, however, that the later extensions of that decision rest on questionable grounds. As for the issue of whether newspaper reporters have an immunity under the First Amendment from having to provide law enforcement authorities with information obtained through confidential sources, it would seem that requiring reporters to supply such information constitutes no per se violation of the First Amendment. Further, the First Amendment does not imply a right of individuals to a media forum. On the other hand, statutory enactments creating such a right are constitutionally permissable provided they involve no per se violations. In this regard, serious questions can be raised about the personal attack and editorializing rules promulgated by the Federal Communications Commission under its Fairness Doc-trine. Indeed, serious constitutional difficulties appear to attend the Fairness Doctrine itself. Finally, it would seem that the First Amendment does not imply a right of access to information.

IV

Free Expression
in the Workplace

In a novel entitled *Scientists and Engineers: The Professionals Who Are Not*, the author, Lewis V. McIntire, presents an extremely negative picture of life as an employee in a large private corporation.[1] Characters in the novel inveigh against management favoritism, cheating inventors out of bonuses, and taking unfair advantage of employees in employment contracts. The fictional employer bears a striking resemblance to DuPont, the company for whom McIntire worked as a chemical engineer from 1956 through 1971, the year the book was published. In 1972 McIntire was fired.[2]

Did DuPont violate McIntire's rights under the First Amendment? The question would appear at first glance to reflect a serious misunderstanding of constitutional adjudication. Every theory generally credited with at least a remote plausibility conceives of the First Amendment as imposing requirements only upon *governmental* bodies. According to this approach, the relationship between an individual, such as McIntire, and a private entity, such as the DuPont Corporation, simply falls outside the scope of the First Amendment. DuPont did not violate McIntire's constitutionally protected right to freedom of expression, so the analysis goes, because it could not. DuPont has no governmental authority.

Some would question the classification of DuPont, and other large corporations, as unequivocally private organizations. Large corporations frequently do extensive government contract work under precise regulations and specifications not unlike those that would apply to a government agency.[3] Noting this point, it has been suggested that in many instances corporate activity amounts to what constitutional lawyers call "state action."[4] That is to say, according to this view, corporate activity frequently takes on the aspect of an act of the state by virtue of the high degree of governmental involvement with it.

The question of how to draw a reasonably clear line between public and private activity has proven extremely vexatious.[5] There is, however, an even more basic question for our purposes. Why insist at all upon the requirement of state action before considering whether First Amendment rights have been infringed? That is, why assent to the virtually universal judgment that First Amendment issues exclusively involve relationships between citizens and the state? The answer is not obvious. No responsible judge would disregard the state action requirement. But this fact, considered alone, hardly moots the foregoing issue. The evolution of First Amendment case law, described in Chapter Two, from *Schenk* v. *U.S.* to *Brandenburg* v. *Ohio*, indicates the possibility of substantial revisions of basic doctrine.[6] If within a sixty-year period the Court completely changed its approach on so crucial a matter as the constitutionality of sedition laws, conceivably it could do so on other important matters as well.[7]

Does intellectual coherence absolutely require arguing state action in order to show that DuPont violated McIntire's First Amendment rights? An answer to this question necessarily involves consideration of whether the theoretical analysis of constitutionally fundamental rights laid down in Chapter One can be extended to encompass not ony the rights of individuals against governmental bodies, but also their rights against each other. In the case of the First Amendment, such an analysis would have to include the following elements:

1. a plausible argument to the effect that the rational contractors would unanimously agree that individuals have a duty not to interfere in various specified ways with the expression of attitudes and beliefs by other individuals, precisely because such interference involves evils analogous to those attending proscribed governmental interferences; and

2. a credible demonstration that this duty admits of reasonably precise specification for the purpose of adjudicating controversies.

If one could make a strong case for both the viability of this analysis and for the contention that it applied to the firing of McIntire by DuPont, then the state action requirement would become superfluous with respect to the question of whether DuPont violated McIntire's First Amendment rights. If, however, neither of these cases could be established, then a state action argument would remain essential in the attempt to bring DuPont's firing of McIntire under constitutional scrutiny.

Furthermore, other important questions would remain, even if one ultimately concluded that McIntire had no valid First Amendment claims. Possibly there are strong grounds for according individuals in McIntire's situation legal protections of a nonconstitutional nature by way of statutes or judicially created remedies. On the other hand, perhaps such a course would seem unwise upon weighing all relevant factors. Or, maybe such legal protections would violate important employer rights, which themselves could be thought of as constitutionally fundamental.

This chapter first concerns itself with whether the First Amendment applies in cases such as the firing of Lewis V. McIntire by DuPont. A theoretical analysis of the kind just described suggests a negative answer to this question. I will proceed, however, to argue for the desirability of according employees in the private sector substantial protection by law, of a nonconstitutional kind, designed to secure for them a right to freedom of expression in the workplace. The exposition of this argument will include grounds for holding that such legal protection would not violate any constitutionally fundamental rights of private employers.

First, a few words are necessary by way of background about the legal situation that confronted McIntire at the time of his firing and that still persists at the present time. Not only would the courts have rejected any constitutional claims he might have put forward under the First Amendment, but in all probability they would not have acknowledged any legal basis whatsoever for him to bring an action against DuPont. For the most part, the common law doctrine of "employment at will" governs employer-employee relations in the private sector. This doctrine looks upon employee and employer as equal partners to an employment contract.[8] Just as employees may resign whenever it pleases them, so also employers may dismiss their employees whenever they desire. This doctrine has been stated forcefully time and again in various court decisions. For example, in *Payne* v. *Western and Atlantic Railroad* the court declared that "employers may dismiss their employees at will . . . for good cause, for no cause, or even for cause morally wrong, without being thereby guilty of legal wrong."[9] Similarly, in *Union Labor Hospital Association* v. *Vance Redwood Lumber Co.* the court said that the "arbitrary right of the employer to employ or discharge labor is settled beyond preadventure."[10] The doctrine of employment at will was recently invoked by the Supreme Court of Pennsylvania to dispose of *Geary* v. *United States Steel Corporation*.[11] In this case Geary, an employee, charged that he was unjustly dismissed by United States Steel after he went outside normal organizational channels to warn a vice-president of the company about defects in the steel tubing that was about to be marketed.[12]

The doctrine of employment at will is sometimes referred to as "Wood's Rule," because it received its classic formulation in H. G. Wood's treatise on the law of master and servant in 1877.[13] Wood's Rule marked a dramatic departure from traditional legal rules regulating the employment relation. According to tradition, when an employment contract specified duration, the courts simply enforced it. If work continued after the expiration date of a specified term, this was taken as implying renewal for an identical period. When no specific duration was mentioned, a judge simply determined the rights of the parties. Wood's Rule radically changed this approach. Under its application, unless duration of employment was specified precisely, the courts simply held that no express provision of the contract dealt with the matter. They then summarily upheld the discharge at issue, with no consideration whatsoever of the equities in the case. In its most pernicious application, Wood's Rule was employed to redefine permanent employment as indefinite and hence terminable at will.[14]

Wood's Rule today remains the dominant approach of most American courts in employee discharge cases. Courts occasionally have upheld suits by discharged employees on grounds of public policy, as when the discharge was for refusal to give perjured testimony,[15] for filing a workman's compensation claim,[16] and for serving on a jury.[17] For the most part, however, courts do not acknowledge even these narrow limitations on the employers' absolute right of discharge. For example, an employee who convinced a jury that he was discharged because he would not vote for certain candidates in a city election was nonetheless barred from recovering damages by the appellate court.[18] Along the same line, a secretary who refused to comply with the order of her superior to indicate falsely that she was not available for jury duty found she had no grounds for recovery when she lost her job. In considering her case the court declared that while the reason for her discharge was "quite reprehensible," "selfish," and "short-sighted," nonetheless "her employer could discharge her with or without cause. . . . It makes no difference if the employer had a bad motive in so doing."[19]

Under the doctrine of employment at will, then, which does not require even minimal standards of just cause for dismissal, most employees in the private sector have no legal remedy if fired for expressing their opinions or attitudes. The situation in the public sector, however, is quite otherwise. Public employees enjoy a substantial right of free expression under the decision of the United States Supreme Court in *Pickering* v. *Board of Education.*[20] This case involved the dismissal of a high school teacher, Pickering, for writing, to a local newspaper, letters that criticized the board of his school in Illinois. Pickering alleged that the board had built an athletic field out of unauthorized bond funds. He charged the board with creating a "totalitarian atmosphere" and of lying to the public to gain support for high school athletics.

Pickering was fired. In his bid for reinstatement he lost in the Illinois courts but ultimately won in the United States Supreme Court. In reviewing his case the Supreme Court first stated that the First Amendment unequivocally applies to public employment. Citing a prior decision, *Keyishian* v. *Board of Regents*, the Court noted that "the theory that public employment . . . may be subjected to any conditions regardless of how unreasonable has been uniformly rejected."[21] Hence, teachers may not be forced to give up the rights they would otherwise have as citizens under the First Amendment to comment on matters of public interest in connection with the schools. The Court did recognize, however, that schools have legitimate interests in regulating employee speech. "The problem . . . is to arrive at a balance between the interests of the teacher as a citizen in commenting upon matters of public concern and the interest of the State, as an employer, in promoting the efficiency of the public services it performs through its employees."[22]

The Court pointed out that Pickering's letter, although sarcastic in tone and occasionally inaccurate, nonetheless only attacked the school board. It did not personally criticize any of the individuals with whom he worked on a day-to-day basis. Thus, it could not be said that to retain Pickering would inevitably lower morale or upset the normal operations of the school where he worked. The Court held that under these circumstances a teacher or, for that matter, any public employee should not be subject to dismissal unless his or her statements were made with knowing or reckless disregard of the truth. As we saw in Chapter Three, the phrase "knowing or reckless disregard of the truth" is precisely the same as the one employed by the Court in *New York Times* v. *Sullivan* with respect to the standard of proof brought by public officials in lawsuits for defamation.[23] Such a standard thus provides nearly absolute protection to public employees in situations similar to Pickering's. Under the rule in *Pickering* v. *Board of Education,* then, courts should focus in most instances upon whether the employee's words so undermined working relationships on the job as to justify the discharge. Applying this test, specific remarks might constitute grounds for discharge in some cases but not in others. Courts should generally look to the specifics of the employment situation rather than concentrating upon the employee's words in and of themselves.

The general approach employed by the Supreme Court in *Pickering* v. *Board of Education* seems entirely appropriate. Indeed, had the Court allowed Pickering's dismissal to stand it would have endorsed an instance of penalization, one of the seven categories of per se violations of the First Amendment. Can one say that constitutionally proscribed penalization obtains not only when done by a governmental body but also by a private business organization? It would seem not. Mill's arguments in *On Liberty* apply directly to situations in which governmental bodies do the penalizing. Penalization is a mode of regulating expression, and Mill's arguments call attention to the grave, long-run social harm that stems from giving a single individual or group power to regulate expression and hence to control thought. Now, while private employers can, and undoubtedly often do, exercise substantial coercive force to discourage their employees from freely expressing themselves, it would seem that no one corporation could exercise the kind of centralized power to control thought of which a strong government would be capable. Accordingly, sanctions by private employers that discourage employees from freely expressing themselves cannot be linked with Mill's arguments in the requisite way to count as penalization.

It would seem that if one does not argue state action, only two possible strategies exist for establishing that a private organization violates the First Amendment by dismissing its employees simply for expressing their opinions or attitudes. First, one may continue to regard Mill's arguments in *On Liberty* as the only philosophically crucial ones for purposes of constitutional theory, and may propose another per se category, in addition to the seven enunciated in Chapter Two, that covers actions such as those taken by DuPont against McIntire. Such an approach seems unpromising. The aforementioned problem with extending penalization to cover sanctions imposed by private parties turns on a general point that appears to undercut any attempts of this kind. Each of the seven per se categories set out in Chapter Two gains its status because it specifies a mode of regulating expression that involves precisely the dangers of thought control by a single individual or group to which Mill calls our attention in *On Liberty*. But since in all likelihood no actions, however pernicious, of any given private organization carry such a danger, the notion of a new per se violation relating such actions to Mill's arguments would seem unconvincing.

The second possible strategy involves (*a*) proposing, in addition to Mill's, another basic philosophical argument with regard to free expression, and (*b*) attempting to demonstrate that dismissal of private employees simply for expressing themselves falls under a per se violation related to this new argument. Such, however, would be a formidable undertaking. Recall that in order for an argument to count as philosophically basic from the standpoint of constitutional theory, it must be the case that rational contractors under a veil of ignorance would unanimously accept it. Not many arguments can satisfy this condition, and even if a given argument succeeds, condition (*b*) remains to be fulfilled. That is, the question of whether one can relate per se violations of the First Amendment to a given philosophical argument is entirely separate from that of whether the argument satisfies the criterion for being philosophically basic, namely that rational contractors would unanimously accept it.

As an example of the difficulties, let us consider various lines of argument. Advocates of free expression in the workplace at times conceive of it as having to do primarily with associated potential benefits to society from increased exposure of corporate corruption, waste, and negligence. The following quotation from *Where the Law Ends* by Christopher Stone exemplifies this approach.

anyone concerned with improving the exchange of information between the corporation and the outside world must pay serious regard to the so-called whistleblower. The corporate work force in America, in the aggregate, will always know more than the best planned government inspection system we are likely to finance. Traditionally workers have kept their mouths shut about "sensitive" matters that come to their attention. There are any number of reasons for this, ranging from peer group expectations, to the employee's more solid fears of being fired . . .

This means that if ethical whistleblowing is to be encouraged some special protections and perhaps even incentives will have to be afforded the whistleblower.[24]

This line of thought, however, does not satisfy the first condition for thinking of a right as constitutionally fundamental—that is, the rational contractors would not unanimously accept it. The reasons for this become clear when one considers the question, "What should happen to whistleblowers who turn out to be wrong?" Following the above approach one would weigh the social benefits and costs associated with corporate whistleblowing. As mentioned above, on the benefit side one can cite the increased exposure of corporate waste, corruption, and negligence. On the cost side, however, one must include the possibility of a general decline in productivity stemming from decreased efficiency as a result of disruptions in the corporate decision-making and administrative routines. In addition, where whistleblowers are mistaken in their allegations about the safety or quality of a product, the affected corporations may unfairly suffer a decline in profits.

A social cost-benefit analysis of corporate dissent not only requires attaching values to the factors involved, but also necessitates an assessment of both the prevalence of antisocial corporate behavior and the nature of its consequences. A person who regards such behavior not only as commonplace but also as gravely harmful would advocate extensive protection for corporate dissenters, holding that the costs associated with mistaken allegations they might make count for relatively little in the balance. On the other hand, if serious corporate misbehavior is looked upon as the exception rather than the rule, then a different view of the matter becomes appropriate. Indeed, depending upon how exceptional one regards it, and how heavily one weighs the costs associated with corporate dissent, it might be reasonable to suggest that such dissent should be thought of by analogy with the common law rules regulating citizen's arrests. Specifically, a person making a citizen's arrest avoids tort liability for unlawful detention only if the person he or she arrested *actually* committed a felony. Reasonable belief is not a defense.[25] By analogy, someone who regards corporate misconduct as exceptional might say that freedom of expression in corporations should only extend to dissenters who turn out to be right.

The prevalence of serious corporate misbehavior, and the nature of its social consequences, are empirical issues lying beyond the scope of this discussion.[26] The point to be noted here, however, is that when one makes the case for freedom of expression in corporations by way of the foregoing approach, the question of *how much* freedom corporate employees should have involves weighing of costs and benefits, a process that essentially depends upon one's beliefs about matters with regard to which rational people may differ substantially.

Another line of argument initially appears more promising. We saw earlier that in chapter three of *On Liberty* Mill contends that certain abilities and capacities, such as observation, judgment, discrimination, firmness of will, and so forth, are the distinctive endowment of a human being.[27] These abilities and capacities, which Mill regards as elements of what he terms individuality, make it possible to discern and desire what is best.[28] Thus, in the proportion to which people have them they become both more valuable to themselves and potentially more valuable to others.[29] Furthermore, Mill contends persuasively that according to any reasonable conception of the good for society, it should be a primary function of social arrangements to facilitate everyone's cultivating his or her individuality, as understood above, to the greatest possible degree.[30] Individuality, so understood, consists in the possession of a variety of different abilities and capacities, all of which can be developed only by exercising them.[31] Without freedom of expression, however, the likelihood for such development on a large scale is extremely low.[32]

Now, the near-unanimous testimony of people with substantial work experience in the corporate world is that business corporations generally tend *not* to be places in which employees feel free to express their beliefs and attitudes. When CBS televised a program on Phillips Petroleum Corporation, William V. Keeler, then its chief executive, said of the employee who deviates from unwritten company rules about dress, manners, or other behavior, "The rest of the pack turns against him."[33] In his review of the program in the *New York Times*, John J. O'Connor noted that at Phillips there was a "direct ratio between the extent of an individual's ambitions and the pressure for conformity."[34] Phillips may be an extreme case, but if so it is an extreme case of a situation common to most large business corporations—namely, the absence of an open atmosphere conducive to free expression by employees.

It would appear then that the corporate workplace tends to stifle the individuality that Mill accords predominant importance. This does not imply, however, that most corporate employees find their day-to-day work environments unbearably oppressive. A great many do enjoy their jobs, and the vast majority find them at least acceptable. Nor does the claim that the work atmosphere in corporations stifles individuality commit one to holding that such an effect may be directly observed by comparing corporate employees with some properly selected contrast group in regard to degree of individuality. The claim is not based primarily upon actual observation of the kinds of personal characteristics people tend to develop, or fail to develop, when employed by large private corporations.[35] Rather, it rests in part on empirical support and in part on theory. One can say, with strong empirical support, that free expression seldom exists in the corporate workplace. The contention that such a state of affairs tends to stifle individuality, however, rests upon Mill's persuasive theoretical analysis to that effect.

One might hold that the foregoing points suggest a new basic philosophical argument with respect to freedom of expression. Mill contends that without freedom of expression a person's individuality remains uncultivated, and that from both an individual and a social perspective the development of this trait should be accorded primary importance. While these observations suggest the undesirability of governmental interference with the expression of beliefs and attitudes, they also constitute a strong argument against anything else that undermines the development of individuality. Mill's arguments in *On Liberty*, which ground the account of the seven per se violations, turn specifically upon the evil that results from according a single person or group the power to regulate expression. Nonetheless, the undesirable condition associated with a denial of free expression to which Mill calls our attention in chapter three of *On Liberty*—that is, the stifling of individuality—can obtain when coercive interference with the expression of beliefs and attitudes stems from a multitude of independent sources.

What matters most is that individuality be fostered on a large scale. Whether a governmental or private body prevents this from happening, the consequences are equally lamentable. Accordingly, governments have not only a negative duty to refrain from restricting expression in ways that tend to undermine the fostering of individuality, but also a positive duty to prevent private organizations from doing so. Accordingly, if one accepts this conclusion, the First Amendment can be thought of as applying to restrictions upon employee expression by private organizations. To the extent that restrictions in the corporate workplace, or any other workplace in the private sector, tend to stifle individuality, it would appear that one has compelling grounds to hold that such restrictions should not exist and that governmental authorities should step in to eradicate them. One obvious means of doing so would be to countenance direct legal action by employees against employers under the First Amendment.

The above argument, which goes substantially beyond those that I have attributed to Mill, incorporates a number of sound points. Nonetheless, it must be rejected. At most it only shows that the notion of a right of employees from restrictions upon their freedom of expression by private employers satisfies the first condition for a right to be deemed constitutionally fundamental. One can cite strong grounds for holding that the notion of such a right cannot satisfy the second condition. In other words, possibly one can say that rational contractors under a veil of ignorance would regard actions by private employers, which have the effect of hindering the development of individuality, with the same disfavor as they would governmental actions which have such an effect. However, the principle that individuals should have a measure of protection against such actions by private individuals would have a status akin to the duty to eliminate inequality cited at the beginning of Chapter One.[36] It was suggested there that this duty only binds governmental authorities, so to speak, *in foro interno*. That is, one can say generally that legislators who willfully or heedlessly disregard the implications of various social policies with regard to their distributional effects should be morally condemned. The notion of a duty to eliminate inequality, however, cannot be articulated with sufficient precision to say over a wide range of specific cases whether legislators have violated it. For that reason the notion of a constitutionally fundamental right to equality of income must be rejected.

A similar problem attends the idea of constitutionally mandated protection of individuals from private activities that tend to undermine the development of individuality. Rational people differ significantly over what actions have such an effect. Consider in this regard the enormous area of disagreement about the best methods of child care and primary schooling. If such extensive disagreement exists in but one domain, consider both the analytical and practical problems that would result from holding governments responsible, as a constitutional matter, for assessing the effects of all relationships among private parties upon the development of individuality. Specifically in regard to the workplace, one can argue that individuality on a wide scale can flourish only under background conditions of general economic well-being. Certain modes of discipline in a work setting, however, are indispensable for the maintenance of efficient production or delivery of services. Accordingly, freedom of expression in the workplace must not extend so far as to undermine seriously the conditions of material prosperity upon which individuality also depends. Rational people nevertheless can differ significantly in specific instances about whether proposed measures to enhance freedom of expression for private sector employees would have such an effect. The seemingly basic cleavage between optimists and pessimists about human nature would manifest itself in disagreements over this matter, no less than it does in other important issues of political and social theory.[37]

The above considerations strongly suggest that, at least in cases involving the First Amendment, the requirement of state action has a genuine theoretical basis. It would seem that the only duties concerning free expression reasonably ascribable from a constitutional standpoint to a government all simply forbid various kinds of actions on its part. The notion of a constitutionally mandated right of individuals to protection from private behavior that undermines the purposes associated with the right to freedom of expression cannot be made plausible.

This still leaves the question of whether the actions of at least some private organizations fall under the state action concept. One widely discussed recent case reached an affirmative conclusion. In *Holodnak* v. *Avco-Lycoming Division*, the rule in *Pickering* was extended to apply in a situation where the employer was a private concern heavily involved in Department of Defense contract work.[38] Michael Holodnak, a skilled employee with nine years' experience, wrote an article in a local newspaper criticizing both management and union leadership at his plant. Holodnak was fired under a company rule that forbade employees from "making false, vicious, or malicious statements concerning . . . the employee's relationship" to the company. Holodnak first went to arbitration, but the decision went against him (the district court later concluded that the union attorney made only a half-hearted attempt to defend him). He next went to the United States District Court of Connecticut, where his dismissal was ruled unjust. The court noted Avco-Lycoming's close relationship to the government, which actually owned most of the land, buildings, and equipment at its plant. In addition, about 80 percent of Avco-Lycoming's production was defense-related. Furthermore, the government maintained a large force on site to oversee operations. Thus, while agreeing that the First Amendment does not apply to a private employer, the court stated that workers at Avco-Lycoming were protected in virtue of the "government presence" at the plant.[39]

Though it is often cited, thus far other courts have declined to follow *Holodnak* v. *Avco-Lycoming Division*. Nonetheless, David Ewing views the *Holodnak* case as enormously important from a theoretical standpoint. If workers at a company with 80 percent sales to government fall under the scope of the First Amendment, Ewing asks, then why not workers at a company with 50 percent or 35 percent government sales?[40] He suggests that *Holodnak* may well lead ultimately to a dramatic reorientation of the judicial approach to employee rights.[41]

Ewing's conjecture may indeed come to pass. One seldom can predict the path of development with regard to legal doctrine in the constitutional domain. Yet a closer look at the concept of state action raises grave questions about whether it would be an appropriate legal basis from the standpoint of intellectual coherence for expanding the right to freedom of expression for employees in the private sector. Essentially, the Supreme Court has applied three separate analyses to determine whether a given act by a private party falls under the concept of state action. None of these approaches, however, applies to the actions of most private employers toward their employees, even in the case of large corporations.

First, the Court has held that state action exists when private parties perform public functions. The leading case in this regard is *Marsh* v. *Alabama* (1946), when the owners of a company town were required to allow Marsh, a Jehovah's Witness, to distribute religious literature.[42] Referring to the various aspects of the town, such as its streets and sidewalks, Justice Black wrote, "Since these facilities are built and operated primarily to benefit the public and since their operation is essentially a public function it [the company town] is subject to state regulation."[43]

Unfortunately, subsequent cases have left highly unclear what counts as a public function and why.[44] The problem is that, on the one hand, a characterization of public functions as activities actually engaged in by governments sweeps far too wide; it includes virtually anything. On the other hand, to characterize public functions as those that as a matter of fact are performed only by governments would be to rule out almost everything. It seems that what one needs to make the notion of a public function viable is a philosophical account of government that provides theoretical reasons for treating certain of its activities as basic. One could then say of private parties who engage in these basic governmental activities that they perform public functions. Now, insofar as such a theory never has been adumbrated for constitutional purposes, not much can be said about salient features. It would appear, however, that when one considers the myriad commercial activities engaged in by various business organizations, it scarcely seems credible to regard most of them as performing *basic* governmental activities.

The second primary mode of analysis the Supreme Court employs in dealing with state action cases may be termed the significant state involvement approach. The basic idea here is that even if ostensibly private activity does not constitute the performing of a public function, nonetheless it may fall under the state action concept in virtue of significant state involvement with it. The Federal District Court of Connecticut appears to have relied upon this approach in *Holodnak* v. *Avco-Lycoming Division*. The court found state action in that case because the government involved itself so extensively with the operation of Avco-Lycoming's plant.[45]

This approach presents the analytical problem of specifying general conditions under which state involvement with private activity may be deemed "significant." As with the public function mode of analysis, here too the Supreme Court has left matters extremely indefinite, as illustrated by the case of *Burton v. Wilmington Parking Authority*.[46] The issue in this case was whether a privately owned and operated restaurant located within a municipal parking facility could be enjoined from refusing to serve blacks. The case occurred prior to passage of the 1964 Civil Rights Act, so the only basis upon which to seek an injunction was that the activities of the restaurant fell under the concept of state action.

Though the Court held that the concept indeed applied, the majority opinion failed to make the reasons for this conclusion perspicuously clear. The opinion first cited seven diverse features noted by the lower court as grounds for denying the applicability of the state action concept.[47] It then, however, cited six other factors that it deemed to override the seven noted by the lower court.[48] The Supreme Court nonetheless explicitly declined to make any general remarks to explain why the six factors it cited should be considered decisive. The majority opinion thus prompted Justice Harlan to complain in a dissent that "the Court's opinion by a process of first undiscriminatingly throwing together various factual bits and pieces, and then undermining the resulting structure by an equally vague disclaimer, seems to me to leave completely at sea just what it is in this record that satisfies the requirement of 'state action.' "[49]

The Court's opinion may not have left matters quite so intellectually chaotic. The following passage, referring to the relationship between the municipal parking authority and the restaurant, I think at least suggests an approach to dealing with the question of what factors count as relevant under the significant state involvement criterion of state action.

The State has so far insinuated itself into a position of interdependence with Eagle [the restaurant] that it must be recognized as a joint participant in the challenged activity, which on that account cannot be considered to have been so "purely private" as to fall without the scope of the Fourteenth Amendment.[50]

This passage suggests that one may think of the intuitive idea behind the significant state involvement test as that of "joint participation" or, better yet, "joint action," that is, the ascription of a single act to two or more persons. In other words, under certain circumstances a governmental body becomes so involved in the acts of a private party that one can rightly ascribe the act to both of them. A question remains, however, about the general nature of such circumstances. In this regard one can say that joint action is not simply a matter of two or more persons contributing to the production of a given effect. Person A may pick up about half the litter in a given area, and then an hour later Person B, entirely unacquainted with A, may pick up the rest of it. Here A and B are jointly responsible for a certain effect, namely, the cleaning of the area. One would not say, however, that they performed a single act together. Such could be said only if the two of them shared the same intention. That is, A and B would both have to intend that *we* (A and B) clean the area.[51]

Taking joint participation, and hence joint intent, as central in applying the significant state involvement approach provides some, though only moderate, assistance. The notion of joint intent itself requires substantial elucidation. The foregoing remarks then do not by themselves provide guidance as to what factors one should focus upon when using the significant state involvement test for state action. Instead, they merely point to the concept whose clarification necessarily must precede a successful account of those factors.

I regret that I have no insights to offer on the conditions for ascription of joint intent. It would seem, however, that one can say at least the following: in any reasonable conception of joint intent, in only a very few cases could activities be thought of as jointly intended by private business organizations and governmental agencies. Possibly, the policies of the restaurant in *Burton* v. *Wilmington Parking Authority* admit of such a construal. In this regard the majority opinion laid considerable stress upon the fact that the parking authority both knew of and benefited from the restaurant's policies. These features strike one as the kinds of things one might point to as indicia of intent, although admittedly in the absence of a general analysis of joint intent such an observation is based entirely upon intuition. Given the facts in the *Holodnak* case, the notion of joint intent may not be out of place. But these cases would seem relatively infrequent. By contrast, when one considers others, such as the firing of Lewis V. McIntire by DuPont, the notion of action jointly intended by a government agency and a private business organization seems highly out of place. This second approach to the concept of state action thus does not provide a broad basis for bringing private business organizations under the scope of the First Amendment.

The third major approach to state action taken by the Supreme Court may be termed the facilitation test.[52] This test applies only in contexts where courts take the undesirability of certain conduct by private parties as given. In such contexts, state action obtains if the government, either through action or inaction, has facilitated the undesirable conduct. In the case of *Reitman* v. *Mulkey* the Supreme Court employed this test to strike down as unconstitutional Article I, section 26 of the California State Constitution, which provided in part that "[n]either the State nor any subdivision or agency thereof shall deny, or abridge, directly or indirectly, the right of any person, who is willing or desires to sell, lease, or rent any part or all of his real property, to decline to sell, lease, or rent such property to such person or persons as he, in his absolute discretion, chooses."[53] The Court maintained that the above provision, which made fair-housing laws unconstitutional under the California State Constitution, had the effect of facilitating racial discrimination.[54]

Justice Harlan, joined by Justices Black, Clark, and Stewart, vigorously dissented.[55] He noted that the provision at issue in this case was adopted by way of a statewide referendum in 1964 as a direct response to the Unruh and Rumford Acts, two state fair-housing measures enacted respectively in 1959 and 1963. To be sure, Justice Harlan observed, the new provision made discrimination in housing easier for private individuals relative to the situation at the time of its adoption. It made discrimination that was illegal under the 1959 and 1963 acts permisable on the basis of race. Harlan, however, regarded this point as irrelevant because these two acts were in no way constitutionally required. In other words, according to Harlan, the fact that the new provision made discrimination easier relative to the situation immediately prior to its enactment could not be regarded as grounds for holding that it unconstitutionally facilitated discrimination. To do so would involve the following anomaly: it would imply that while the Constitution does not require enactment of state fair-housing laws, nonetheless, once enacted, it forbids repealing them. Harlan went on to pose the real issue—whether the provision facilitated discrimination relative to the situation *prior* to the passing of the two state fair-housing laws. He maintained that indeed it did not. That is, under the new provision racial discrimination in housing was not easier to accomplish than under a situation where no state fair-housing laws exist. For this reason Harlan concluded that the provision at issue could not be said to facilitate discrimination.

Justice Harlan's dissenting opinion reveals a crucial aspect of the facilitation test. To say that certain governmental action, or inaction, facilitates undesirable private conduct is to say that it makes it easier to accomplish. But easier as compared with what? In this regard one must have a standard of comparison in mind. Suppose one proposes to bring the area of free expression in the private workplace within the constitutional sphere by maintaining that governmental inaction facilitates actions of private employers that discourage employees from freely expressing themselves. This would be to suggest that such inaction makes the above undesirable activities of private employers easier for them. Again, compared with what?

One cannot take the conditions that normally obtain as one's standard of comparison. As noted earlier, the doctrine of employment at will still remains the dominant legal rule pertaining to employee-employer relations in the private sector. Suppose, then, one adopts as a standard of comparison the conditions that one believes *ought* to obtain. To take this tack unfortunately involves an indirect yet vicious circularity. That is, if one takes the circumstances that obtain when the government does what one takes to be its duty as the standard of comparison in applying the facilitation test, then the argument for bringing private employers under the First Amendment may be rendered as follows:

1. The government has a constitutional duty to prevent activities by private employers that discourage employees from freely expressing themselves only if the concept of state action applies to such activities.
2. The concept of state action indeed applies, because governmental failure to prevent the above kind of undesirable behavior by private employers constitutes facilitation of it.
3. Such inaction constitutes facilitation of the above type of undesirable behavior by private employers, because it makes it easier for them to do it than would be the case if the government fulfilled its constitutional duty to prevent such behavior.

Government therefore has a constitutional duty to prevent activities by private employers that discourage employees from freely expressing themselves.

As is evident, the third premise of the above argument presupposes the conclusion. It would seem then that the facilitation test cannot be employed to bring the area of free expression in the private workplace under the concept of state action.

To summarize the ground covered thus far, three possible strategies for extending the First Amendment to cover employer-employee relations in the private sector have been considered and found to have serious problems. First, one cannot maintain that there exists a per se category of First Amendment violation related to Mill's arguments in *On Liberty* that applies to restrictions upon freedom of expression in the private sector. Second, it seems unlikely that one can advance a new philosophical argument and then demonstrate that dismissal of private employees for expressing themselves falls under a per se violation related to that new argument. Finally, no matter which mode of analysis one considers with regard to the concept of state action, limitations by private employers upon freedom of expression of their employees do not fall under the concept.

It would appear then that one must reject the idea of a constitutionally protected right to freedom of expression in the private workplace. This by no means, however, necessarily implies rejecting the possibility of creating such a right through nonconstitutional means, for example, by way of judicial decisions or statutes. Constitutional argument must satisfy extremely strong constraints not applicable to legal rulemaking in case law or statutory contexts. As we have seen, a constitutional argument, in the first instance, must be such that rational contractors under a veil of ignorance would unanimously accept it. By contrast, nonconstitutional judicial decisions or policy arguments for a statute need not satisfy such a strict standard. Precisely what standards they should satisfy is not easy to say. Nonetheless, it would seem that these standards bear a relationship to the conditions of adequacy for constitutional argument akin to that between the "preponderance of the evidence" standard of proof in civil litigation and the "beyond a reasonable doubt" standard in criminal law. In other words, one makes one's case for enactment of a statute by arguing persuasively that on balance the points in favor of it outweigh those against it. The situation with respect to introducing a new rule judicially is somewhat more complex, because judges have an institutional duty in civil litigation to decide the cases before them in ways that cohere reasonably with the accumulated body of precedent. As remarked by many and diverse legal theorists, however, this duty leaves room for an extremely broad exercise of discretion in numerous cases. Subject then to the constraint of institutional duty, one justifies judicially created rules by appeal to the same standard one applies with respect to statutory enactments, namely, that the advantages of introducing a new rule on balance outweigh the disadvantages.

When we considered whether any other constitutionally sufficient arguments for freedom of expression exist besides Mill's, strong grounds emerged for holding that many work environments in the private sector tend to stifle individuality.[56] While such an observation does not support the notion of a constitutionally based duty of government to counteract this state of affairs, it does suggest that, to the extent governmental action can do so without undermining equally important interests, it should make the effort. In this regard the Supreme Court's approach in *Pickering* v. *Board of Education* to public sector employer-employee relations would seem equally appropriate for private employment contexts. Under *Pickering* employees may say whatever they wish as long as (*a*) they do not knowingly or recklessly disregard the truth and (*b*) their acts of expression do not irretrievably undermine working relationships. Such an approach seems to accommodate reasonably the most important interests at stake. The approach fosters individuality by way of according private employees considerable latitude for expressing themselves. Efficiency and morale remain protected, however, by the proviso that Courts may uphold a dismissal or other sanction against an employee when his or her words have a severely deleterious effect upon the relationships of individuals who must work together.

In light of such an approach, an executive would not be compelled to continue working with a secretary who had publicly denounced him or her. On the other hand, if the denunciation was made, let us say, by an employee in the mailroom, with whom the executive had little or no contact in the normal course of events, then dismissal would not be allowed.[57] Along the same lines, the *Pickering* approach applies in a reasonable way to the situation of small businesses. In such cases highly critical remarks by employees could very possibly damage working relationships with the employer to an extent that would justify dismissal.[58]

Over the past decade or so a voluminous literature has emerged concerning alternatives to the doctrine of employment at will. If the *Pickering* approach were extended to the private sector, any number of these alternatives could be introduced to provide the appropriate legal remedies for employees who suffer at the hands of their employers simply because they expressed their beliefs and attitudes. In this regard Lawrence E. Blades has proposed that the law recognize a new cause of action, which he terms "abusive discharge," pertaining to cases where employees suffer as a result of unjust dismissals.[59] Blades sees such an approach as a natural extension of basic principles in the law of torts. In his words, "If the employer invades legally protected rights of the employee, for instance, by the infliction of bodily injury or by defamation, the existence of the employment 'contract' does not stand in the way of determining employee rights under the law of torts. Since analogous interests are at stake when the employer unreasonably attempts to interfere with his personal freedom, it seems reasonable to bypass the law of contracts and its unyielding requirement for consideration by turning to the more elastic principles of tort law for a suitable basis upon which to predicate the discharged employee's suit for damages."[60]

Blades notes that remedies for abusive discharge similar to those he advocates already exist under various statutes. The National Labor Relations Board, for example, is empowered to grant damages, in the form of back pay and reinstatement, to employees discharged for involvement in union activities. In a similar fashion, various civil rights and fair-employment practices commissions have responsibility for protecting against discriminatory practices in hiring and firing. The Federal Automobile Dealer Franchise Act of 1956 provides a remedy to wrongfully disenfranchised dealers. This law provides a particularly interesting parallel to employee discharge cases because in drafting it, Congress responded to a problem not unlike the one that obtains in most employer-employee relationships, namely, the ability of the manufacturer to take unfair advantage of the dealer in virtue of its power to terminate the relationship.

Blades points to the tort of abuse of process as providing a useful analogy in many respects for conceiving of a new cause of action for abusive discharge. In this regard he writes. "[i]t can be said the discharge at the will of the employer, like resort to legal procedures, is in its essence lawful. It can also be said, as with the right to invoke the processes of the law, that the employer's right of discharge is too valuable a right to be encumbered with unnecessary limitations. But as with any individual's right to bring legal action, the law should not allow the employer to exercise his right of discharge in order to effectuate a purpose ulterior to that for which it was designed."[61]

Taking a different approach than Blades, J. Peter Shapiro and James F. Tune have argued that courts should recognize implied contract rights to job security.[62] They suggest that such an approach is implicit in two important Supreme Court cases, *Board of Regents* v. *Roth* and *Perry* v. *Sindermann*.[63] In *Roth* a newly employed college teacher, who had a nine-month memorandum contract, was not rehired for the succeeding year. He was given no reason for this action and denied a hearing with respect to it. The Supreme Court rejected the claim that the lack of a hearing and statement of reasons for Roth's nonrenewal violated his Fourteenth Amendment right to due process. The Court noted that Roth had no job security rights either under his contract or under state statutes. Hence, any property right he claimed in his job had to be determined from the circumstances of the appointment. The Court, however, found nothing in these circumstances to support such a claim.

Perry v. *Sindermann* involved dismissal without stated reasons or a hearing of a teacher, Sindermann, who had taught full time for ten years. Since the school at which he taught did not have a tenure system Sindermann did not enjoy formal job security. The school's faculty guide, however, stated that a faculty member's job was secure as long as his or her services were satisfactory. Unlike in *Roth*, the Court here held that given these conditions it was an open question whether or not Sindermann had a property right in his job. If so, then he was entitled at least to a statement of reasons for dismissal and a hearing with regard to them. If not, then he was not. The Court thus remanded Sindermann's case to the lower court to resolve the question of whether Sindermann had a property right in his teaching job.

Shapiro and Tune suggest that the *Roth* and *Sindermann* cases point by implication to an implied contractual right to job security. The factors for determination of whether such a right obtains in particular circumstances relate primarily to the employment situation. The *Sindermann* case involved some such factors, namely length of service and stated policies of the employer. According to Shapiro and Tune, however, others should be considered as well. Among these they cite the following:

1. Separate consideration: did the employee confer some additional benefit upon the employer in taking the position at issue, such as making financial contributions to the employer's business? Or, did the employer induce special reliance by the employee so that the latter passed up valuable opportunities in choosing to work for the former? In this regard, the mode of recruitment—i.e., "hard sell or soft sell"—may be crucial.
2. Nature of the job: does the job at issue, by its very nature, imply a definite duration? In this regard, some positions involve a clear tacit understanding of terminability at will, e.g., a church congregation's employment of a minister.
3. Common law of the industry: the general practice with regard to employment in a particular line of work may be considered an implied part of the bargain, especially when an employer expects or encourages this understanding.

Although Shapiro and Tune do not discuss free expression for private employees, their broad approach would provide it substantial protection.

Blades and Shapiro and Tune favor eliminating the doctrine of employment at will through judicial action. By contrast, Clyde W. Summers believes that an overwhelming case exists for comprehensive state laws to protect employees from unjust dismissal.[64] He contends that despite the variety of plausible legal theories available for developing such protection, on the whole courts have declined to employ them on the ground that doing so would initiate a perilous journey into "uncharted territory."[65]

Comprehensive state statutes thus seem to Summers the most effective and practical means of protecting workers against unjust dismissal. Contrary to prevailing judicial opinion, Summers maintains that enacting such statutes would not involve traveling into uncharted territory. Indeed, a mature set of basic principles for unjust dismissal cases has evolved out of the accumulated experience of labor arbitrators. Summers notes that for at least the past two decades, arbitration of grievances under collective bargaining agreements has primarily involved applying these principles to specific cases. Moreover, in drafting comprehensive statutes, states could draw upon the experiences of many countries throughout the world, including England, Germany, France, and Sweden, which already have laws in place providing for the adjudication of employee grievances.

Summers thus proposes statutes reaching all forms of disciplinary action in the workplace and covering all employees, both public and private, with perhaps an exception for very small enterprises. He believes that such statutes can best be built upon the standards of the existing arbitration system. Thus, the term "just cause" should not be statutorily defined, for the existing body of precedent has already given it a definite yet flexible content. Claims under the statute would be submitted to arbitration. One possible procedure would provide that if the parties were unable to agree on an arbitrator, one would then be selected from a panel maintained for that purpose by the state. Arbitrators under the statutes Summers proposes would have the same scope and flexibility in determining remedies as do arbitrators under collective bargaining agreements.

It would seem that on balance a strong case exists for introducing the foregoing kinds of measures in order to promote freedom of expression in the private workplace. Such a judgment, however, is not, as Bernard Gert would say, required by reason.[66] In other words, though the judgment seems highly plausible to me, it may not seem at all plausible to other rational people. Indeed, for this reason one cannot regard the above kinds of measures as constitutionally required. Nonetheless, belief in their desirability, all things considered, constitutes sufficient ground to advocate in good faith their adoption through nonconstitutional means, such as statutory or judicial rulemaking.

This last point, in all likelihood, would be vigorously disputed in certain quarters. Some writers might well argue that if put into effect the proposals advanced by Blades, Shapiro and Tune, or Summers would violate rights of employers so basic as to merit constitutional status. Such a viewpoint seems implicit in Robert Nozick's influential book *Anarchy, State, and Utopia*.[67] Nozick devotes himself in part one of this book to demonstrating that governmental institutions, which perform only the functions of enforcing contracts and protecting citizens against force, theft, and fraud, would emerge out of the state of nature, as conceived of by John Locke, and they would do so in a way that involved no morally impermissable behavior on anyone's part.[68] Nozick refers to a government whose activities are limited to carrying out the above functions as "the minimal state."[69] He then begins part two of his book with the following statements: "The minimal state is the most extensive state that can be justified. Any state more extensive violates people's rights."[70]

Nozick would most likely regard measures to facilitate freedom of expression of employees in the private sector as going beyond the legitimate functions of government. Of course, one might note that to include the protection of citizens from force in a list of basic aims of government, by itself, leaves open what falls under this concept. Nozick nowhere explicitly denies that an action such as the firing of McIntire by DuPont counts as using force according to his understanding of the term. Nonetheless, he emphasizes the narrowness of legitimate governmental activity on his view with such strenuousness that one can only suppose that, no matter how Nozick understands force, it does not encompass sanctions by private employers against their employees solely for expressing themselves.

Though perhaps the issue could be jointed with Nozick at this point, there is another, more fundamental, problem. Presumably, according to his approach, measures such as those advocated by Blades, Shapiro and Tune, or Summers would, if put into effect, violate the basic moral rights of employers.[71] But precisely what basic moral rights? Unfortunately, Nozick's book provides no definite answer to this question.[72] One can only speculate upon his likely response. In this regard, one sometimes hears other supporters of Nozick's general outlook in political philosophy express a broad principle of freedom of association, to the effect that one should be free from governmental interference to enter into any kind of voluntary association with others, as long as doing so violates no one else's basic moral rights.[73] Perhaps then, some such principle as this is the presumed basic moral right which a Nozickian would cite as the one infringed by statutory or judicial rulemaking to facilitate freedom of expression for employees in the private sector.

The idea of a basic moral right to such a broad freedom of association is closely related to the idea of an even broader moral right, namely, the right to do whatever one wants as long as so doing violates no basic moral rights of others. This latter right implies the former, and the former, though not logically implying the latter, has as one of its consequences that, provided no one's basic moral rights are violated in the process, one has a right to perform any activity jointly that one might do alone.

Those in Nozick's camp thus often posit two closely related basic moral rights. The first is a right to freedom from governmental interference to enter into any kind of voluntary association, on condition that doing so violates no one else's basic moral rights. The second is an even broader right to do whatever one wants, again, as long as one avoids violating the basic moral rights of others. Noting the close connection between these two concepts of moral rights helps to illustrate the major difficulties that attend the first of them. For convenience, I will set out these difficulties in connection with the latter notion of a basic moral right to do whatever one wants. The exposition in this regard, however, should make it clear that identical difficulties beset the former notion.

To begin, the proviso conditioning freedom to do as one pleases upon a requirement that one not violate the *basic* moral rights of others poses the following problem: it makes application of any given basic moral right to specific situations highly uncertain in the absence of a well-articulated philosophical theory of such rights. The situation here resembles that in connection with the notion of vagueness and overbreadth as per se violations of the First Amendment. As noted in Chapter Two, objecting to a law as too vague or too broad presupposes for intelligibility precise standards of vagueness and overbreadth. By the same token, the principle that one may do whatever one pleases on the condition that in doing so one not violate the basic moral rights of others has virtually no content unless backed up by a philosophically adequate and reasonably workable conception of basic moral rights. Although one can hardly dismiss the possibility of such a conception, as far as I am aware, none as yet exists.[74]

More seriously, on any reasonable conception of basic moral rights, one can imagine an enormous number of counter-examples to the principle that governmental restrictions upon behavior that violate no basic moral rights are fundamentally unjustifiable. In this regard, consider the following very partial list:

1. municipal ordinances that forbid playing musical instruments in apartment buildings after 10:00 P.M.,
2. ordinances limiting the areas in which one may walk dogs in public parks,

3. park regulations that limit use of tennis courts to one hour when others want to play,
4. legal rules that have the effect of imposing liability upon a person for negligently spilling coffee on another person's suit,
5. legal rules requiring railroad companies to compensate farmers for crop damage by railroad train sparks, and
6. legal rules that impose liability in an automobile accident involving fender damage upon the party who did not have the right-of-way.

While all the above rules, imposing either direct or indirect restrictions upon conduct, appear eminently justifiable, none can be thought of plausibly as protecting basic moral rights of individuals. The notion that one has such *basic* moral rights as freedom from the absence of canines in certain designated areas, assurance of court time on public tennis courts, freedom from negligent soiling of one's clothes by others, and so forth, seems counterintuitive, to put the point conservatively. One might object that violations of the foregoing rules would indeed infringe basic moral rights, but of a highly general nature. The first three rules involve potential conflicts with respect to the use of a common space. Accordingly, so this objection would have it, these rules all in diverse ways protect the right to fair treatment. Along similar lines, the second three rules involve negligent conduct. For this reason they could be deemed to protect another general basic moral right, namely, the right not to suffer harm from the negligence of others.

The foregoing response, however, does not suffice. Writers such as Nozick, for whom the notion of basic moral rights looms large, invariably contrast judgments concerning them with judgments that compare various courses of action with respect to net social benefit. The former kind of judgment, according to their view, sets the boundaries, so to speak, within which one may act upon judgments of the latter kind.[75] In other words, one may act on calculations of net social benefit only so long as doing so violates no one's basic moral rights. Now it would seem that the distinction between these two kinds of judgments collapses should it turn out in a given case that one can determine whether basic moral rights have been infringed only by assessing which of the possible ways of dealing with it maximizes the net social benefit.

Such, however, would appear to be precisely the case with the above six rules. In the first three, fairness, as it pertains to adjudicating or mediating potential conflict over use of a common space, really amounts to nothing more than determination of which pattern of uses maximizes social benefits. At any rate, individuals who bear responsibility for such decisions characteristically approach them this way. More important, they conceive of themselves as trying to be fair precisely insofar as they weight costs and benefits impartially. To be sure, in all but the simplest of cases, such an approach seldom yields determinate conclusions.[76] But this simply indicates the existence of an enormous gray zone with respect to questions of fairness in this domain within which rational people can differ in good faith. The notion of a body of principles applicable to questions of fairness in the resolution of potential conflict over uses of a common space, which completely eschews social cost-benefit analysis, would thus seem implausible.

We have a similar situation with the second three rules. Negligent behavior essentially involves failure to exercise reasonable care. But how does one determine reasonableness in this regard? Overwhelmingly, legal theorists treat the answer to this question as intimately bound up with assessment of social benefits and costs. Learned Hand succinctly expressed the dominant train of thought on this matter in the case of *U.S.* v. *Carroll Towing Company*.[77] The issue in that case was whether the owners of a vessel were negligent in not having a hand on board to prevent the vessel from breaking loose of her moorings. In the following now-famous passage Hand formulated the basic analytical framework for dealing with this question:

Since there are occasions when every vessel will break away from her moorings, since if she does, she becomes a menace to those about her, the owner's duty, as in other similar situations, to provide against resulting injuries is a function of three variables: (1) the probability that she will break away; (2) the gravity of the resulting injury, if she does; (3) the burden of adequate precautions. Possibly it serves to bring this notion into relief to state it in algebraic terms: if the probability be called P, the injury L, and the burden B, liability depends upon whether B is less than L multiplied by P; i.e, whether B is less than PL.[78]

To paraphrase, the law deems a person negligent in a given case for failure to adhere to the standard of care required of a reasonable person. It determines what reasonable care amounts to in a particular situation by comparing the costs associated with preventing harms that possibly attend situations of the same kind with the expected value of suffering such harms. Richard Posner explains this approach succinctly as follows in connection with our fifth case above, that of sparks from a railroad train causing damage to crops planted along the tracks:

The economic goal of liability rules in such a case is to maximize the joint value of the interfering activities, railroading and farming. To identify the value-maximizing solution requires a comparison of the costs to the railroad of taking steps to reduce spark emissions to various levels, including zero, and the costs to farmers of either tolerating or themselves taking steps to reduce the damage to their property from the sparks. . . . The railroad will be adjudged negligent if the crop damage exceeds the cost to the railroad of avoiding that damage. But the farmer will still not prevail if the cost of the measures *he* might have taken to avoid the damage to his crops is less than the crop damage; this is the rule of contributory negligence.[79]

The Hand formula thus recommends, in effect, that we place liability upon the party who can avoid a given kind of mishap at the least cost. Borrowing Professor Guido Calabresi's terminology, we can say that the Hand formula calls for placing liability on the "least cost avoider"—that is, the party whom placing liability upon minimizes the costs associated with a kind of mishap, all things considered.[80] If the burden of prevention is less than the expected costs of a mishap, then the party in the best position to take such precautions qualifies as the least cost avoider, and should have liability placed upon him or her. Similarly, if PL is less than B, one minimizes costs by lettng them fall on the individual suffering as a result of the mishap.

The foregoing analysis tends to become enormously complicated when one departs from two-party situations. Indeed, most interesting cases are so complicated that a rule advising one to place liability on the least cost avoider has only slightly more practical content than St. Thomas Aquinas's famous statement of the first principle of natural law, Do good and avoid evil. A brief summary of Calabresi's distinction between three different kinds of measures to reduce the costs of accidents indicates the problems in this regard. Calabresi first notes what he terms *primary accident cost reduction measures*. These are measures to prevent accidents from occurring in the first place. *Secondary accident cost* reduction measures, his second category, aims to lower the costs associated with accidents after they occur. They consist primariy in different techniques for spreading such costs or shifting them from one party to another. *Tertiary accident cost* reduction is a very broad category that encompasses all measures to reduce the overhead, so to speak, associated with primary and secondary accident cost reduction measures.

Now, questions about how to effect the foregoing kinds of accident cost reduction measures pose an enormous diversity of problems. Most prominently, answers to such questions call for a great deal of factual information that is often difficult to obtain. For example, consider the primary accident cost reduction measure of banning or penalizing certain activities. Questions such as whether an activity should be banned, whether it should be penalized rather than banned outright, if it should be penalized then how much, and so forth, often require difficult-to-obtain facts and figures for their intelligent resolution.

Even more troublesome, as Calabresi notes, is the fact that his three kinds of accident cost reduction measures frequently conflict with each other. To cite an extreme illustration, a decision to spread the costs of accidents as widely as possible clearly conflicts with most measures to effect primary accident cost reduction. This is because these latter kinds of measures, in one way or another, tend to involve imposing the costs of accidents primarily upon people who engage in those activities ascertained to involve the most significant risk of causing harm. To cite another example, the primary accident cost reduction measure of distinguishing different categories of individuals with respect to their accident-proneness for the purpose of charging them differential insurance premiums requires substantial research in order to arrive at a reasonable set of categories. But the (tertiary) costs associated with such research conceivably could exceed any gains in primary accident cost reduction resulting from it.

In short then, the issue of which party is the least cost avoider often involves difficult policy questions as well as difficult factual ones. It requires facing the question of what mix of primary, secondary, and tertiary accident cost reduction measures one finds most desirable, all things considered. The statement that one should place liability on the least cost avoider is thus, for most practical purposes, a formulation of the problem rather than a principle for application in resolving it. Still, for all that, the statement has theoretical significance. It may be taken as underscoring that in attempting to formulate fair standards for assigning liability one really has no satisfactory alternative but to weigh costs and benefits impartially from the broadest standpoint.[82]

Accordingly, the judgment that a person acted negligently in a given case involves decisions about the appropriate standard of reasonable behavior for like cases requiring assessment of social costs and benefits. One cannot then accept the idea of a basic moral right not to be harmed through the negligence of others functioning as a constraint upon social action guided by cost-benefit analysis.

The objection implicit in Nozick's political philosophy to creating rights of free expression for employees in the private sector through statutes or judicial decisions thus presupposes an unacceptably vague conception of basic moral rights. We have considered a commonly advanced proposal for rendering this conception more precise and found it theoretically unsound. Another writer, Roger Pilon, has gone beyond Nozick in articulating a philosophical theory of basic moral rights intended to generate the kinds of conclusions Nozick endorses in *Anarchy, State, and Utopia*—e.g., the unjustifiability of anything besides the "minimal state."[83] Pilon distinguishes two categories of rights, general and special. The former are the basic moral rights held by everyone with respect to everyone else, while the latter arise out of specific voluntary associations among specific individuals.[84] The most basic general right, according to Pilon, "for it is logically prior to all other rights . . . is the right to non-interference, which may be variously described as the right to be free, the right to be left alone, the right against trespass, and so forth."[85] Pilon maintains further that as long as we do not violate this basic moral right,

each of us has a general right to associate with others, provided we do so with their consent. If A and B want to associate with each other and want to order that association by creating special rights and obligations between themselves, then they have a general right to do so, a right against third parties; these third parties have a correlative general obligation not to interfere with A and B, an obligation not to take or prevent those actions of A and B that will bring about this special relationship.[86]

Pilon brings the above conception of basic moral rights to bear specifically upon the subject of rights of employees in the private sector:

Nowhere perhaps [do the above principles] come more clearly into focus than in cases involving the "terminable at will" doctrine where either employer or employee may terminate the association "at will," i.e., without cause "just" or otherwise. . . . Many of these cases are odious . . . But here . . . we have to distinguish between what it would be good for the employer to do and what he has a right to do. The employee enjoys no general right to a job because there is no right to forced association. Accordingly, when employer and employee come together, they do so only insofar as the agreed upon terms of the association specify. If these terms include the option to terminate the association without cause then there really is nothing more to say on the matter.[87]

As noted above, Pilon's contention that the doctrine of employment at will is grounded in basic moral rights presupposes the idea of the right to noninterference. Should the idea of this right prove confused, then his entire analysis founders. Now it will not do to think of the right to noninterference as universal in scope, for such a viewpoint would generate contradictions. If Smith and Jones live in adjoining apartments Smith cannot have an unconditional right to freedom from noninterference when he plays his stereo, and Jones have an equally unconditional right not to be interfered with when napping. The notion of a right to freedom from interference is coherent only if one precisely specifies its domain.

Pilon recognizes the above problem and proposes to deal with it in the following way. He maintains that the basic moral right to noninterference ranges only over those things we own.[88] This answer, in turn, generates a new problem. Pilon conceives of the right to noninterference as absolutely fundamental from a moral standpoint; that is, as logically prior to all other rules.[89] Ordinarily, however, we think of legal rules as providing the basis for distinguishing, as Hobbes might have said, mine from thine.[90] Pilon's theory thus requires that he explicate the notion of ownership, presupposed by the right to noninterference, in a way that makes no reference to legal rules.

Again, Pilon realizes this difficulty, and goes on to explain the relevant conception of ownership thus.[91] He begins by following Nozick's "historical or entitlement theory of justice on holdings, according to which a set of holdings is justly distributed if the process by which the distribution . . . arose violated no one's rights. Holdings [according to this view] justifiably arise by (1) voluntary acquisition (of unheld things in the state of nature), (2) voluntary transfer, and (3) redistribution in rectification of violations of the rules that apply in (1) and (2)."[92]

This theory crucially depends upon the notion of original acquisition. How does one acquire rights of ownership under circumstances where no legal conventions exist for creating such rights? Pilon addresses this question in the following way. Referring to a group of individuals under hypothetical circumstances where each enters the world in different, specific, spatio-temporal regions he writes:

the question arises by what right are these individuals where they are in this theoretical world? They are *ex hypothesi,* standing at some spot on the earth. Why aren't they trespassing? The answer, I should argue, is that no one *else* has a prior claim to be where any other individual is. And indeed, if such a claim should be made, the burden would rest upon the *claimant* to make his case.[93]

These remarks, nonetheless, fail to answer satisfactorily the question Pilon poses for himself at the outset of the above passage. He invites us to imagine a hypothetical situation where, so to speak, *ex nihilo* individuals come into the world occupying particular spatio-temporal regions. Pilon urges that they each have the right to occupy their respective regions because "no one else has a prior claim." But this hardly suffices. Assume that X is a region occupied by an individual A under Pilon's hypothetical conditions. Pilon maintains that A has a right to stand there rather than B, another individual, because B has no prior claim to stand at X. *By the same token, however, neither does A.* Under Pilon's hypothetical conditions the situation of A and B with respect to X would appear identical. In other words, while no one else has a better claim to X than A, neither does anyone else have a worse claim.

The foregoing difficulty vitiates Pilon's further explanation of how one originally acquires property beyond that directly under one's feet. His account of this latter issue exactly resembles his analysis of original acquisition with respect to one's initial location. That is, according to Pilon, a person originally acquires the land adjacent to one's starting point simply by claiming it.[94] But again, one can ask, why should any given person's claim count for more than anyone else's under the conditions hypothesized by Pilon? It would seem then that Pilon has failed to explain satisfactorily how individuals can come to own real or personal property under hypothetical circumstances where no prior rules creating rights in these regards exist. Yet Pilon's analysis of the notion of a basic moral right to noninterference constitutes the most philosophically rigorous attempt to explicate it, at least in recent years. That such serious problems attend his account suggests that the notion itself is untenable.

Bernard Siegan recently has advanced arguments that conceivably could be invoked to question the constitutional validity of statutory or judicially created protection of free expression for employees in the private sector. These arguments bear scrutiny because they appear not to depend upon suspect ideas concerning basic moral rights. In his book *Economic Liberties and the Constitution*, Siegan advocates that courts employ the due process clauses of the Fifth and Fourteenth Amendments to strike down certain kinds of governmental economic regulations.[95] By way of background, during a period that ran roughly from 1890 to 1935 the Supreme Court repeatedly invoked these amendments to invalidate federal and state legislation pertaining to economic affairs.[96] By the mid-1930s, however, the Court abruptly shifted gears and adopted an approach, which more or less predominates today, whereby it upholds all such legislation on the minimal condition that it have some rational basis, however slim.[97] On the other hand, as noted frequently throughout this book, if the Court regards a right as fundamental then, for all practical purposes, any legislation infringing upon it is deemed constitutionally invalid.

In arguing for his viewpoint Siegan explicitly criticizes this dichotomy in the standards of constitutional review:

Government supervision over private activity is commonly referred to as *censorship* when applied to the press and *regulation* when implemented elsewhere. However, these labels becloud the similarities. A robust un-inhibited press is far from trouble free, but it is preferable to censorship; and the same logic can be applied to economic activity.[98]

Siegan contends then that the case for freedom of expression applies with equal force to freedom of buyers and sellers from governmental regulation. His arguments, however, fail to provide adequate support for this position. Siegan cites a passage from Thomas Emerson's essay "Toward a General Theory of the First Amentment," which enumerates a variety of evils associated with press censorship.[99] He then observes that for him "Emerson's observations are not merely theory. In more than two decades as a practicing attorney I [Siegan] appeared many times before zoning authorities and other regulatory bodies. During these years I constantly encountered acts comparable to those he [Emerson] describes."[100]

This personal observation of Siegan's fails to persuade because the passage he cites from Emerson does not mention either of the basic philosophical arguments for freedom of expression formulated by Mill in chapters two and three of *On Liberty*.[101] Thus, nowhere does Siegan discuss whether government regulation of economic affairs opens the door to thought control or seriously undermines the development of individuality. For this reason, his comparison of press censorship with economic regulation does not touch upon the most crucial considerations for deciding whether one can think of the two as relevantly similar.

In addition to recounting his personal experience Siegan enlists the support of other writers for his position. In this regard he quotes the following passage from F. A. Hayek's book *The Constitution of Liberty*:

To extol the value of intellectual liberties at the expense of the value of the liberty of doing things would be like treating the crowning part of an edifice as the whole. We have new ideas to discuss, different views to adjust, because those ideas and views arise from the efforts of individuals in every new circumstance, who avail themselves in their concrete tasks of the new tools and forms they have learned.[102]

Siegan believes Hayek's points to be so straightforward in support of the position he favors that one must look for a special explanation of why so many writers have apparently failed to regard freedom of expression and freedom of businesses from governmental economic regulation in the same light. In this connection he cites with approval the following remark by Ronald Coase:

The market for ideas is the market in which the intellectual conducts his trade. Self-esteem leads the intellectuals to magnify the importance of their own market. That others should be regulated seems natural, particularly as many of the intellectuals see themselves as doing the regulating. But self-interest combines with self-esteem to ensure that, while others are regulated, regulation should not apply to them. And so it is possible to live with these contradictory views about the role of government in these two markets. It is the conclusion that matters. It may not be a nice explanation, but I can think of no other for this strange situation.[103]

Both of these questions require comment. The one from Hayek

seems consistent with Siegan's viewpoint when considered by itself. A close reading of the *Constitution of Liberty*, however, indicates that Siegan erred in relying upon Hayek's political philosophy for support. Siegan's passage from Hayek appears almost at the outset of *The Constitution of Liberty*. It constitutes an extremely broad statement of Hayek's general orientation and is refined substantially in ensuing chapters, which contain the systematic development of his political philosophy. While an extensive summary of Hayek's philosophy cannot be undertaken here, the following quotation, which appears in the text nearly two hundred pages after the passage Siegan quotes, indicates, I think, considerable divergence from Siegan's position. Indeed, this quotation expresses a viewpoint about the constitutionality of economic legislation virtually identical with Justice Holmes's as stated in his famous *Lochner* dissent:[104]

a free system does not exclude on principle all those general regulations of economic activity which can be laid down in the form of general rules specifying conditions which everybody who engages in a certain activity must satisfy. They include, in particular, all regulations governing the techniques of production. We are not concerned here with the question of whether such regulations will be wise, which they probably will be only in exceptional cases. They will always limit the scope of experimentation and thereby obstruct what may be useful developments. They will normally raise the cost of production or, what amounts to the same thing, reduce overall productivity. But if this effect on cost is fully taken into account and it is still thought worthwhile to incur the cost to achieve a given end, there is little more to be said about it. The economist will remain suspicious and hold that there is a strong presumption against such measures because their over-all cost is almost always underestimated and because one disadvantage in particular—namely the prevention of new developments—can never be fully taken into account. But if, for instance, the production and sale of phosphorous matches is generally prohibited for reasons of health or permitted only if certain precautions are taken, of if night work is generally prohibited, the appropriateness of such measures must be judged by comparing the over-all costs with the gain; it cannot be conclusively determined by appeal to a general principle.[105]

As for the quotation from Coase, it would seem that were one to call the just-quoted remarks by Hayek to Coase's attention, he would have no response except perhaps "Et tu, Hayek." This is hardly surprising, for the notion that "intellectuals" unjustifiably elevate freedom of expression above other equally important "economic" liberties is deeply confused. To begin, if one uses the term *intellectual* in a broad way to refer to highly literate people, then it simply seems false that the overwhelming majority of intellectuals attach predominant importance to freedom of expression, at least as I have analyzed it in this book. The American Civil Liberties Union lost hundreds of thousands of dollars in contributions and membership fees from its highly literate supporters when it defended the right of a group of Nazis to march in Skokie, Illinois.[106] In the same way, when the Justice Department sought to enjoin *The Progressive* from publishing Howard Morland's article about hydrogen bomb technology, for the most part the press remained silent.[107] During the McCarthy period eminent academics called for a purge of all communists teaching in colleges and universities. Highly literate clergy of the Catholic Church for generations prepared the *index prohibitorum*. Instances of disregard by intellectuals of the principles of free expression can be found all too readily.

Furthermore, one hardly need posit overweening hubris to account for why some people accord freedom of expression fundamental status but deny it to freedom of business from governmental regulation.[108] They may be thought of as basing this outlook upon the belief that limitations of the first freedom involve unique dangers of thought control and stifling of individuality that do not obviously attend limitations of the latter freedom. It would appear then that Siegan's general position cannot be sustained.[109] The primacy of place accorded freedom of expression would appear to have a solid basis.

With these observations I conclude this essay on the philosophy of free expression and its constitutional applications. Much of importance remains unexamined. My purpose, however, was not to write a comprehensive treatise, but instead to suggest a new framework for thinking about the right to free expression. I have presented a unified approach that, I think, yields reasonable positions by appeal to a small number of principles, on a wide variety of issues that many writers have tended to regard as irreducibly disparate. But whatever my degree of success in this regard, the right to free expression is so profoundly important that one cannot question the value of attempting to illuminate it. The foregoing contrast between the right to free expression and the right to other kinds of freedoms, such as economic liberty, thus has special appropriateness as a final topic of discussion. It underscores again the fundamental status of the right to free expression.

Appendix I
Does Judicial Review
Protect Fundamental Rights?

A few words are in order about the measure of protection I conceive judicial review by courts to provide against violations of fundamental rights. Learned Hand regarded such review not only as unjustifiable but also as either unnecessary or ineffective. In this regard he wrote: "Liberty lies in the hearts of men and women; when it dies there, no constitution, no law, no court can save it; no constitution, no law, no court can even do much to help it. While it lies there it needs no constitution, no law, no court to save it."[1] This dichotomy, however, greatly oversimplifies matters. A government may generally respect the fundamental rights of its citizens, at least relatively speaking, and nonetheless in some instances severely violate them. Moreover, just as a person's moral character can change from good to bad when repeated minor breaches of morality pave the way for more serious ones, so also a just society can slide into tyranny with continued violations of fundamental rights. Hence the desirability of an institutional means for upholding them.

As a practical matter, I think that on the whole judicial review has worked to uphold fundamental rights more effectively against infringements by the states than by Congress. This is hardly surprising since Congress, with its constitutionally mandated authority under Article III to define the jurisdiction of federal courts, has at its disposal overwhelming coercive power not available to the states, which it could bring to bear in a major struggle with the Supreme Court. Thus, with respect to the First Amendment, cases advancing the cause of free expression almost invariably pertained to state statutes or the actions of state officials. By contrast, the Court has been far more circumspect in First Amendment cases involving Congress.[2] Accordingly, to view the Supreme Court as having ombudsmanlike power to overrule both the states and Congress when they violate fundamental rights is unrealistic.[3] Nonetheless, the Court has provided a substantial measure of protection to citizens from infringements of their fundamental rights by the states. In addition, one may always hope that valid principles enunciated by the Court in cases involving the Bill of Rights become so deeply entrenched over time as to exert a powerful though indirect or, if you will, moral influence on Congress.

The above remarks raise yet another important issue concerning the measure of protection judicial review provides against infringements of fundamental rights. Under favorable conditions— that is, when most judges apply a sound background theory— judicial review affords considerable support for the exercise of fundamental rights. But what about when such conditions do not obtain? In the case of *Lochner* v. *New York*, decided in 1905, the Supreme Court struck down a New York State statute mandating maximum working hours for bakers on the ground that it infringed upon a supposed fundamental right of "freedom of contract." Although it is mentioned nowhere in the Constitution, the Court declared this right protected by the Fourteenth Amendment Due Process Clause.[4] This case came to symbolize an entire era of constitutional adjudication spanning roughly the period 1900–32 during which the Supreme Court repeatedly struck down progressive state legislation of which a majority of the justices personally disapproved.[5] Typically, in such cases the majority opinion proclaimed, with no supporting argument whatsoever, that the statute in question infringed upon fundamental rights. Disturbed by this proclivity, Justice Holmes complained in a famous passage from his dissent in *Lochner* v. *New York* that

this case is decided upon an economic theory which a large part of this country does not share . . . A constitution is not intended to embody a particular economic theory, whether of paternalism and the organic relation of the citizen to the state, or of *laissez faire*. . . . The Fourteenth Amendment does not enact Mr. Herbert Spencer's *Social Statics*.[6]

Thus, while judicial review in cases involving the Bill of Rights serves to protect fundamental rights when judges apply a sound background theory, if they do not it then opens the door to precisely the kind of judicial meddling in social policy that makes cases like *Lochner* v. *New York* objectionable.

The foregoing point can neither be minimized nor dealt with in short order. Only a candid and reasonably accurate appraisal of the costs and benefits associated with judicial review under the Bill of Rights will suffice in addressing it. The *Lochner* period clearly illustrates one serious cost. For an entire generation the Supreme Court applied gravely misguided standards in dealing with major constitutional issues.[7] One would overstate the social costs incurred during the *Lochner* era, however, by describing it as a period of *absolute* judicial tyranny. Had enough people in enough states objected deeply enough to the *Lochner* era decisions, then they could have been reversed either through congressional legislation or a constitutional amendment. This observation is not meant to minimize the evil of unwarranted judicial legislation by suggesting that the American scheme of government provides regular procedures for dealing with it. The remedial measures in this regard are clearly extraordinary. I only note that in realistically assessing the costs of the *Lochner* era one must remember that such remedies always existed in the background.

A second cost, or possible cost, of judicial review under the Bill of Rights was repeatedly stated by Felix Frankfurter in his many writings both on and off the bench.[8] Frankfurter maintained that by justifying judicial review in terms of its efficacy in protecting fundamental rights, one countenances a view of courts that allots them the function of exercising a paternalistic guardianship over the public that lifts from its shoulders the responsibility of protecting itself from violations of fundamental rights. Frankfurter believed that insofar as all paternalistic guardianships that extend indefinitely in time stunt the capacities to think and act of those guarded, so also this one would ultimately sap the ability of the public to understand the stakes when fundamental rights were violated and to combat such violations effectively.

So much then for the costs associated with judicial review under the Bill of Rights. What about its benefits? These are best brought out through a somewhat indirect line of inquiry. What consequences would flow from abolishing judicial review in cases involving the Bill of Rights? Most obviously, fundamental rights would no longer enjoy judicial support. Other means for their protection would have to suffice. Serious problems emerge, however, when one considers what this entails. Both Hand and Frankfurter appear to have recommended that we rely primarily for the protection of fundamental rights upon such traditions of respect for liberty as American society can be said to possess. Adopting this course, I suppose one would proceed in the hope that violations of fundamental rights occuring in the future would be infrequent and have no long-lasting effects.

Although one cannot dismiss such hope as absolutely unrealistic, I for one do not share it. It seems to me that our traditions of liberty can be regarded at best as still developing rather than as well entrenched.[9] Circumstances that seriously threaten the enjoyment of fundamental rights are not really so implausible. Under such conditions it would seem that Supreme Court decisions can help to shape the public consciousness in a way that strengthens respect for fundamental rights.[10] I think it reasonable to believe, for example, that by proclaiming, as it did in *Near* v. *Minnesota* and the *Pentagon Papers* case, that prior restraints on publication contravene the law of the land, the Supreme Court substantially furthered the cause of free expression.[11]

Aside from traditions of respect for liberty, only two other social mechanisms for the protection of fundamental rights besides judicial review come to mind, namely civil disobedience and heroic efforts by individuals. Obvious problems, however, attend placing primary reliance upon either of these. Civil disobedience is justified at times even in a just, democratic society. But it severely strains the social fabric when engaged in frequently by many diverse groups. It would seem that justified civil disobedience may be undertaken only as a tactic of last resort to protest very serious violations of fundamental rights.[12] As for the hope that strong individuals will always be there to come forth and fight the good fight, this seems highly unrealistic. The particular combinations of virtues possessed by people who made a difference, such as Dr. Martin Luther King, Jr., or Clarence Darrow, are so out of the ordinary that in retrospect the existence of these individuals, let alone their emergence as public figures, seems an enormously fortunate improbability.

To sort out some of the foregoing observations, when one compares the social costs of retaining judicial review under the Bill of Rights with the social costs of giving it up altogether, the following factors emerge as those to be weighed in the balance.

By retaining judicial review we run a substantial risk that courts will indulge unjustifiably in judicial legislation. Should they go to extremes in this regard, however, our governmental scheme provides remedies, albeit in the form of very strong medicine, which most of us would be reluctant to administer. On the other hand, by abolishing judicial review society would deprive itself of an effective, though admittedly far from perfect, means of protecting fundamental rights, *with no reasonable assurance that other means could take up the slack*. Viewed in this light, I think the scale tips in favor of retaining judicial review, the *Lochner* era notwithstanding.

It remains to address Frankfurter's point that reliance upon judicial review for the protection of fundamental rights works against the development of more broadly based social support for them. I agree that as constitutional adjudication under the Bill of Rights increasingly comes to be looked upon primarily as a specialized field of law, the general public—even the highly educated general public—tends to have less interest in and understanding of constitutional questions involving fundamental rights. Such a development is indeed unfortunate. I would not, however, trace its origins to the inherent nature of judicial review, but rather to other factors. Perhaps the most important of these is a seemingly ineluctable tendency in the United States for all bodies of law to grow at enormous rates in both size and complexity.[13]

I have no new insights to offer with respect to this general phenomenon but only note the following. Constitutional adjudication under the Bill of Rights as I have characterized it in this book should be treated as a form of applied philosophy whereby broad principles of social morality are brought to bear upon concrete cases. According to this view, such adjudication essentially involves moral reasoning accessible to everyone rather than arcane legal analysis. I contend that judicial review under the Bill of Rights need not inevitably develop into a complex specialized field of law totally beyond the layperson's reach. The basic principles in this domain, and their most important applications, can and should be widely understood. In a small way this book thus constitutes an attempt to generate the kind of broad-based support for constitutionally guaranteed fundamental rights that Frankfurter correctly identified as their ultimate protection.

Appendix II
Some Interpretations of
On Liberty, *Chapter Three*

To understand Mill's conception of individuality, and the argument he based upon it in chapter three of *On Liberty*, one must begin by addressing some widespread misconceptions about it illustrated by the following remarks. First, Robert Paul Wolff has written:

we must now confront directly the doctrine of individuality, or as we may somewhat facetiously label it, the doctrine of the Sanctity of Idiosyncrasy. Immediately we encounter a difficulty which crops up repeatedly in the writings of Mill: his noblest and most inspiring thoughts are almost invariably those which cohere least well with his professed utilitarianism.[1]

Second, Isaiah Berlin declares more sympathetically but in the same vein:

At the center of Mill's thought and feeling lies not his utilitarianism . . . but his passionate belief that men are made human by their capacity for choice—choice of good and evil equally.[2]

Both Wolff and Berlin then seem to believe that Mill's primary defense of liberty in chapter three turns upon the premises that (1) liberty is necessary for the fostering of individuality, and that in turn (2) individuality is properly considered to be a good in itself; that is, its value stands in need of no justification. Unquestionably, premise (2) conflicts with Mill's professed utilitar-

149

ianism. Indeed, in *On Liberty* itself, Mill underscores his commitment to utilitarianism in two places. First, in a much-quoted passage in the introduction, Mill explicitly declares that he will only appeal to considerations of utility "in the largest sense, grounded in the permanent interests of man as a progressive being."[3] Second, having just completed his clearly utilitarian defense of freedom of thought in chapter two, Mill begins chapter three by posing the question of whether the *same* considerations also militate in favor of freedom of action.[4]

That Mill begins chapter three in this way is significant, because it suggests he conceived himself as putting forward arguments in chapter three no less utilitarian than those in chapter two. The view shared by Wolff and Berlin entails a perception that Mill began the very chapter in which he most radically departed from utilitarianism by reaffirming his commitment to it. To be sure, in some quarters Mill is not regarded as having placed a great value on logical consistency. Nonetheless, one wonders how anyone could be so glaringly inconsistent as Wolff and Berlin would have Mill to be. Accordingly, it would seem wise to place their view under strict scrutiny before judging in its favor.

Wolff is understandably facetious toward the view that one should regard uniqueness of character and personality per se as a paramount human good.[5] Mill's account of individuality, however, does not involve this view. He does devote most of chapter three to explaining forcefully the evils of conforming to custom "merely as custom."[6] It is, however, a *non sequitur* to hold that someone who opposes conforming to custom merely as custom must also believe that people should be encouraged to be idiosyncratic simply for the sake of being idiosyncratic. In one passage of chapter three Mill pleads in behalf of uniqueness of character and personality, but the pleading is distinctly limited. The passage in question strongly suggests that uniqueness of character and personality have value per se solely in circumstances where the primary source of standard for thought and conduct is a mediocre and tyranical public opinion.[7] The nonconformity of the more intelligent and independent members of society in such circumstances has value, according to Mill, because it illustrates to the rest, however little they may desire such illustrations, that public opinion need not be unquestionably followed. Were the public to become more enlightened and tolerant—that is, were the individuals comprising it to become more intelligent and independent, perhaps over many generations—then the "mere refusal to bend the knee to custom" would no longer be a service. Toward the close of the paragraph in question Mill says that where strength of character, genius, mental vigor, and moral courage have abounded, so also has eccentricity. His point here, however, seems to be that eccentricity is, as it were, ephiphenomenal to these highly desirable things rather than a fundamental constituent of them. In a society of intelligent and independent individuals there will be much eccentricity, so one need not worry about having to cultivate it. But one cannot foster strength of character, genius, mental vigor, and moral courage simply by encouraging everyone to be eccentric.

For Isaiah Berlin, chapter three of *On Liberty* underscores the unconditional and ultimate value of the human "capacity for choice."[8] In this connection Berlin writes of Mill: "He believed that it is neither rational thought, nor domination over nature, but freedom to choose and to experiment that distinguishes men from the rest of nature: of all his ideas, it is this view that has ensured his lasting fame."[9] At least one passage in chapter three, however, indicates that Mill did not regard all situations in which the capacity for choice is exercised as equal in value. In this passage he says that the capacity for choice is of negligible value to individuals whose opinions or feelings are not of "home growth" or "properly one's own."[10] Just what makes an opinion or feeling "properly one's own" according to Mill is not easy to explain, since he does not explicitly state how this phrase should be taken.[11] The above-mentioned passage nevertheless strongly suggests that Mill did not consider the human capacity for choice, in itself, to be an unconditional good.

Of equal importance, several other important passages in chapter three can only be taken as implying that Mill did not consider the capacity for choice, in itself, as an ultimate good. For example, he writes, "in proportion to the development of his individuality each person becomes more valuable to himself and others."[12] Similarly, he also declares:

Having said that individuality is the same thing with development, and that it is only the cultivation of individuality which produces, or can produce, well-developed human beings, I might here close the argument; for what more or better can be said of any condition of human affairs than that it brings human beings themselves nearer to the best thing they can be.[13]

These passages suggest that Mill attached the greatest importance not to the mere exercise (or existence) of the capacity for choice, but to certain states of affairs and conditions that he believed are the consequence, under favorable conditions, of its free exercise. That is, for Mill the cultivation of individuality "brings human beings themselves nearer to the *best* thing they can be" and it "makes every individual more *valuable* to himself and others." In these passages Mill seems to be presupposing some prior ideal of excellence for human beings further realized by allowing liberty of action and thought. Hence, it would appear that he did not consider the capacity for choice, in itself, to be an ultimate good.

Cognizant of the above points, Albert William Levi notes that Mill's presupposed ideal of excellence for human beings is identical with Aristotle's in the *Nichomachean Ethics*.[14] Indeed, Levi maintains that in *On Liberty* Mill moves away from utilitarianism altogether toward an explicitly Aristotelian moral philosophy.[15]

Such an interpretation deserves careful attention, for there are many passages from chapter three that appear to support it. For example, Mill writes: "to conform to custom merely as custom does not educate or develop . . . any of the qualities which are the distinctive endowment of a human being."[16] In the same vein he also insists, "It really is of importance, not only what men do, but also what manner of men they are that do it. Among the works of man which human life is rightly employed in perfecting and beautifying, the first in importance surely is man himself."[17]

The essentials of the Aristotelian position that Levi finds in Mill's argument in chapter three are, I think, (a) the proposition that an important part of the ideal of excellence for human beings is to be highly capable of rational activity, and (b) the proposition, entailed by Aristotle's essentialist presuppositions, that the reason why being highly capable of rational activity is a key part of the ideal of excellence for human beings is that a fully developed human being just is one who, among other things, has this characteristic. Now while Levi makes a persuasive case for (a) he does not do so for (b). There is strong textual evidence that Mill conceived the ideal of excellence for human beings in a manner not unlike that suggested by Aristotle in the relevant portions of the *Nichomachean Ethics*. Had Mill believed, however, that the basis for embracing this ideal is that it specifies an inherent ideal of perfection for human beings, he would have had to accept the essentialist assumptions that seem to underlie Aristotle's ethical thought, viz., that there are certain states whose attainment by a human being constitutes their full development as human beings, and that the attaining of full development as human beings is the ultimate ideal of excellence for such beings. The text of chapter three, however, provides no evidence that Mill accepted these assumptions, and there are independent grounds for supposing that he rejected them.

A true Aristotelian would answer the question "Why is the attainment of great capacity for rational activity an important part of the ideal of excellence for human beings?" by asserting that fully developed human beings are those who, among other things, have this characteristic. It is unlikely, however, that Mill would have felt comfortable with such an answer. It is not only at odds with his utilitarianism, but also with his conception of scientific method. Underlying Aristotle's moral philosophy is his teleological conception of nature according to which natural phenomena have ends toward which they tend, and only in terms of which their salient features can be understood. The incongruity of such a view with Mill's empirical philosophy of science is evident.[18] Thus on Levi's Aristotelian interpretation of chapter three, we must imagine not only that Mill shifted to an Aristotelian standpoint in moral philosophy but also that he did so in the philosophy of science. There is, however, no independent evidence of such a shift on his part in this latter domain.

Levi grasps the important point that Mill's defense of liberty of action in chapter three involves appeal to an ideal of excellence for human beings that is similar to Aristotle's. His conclusion from this, however, that in chapter three Mill moves "toward the explicit standpoint of an Aristotelian moral philosophy," is unwarranted by the text. In the relevant passages Mill appeals to an Aristotelian ideal of excellence for human beings but does not explicitly state what he considers to be the basis for regarding it as such. The account of this matter in Aristotle's own moral philosophy is one but not the only possible such account. One might hold that there is a more comprehensive standard of goodness that when applied to human beings yields the Aristotelian ideal of excellence. Such indeed is the position I attribute to Mill.

Appendix III
Scanlon on Autonomy and Free Expression

Thomas Scanlon's increasingly influential article, "A Theory of Freedom of Expression," places great emphasis on the connection between freedom of expression and personal autonomy.[1] Now, insofar as the concept of individuality, under a Millian analysis of it, coincides with the notion of self-direction, so also it relates to the concept of autonomy as well. Indeed, Mill's account of individuality may be thought of as explaining how this latter concept specifically pertains to the philosophical basis of free expression.

Failure to recognize this point creates substantial problems for Scanlon. He postulates first a proposition he terms "the Millian Principle" that presumably embodies our (or, at least, Scanlon's) central beliefs about free expression.[2] Speaking of this principle he then says,

I will defend the Millian Principle by showing it to be a consequence of the view that the powers of a state are limited to those that citizens could recognize while still regarding themselves as equal, autonomous, rational agents. Since the sense of autonomy to which I will appeal is extremely weak, this seems to me to constitute a strong defense of the Millian Principle as an exceptionless restriction on governmental authority.[3]

Scanlon immediately goes on to enunciate a conception of personal autonomy that, as he says, is "extremely weak." He then argues that allowing a state to violate the Millian principle would grant it power to undermine the citizen's personal autonomy. This, however, Scanlon assumes is something that no rational person, on more or less equal terms with his fellow citizens, would ever permit.

For my purposes it will not be necessary to recount Scanlon's arguments attempting to show that violations of the Millian principle undermine personal autonomy. Rather, my points have to do solely with the conception of personal autonomy Scanlon puts forward. They are perhaps best brought out by taking a more careful look at his strategy for defending the Millian principle. First, Scanlon assumes that autonomy, in his sense, is something that all rational people regard as extremely valuable. Second, he argues that violations of the Millian principle interfere with this autonomy so that such violations ought not to take place.

This schematic reformulation of Scanlon's argument is useful since it highlights the extent to which the burden of his defense of freedom of expression rests upon his account of personal autonomy. Clearly, this sort of argument has no force unless one can explain what personal autonomy is and why it is valuable.

As Scanlon says, his own conception of personal autonomy is extremely weak. To quote him again:

> To regard himself as autonomous in the sense I have in mind, a person must see himself as sovereign in deciding what to believe and in weighing competing reasons for action. He must apply to these tasks his own canons of rationality and must recognize the need to defend his beliefs and decisions in accordance with these canons. This does not mean that he must be perfectly rational, even by his own standard of rationality, or that his standard must be exactly ours. . . . An autonomous person cannot accept without independent consideration the judgment of others as to what he should do. He may rely on the judgment of others, but when he does so he must be prepared to advance independent reasons for thinking their judgment likely to be correct, and to weight the evidential value of their opinion against contrary evidence.[4]

For Scanlon, then, to regard oneself as autonomous is simply to consider one's own judgment about what to do and believe as ultimately authoritative. Being autonomous in this sense is compatible with decision-making of extremely poor quality. That is, a person who is autonomous in Scanlon's sense could habitually

make decisions in ways that were ignorant, narrow-minded, un-
creative, self-deceptive, weak-willed, or any combination thereof.

This fact, however, raises some serious questions. If being
autonomous in Scanlon's sense is compatible with making such
choices, just what is so valuable about personal autonomy? Why
would we not be better off if things were arranged so that those
who are very good at making decisions about what to do and
believe did so for the rest of us?

Scanlon's response to this query is that placing so much power
in the hands of a few people would almost surely lead to disaster.
In this connection Scanlon maintains that while a rational person
might give up his autonomy for a limited time and for limited
purposes, it is out of the question that he or she would do so
permanently; this is roughly because no rational person could have
the degree of confidence in another person's judgment and goodwill
that would be needed in order to consent to such an arrangement.[5]
This response, however, does not go far enough. Most defenders
of freedom of expression who rest their defense on its link with
personal autonomy would feel that even if (assuming the impossible)
there were some individual in whose judgment and goodwill we
could have unbounded confidence, there would still be something
very wrong about a set of social arrangements that allowed him
or her to act in ways that ruled out the possibility of autonomy.
Scanlon's account of autonomy, however, is too sparse to justify
this conviction.

By contrast, when one identifies personal autonomy with individuality, as explicated by Mill, then its connection with freedom
of expression is straightforward. As we have seen, achieving a
high degree of personal autonomy is one of the most important
goods. On any reasonable conception of the good for society it
should be a primary function of social arrangements to facilitate
everyone's becoming as autonomous as he or she possibly can.
As it has been explicated, personal autonomy, being identifiable
with reason, consists in the possession of a variety of different
abilities and capacities, all of which can be developed only by
exercising them. But if freedom of expression is severely abridged,
the likelihood that significant numbers of people would grow in
personal autonomy is quite low. Thus even if the decision not to
abridge freedom of expression can sometimes lead to serious harm,
this must be borne as the cost of making it possible for a society
to develop in which large numbers of people have a high degree
of personal autonomy.

Notes

Chapter One

1. The above issues figured in too many cases for convenient listing. I will take up all of them, however, in subsequent chapters and cite the pertinent cases accordingly.

2. The First Amendment of the United States Constitution is extremely brief. The following constitutes its entire text: "Congress shall make no law respecting an establishment of religion, or prohibiting the free exercise thereof, or abridging the freedom of speech or of the press; or the right of the people peaceably to assemble, and to petition the Government for a redress of grievances."

3. For the definitive exposition of the triadic account of freedom, see Gerald C. MacCallum, "Negative and Positive Freedom," *Philosophical Review* 76 (1967):312–33.

4. 249 U.S. 47 (1919).

5. *Near* v. *Minnesota*, 283 U.S. 697 (1931).

6. *Roth* v. *United States*, 352 U.S. 964 (1957), *N.Y. Times* v. *Sullivan*, 376 U.S. 254 (1964).

7. *Branzburg* v. *Hayes* 408 U.S. 664 (1972).

8. This point will be developed more in subsequent chapters.

9. *Branzburg*, p. 664.

10. U.S. House of Representatives, Subcommittee Number Three of the Committee of the Judiciary. Hearings on H.R. 717, Ninety-Third Congress, U.S. Government Printing Office, 1973.

11. The phrase "Bill of Rights" is generally taken by constitutional lawyers as referring to the first ten amendments to the United States Constitution and the due process and equal protection clauses of the Fourteenth Amendment.

12. 424 U.S. 1 (1975).

13. Ibid., pp. 39–59.

158   NOTES

14. The Court considered and set aside two other points that the government advanced to justify constitutionally the expenditure limitation provisions. The first of these was that the provisions aim to equalize the amounts spent by various candidates. The Court, however, questioned whether the provision would actually accomplish this purpose. The observations immediately following in the text thus apply only to the Court's remarks to justify the expenditure limitations on the ground that they will prevent political corruption. The second point was that expenditure limitations will help to control the escalating costs of federal election campaigns. In this regard, the Court simply declared, with no supporting argument, that such a purpose "provides no basis for government restrictions on the quantity of campaign spending."

15. Herbert A. Wechsler argues that insofar as the Supremacy Clause of Article VI establishes the superiority of federal to state courts it implies a power of judicial review on the part of the former, because such a power has been acknowledged to reside in the latter, for example, in section 25 of the Judiciary Act of 1789. (See Wechsler, *Principles, Politics and Fundamental Law* [Cambridge, Mass.: Harvard University Press, 1961], p. 7.) As Alexander Bickel pointed out, however, Wechsler's argument is question-begging because the *constitutional* basis of this latter acknowledgment is as questionable as would be the acknowledgment of such a power with regard to federal courts. (See Bickel, *The Least Dangerous Branch* [Indianapolis: Bobbs Merrill, 1962], p. 13.)

16. The evidence of this matter is reviewed dispassionately by James Bradley Thayer in his article "The Origin and Scope of the American Doctrine of Judicial Review," *Harvard Law Review* 7 (1893): 129–56.

17. 1 Cranch 137 (1803), also reprinted in Gerald Gunther, *Constitutional Law, Cases and Materials* (Mineola, N.Y.: Foundation Press, 1975), p. 3.

18. 1 Cranch, p. 178: Gunther, *Constitutional Law*, p. 11.

19. *Marbury* v. *Madison* dealt with the power of the U.S. Supreme Court to overturn acts of Congress on constitutional grounds. It thus did not even pertain to the other major context in which constitutional questions under the Bill of Rights arise, namely, the overturning of enactments of a state legislature by the Supreme Court. The case generally cited as establishing the power of the Court in this regard is *Fletcher* v. *Peck*, 6 Cranch 87 (1810). Marshall's majority opinion, however, simply assumed without argument the Court's power to invalidate state laws on constitutional grounds. Accordingly, the opinion in no way bears upon whether the Court has this power specifically in regard to the Bill of Rights. For further discussion, see Robert G. McCloskey, *The American Supreme Court* (Chicago: University of Chicago Press, 1960), pp. 48–53.

20. Learned Hand, *The Bill of Rights* (Cambridge, Mass.: Harvard University Press, 1958), p. 73.

21. Felix Frankfurter, "John Marshall and the Judicial Function," re-

printed in P. Kurland, ed., *Felix Frankfurter on the Supreme Court* (Cambridge, Mass.: Harvard University Press, Belknap Press, 1970), p. 545.

22. In this regard see the discussion that follows immediately.

23. Ronald Dworkin, "Taking Rights Seriously," in *Taking Rights Seriously* (Cambridge, Mass.: Harvard University Press, 1977), p. 184.

24. Hand, *Bill of Rights*, p. 23.

25. John Rawls, *A Theory of Justice* (Cambridge, Mass.: Harvard University Press, 1971).

26. One must distinguish between the weak-value propositions *presupposed* by Rawls's theory, and the strong-value propositions his theory *entails*. On the distinction between presupposition and entailment generally, see J. L. Austin, *How To Do Things With Words* (London: Oxford University Press, 1962), pp. 47–54.

27. Rawls, *Theory of Justice*, p. 4.

28. While it is impossible to present a detailed analysis of the concept of rationality as it functions in Rawls's theory, it can be said that in the above thought experiment the rational individuals must be conceived of as having the following characteristics: (a) no irrational beliefs or desires of long-standing character, e.g., the desire to disable oneself, deprive oneself of pleasure, frustrate one's own aims, etc; (b) consistency in adopting the means that are best suited to realizing one's ends; and (c) transitivity of preferences; that is, preferring *a* to *c* if it is the case that one prefers *a* to *b* and *b* to *c*. With regard to the above conditions, Rawls explicitly mentions only (b) and (c). Condition (a), however, is crucial to avoid patent counterexamples. (See Bernard Gert, *The Moral Rules* [New York: Harper & Row, 1970], chap. 2.)

29. A variant of this approach has been employed by Bernard Gert to elucidate the notion of morality as it applies to interpersonal relations, that is, to activities of individuals conceived of so generally as not to presuppose any institutional background. (See Gert, *Moral Rules*.)

30. Rawls, *Theory of Justice*, p. 137.

31. Ibid.

32. Ibid., p. 136.

33. Thomas Hobbes, *Leviathan*, Michael Oakeshott, ed. (New York: Collier Macmillan, 1962), chaps. 13–17.

34. For the immediate purpose a summary of Rawls's derivation of this duty is unnecessary. For further discussion, see *A Theory of Justice*, pp. 150–83. Also, it should be noted here that I have paraphrased Rawls's ideas in somewhat different terminology than he employs. Specifically, he does not speak of the principles of justice as duties of governments. Nonetheless, I think this formulation is consistent with his position. For an account of morality as it pertains to social institutions that is closely akin to Rawls's and employs the notion of duties of governments, see Gert, *Moral Rules*, chap. 11.

35. Admittedly there exists a voluminous body of constitutional law

pertaining to the contours of the concept of due process. Despite this, I conceive the essentials of the notion as relatively clear. Governments may not deprive a person of life, liberty, or property without first charging him or her with a definite legal offense and then publicly presenting proof that persuades rational, unbiased people that the person in question committed the offense. The idea of due process is sufficiently precise that one can think of a government's duty in this regard as exemplifying the first characteristic noted above, namely that widespread agreement exists, at least about the kinds of considerations pertinent for deciding whether a violation has occurred. As for the second characteristic, a workable means of preventing or remedying violations, the rules of criminal procedure that specify grounds for appeal can be framed so as to incorporate directly various means of protecting individuals from violations by a government of its duties of due process.

It should be noted here, however, that the above remarks pertain to what constitutional lawyers call "procedural due process," that is, due process as a constraint upon the procedures whereby the state seeks to deprive someone of life, liberty, or property. The notion of so-called substantive due process, that is, due process as a constraint upon the actual content of laws, is far from clear. Fortunately, this topic lies beyond the scope of my discussion.

36. How might a society go about doing this? Making opposition against or failure to support measures for the reduction of inequality an impeachable offense would not work. Aside from difficulties in distinguishing the good-faith opposition from genuine violators of their duty, what if most members of the legislature fall into the latter category? In such a circumstance no movement to impeach a given legislator could succeed. The only remaining way would be to fix relative income levels or establish a minimum income as a matter of constitutional law by way of express amendments. Sound economic planning over a year or two, however, is a difficult enough business. Incorporating a specific economic plan into the Constitution to have effect in perpetuity would be out of the question, proponents of a balanced budget amendment notwithstanding.

37. See Hobbes, *Leviathan*, chap. 15.

38. For further discussion, see my paper, "In Defense of a Hobbesian Conception of Law," *Philosophy and Public Affairs*, vol. 2, no. 9 (1980): 134–59, esp. 151–57.

39. Discussion of the coincidence between the abstract philosophical conception of fundamental rights and widely shared intuitive beliefs about them admittedly raises questions about the scope of the philosophical conception. Is it intended to apply with respect to all societies or merely some? And if the latter, then to which? Rawls answers these questions by saying that the philosophical conception need be taken as applicable only to our own society and others similar to it. He notes that even with this limitation the enterprise of articulating such a conception is highly

significant. See Rawls, "Kantian Constructivism in Moral Theory: The Dewey Lectures 1980," *The Journal of Philosophy*:77 (September 1980): 515–72, esp. 516–19.

40. The following passage from Justice Jackson's opinion in *West Virginia State Board of Education* v. *Barnette*, 319 U.S. 624, 638 (1943), is illustrative: "One's right to life, liberty, and property, to free speech, a free press, freedom of worship, and assembly, and other fundamental rights may not be submitted to vote; they depend on the outcome of no elections." Justice Goldberg's opinion in *Griswold* v. *Connecticut*, 381 U.S. 479, 496 (1965), contains a strong statement that echoes the above viewpoint: "while I quite agree . . . that a state may serve as a laboratory and try novel social and economic experiments, I do not believe that this includes the power to experiment with the fundamental liberties of its citizens."

41. See W. V. Quine and J. S. Ullian, *The Web of Belief*, 2nd ed. (New York: Random House, 1978), pp. 35–49.

42. *De Corpore*, Molesworth, ed., p. 8.

43. Rawls discusses this conception of justification in moral theory in *A Theory of Justice*, pp. 17–22. For a parallel approach concerning the justification of principles of deductive and inductive inference, see Nelson Goodman, *Fact, Fiction and Forecast*, 3rd ed. (Indianapolis: Hackett Publishing Co., 1973), pp. 62–66.

44. Ibid., p. 64.

45. It should also be mentioned that Rawls's account of the principles of social justice illustrates the conceptual linkage between our notion of social justice and important aspects of our ideas of what it is to be a rational, self-directed person. For further discussion, see Rawls's "Kantian Constructivism: Dewey Lectures," pp. 515–72.

46. See David Hume, *A Treatise of Human Nature*, L.A. Selby-Bigge, ed. (Oxford: Clarendon Press, 1888), pp. 268–69.

47. It should be noted that the argument for judicial review need merely show that it works well *for us*. One need not show that it is the only possible means of protecting fundamental rights.

48. Alexander Bickel, *The Morality of Consent* (New York: Yale University Press, 1975), p. 57.

49. Bickel wrote voluminously on constitutional subjects for various periodicals, most prominently *The New Republic*.

50. In this regard Bickel criticised Herbert A. Wechsler's idea that constitutional theory requires "neutral principles." Bickel objected that no principles satisfying Wechsler's conditions of neutrality could be genuinely serviceable for constitutional adjudication. See Bickel, *Least Dangerous Branch*, pp. 23–28.

51. Ibid., chap. 4, "The Passive Virtues." An issue is moot when the specific grievance of the plaintiff in the suit has either been resolved or terminated prior to the final outcome of the litigation. Thus, the Court declined to hear *DeFunis* v. *Odegard*, the first case brought before it

involving the constitutionality of affirmative action programs, on the ground that DeFunis, the plaintiff, would have already graduated from law school by the time the Court rendered a decision. A case is unripe when a party requests the Court to rule on an issue before he or she has a specific grievance. Thus, the Supreme Court will not issue advisory opinions in constitutional cases.

In the above-cited chapter of *The Least Dangerous Branch*, Bickel also proposed vagueness and the "political question" doctrine as grounds for the Court to avoid exercising its discretion to decide. The former ground, however, seems to me inseparable from a decision on the merits. That is, judgments that a statute is *impermissably vague from a constitutional standpoint* must be based upon a belief that the statute touches matters that involve the exercise of fundamental rights. As for the political question doctrine, this was rendered moot, so to speak, by *Baker* v. *Carr*, 369 U.S. 186 (1962), the landmark reapportionment decision. That is, this case severely narrowed the scope of the doctrine to a point where it now has relatively little value as a device for the Court to avoid deciding issues.

52. Ibid., pp. 23–28.

53. See J. H. Ely, *Democracy and Distrust* (Cambridge, Mass.: Harvard University Press, 1980), p. 58.

54. Ibid., p. 87.

55. Ibid., pp. 102–3.

56. Raoul Berger, *Government by Judiciary* (Cambridge, Mass.: Harvard University Press, 1977).

57. According to Berger, the framers of the Fourteenth Amendment *specifically intended* that it not apply to segregated schools, voting rights, and malapportioned legislative districts. In addition, he maintains they specifically rejected the view that the Fourteenth Amendment incorporates the first ten amendments and makes them applicable to the states.

58. Berger does, however, say that at this point it would be inadvisable for the Court to overrule itself on the matter of segregated schools. In this regard see *Government by Judiciary*, pp. 412–13.

59. See, e.g., Justice Black's dissenting opinion in *Adamson* v. *California*, 332 U.S. 46, 68 (1947); Alexander Bickel, "The Original Understanding of the Segregation Decision," *Harvard Law Review* 69 (1955): 1–65, esp. 57–65; William Van Alstyne, "The Fourteenth Amendment, The Right to Vote, and the Understanding of the Thirty-Ninth Congress," *Supreme Court Review* (1965): 33–85. Paul Brest, "Berger v. Brown et al.," *New York Times Book Review*, (Dec. 11, 1977), p. 10; W. F. Murphy, "Constitutional Interpretation: The Historian, Magician, or Statesman?" *Yale Law Journal* 87 (1978): 1725–71.

60. Also, of course, according to this assumption the thesis that the Fourteenth Amendment was originally intended to incorporate the first ten amendments making them applicable to the states would be false as well.

61. Berger, *Government by Judiciary*, pp. 363–72. This text spans 483 pages. The above matter is treated directly in a single ten-page chapter entitled "Why the Original Intention?"

62. Ibid., p. 364.

63. Conversation with Aaron Snyder was especially helpful in aiding me to see this point. Obviously, however, I must assume full responsibility for its exposition here.

64. Problems about ascertaining the framers' intent loom large. See Murphy's review of *Government by Judiciary*, "Constitutional Interpretation," pp. 1764–68. See also James Nickel and Stephen Munzer, "Does the Constitution Mean What It Always Meant?" *Columbia Law Review* 77 (1977): 1029–62.

65. See notes 20 and 21, chap. 1.

66. See discussion at pp. 18–20.

Chapter Two

1. The idea for using this quotation from Holmes as the basic formulation of the philosophical problem about freedom of expression comes from Thomas Scanlon, "A Theory of Freedom of Expression," *Philosophy and Public Affairs*, vol. 1, no. 2 (1972):204.

2. 250 U.S. 616 (1919).

3. Holmes, of course, went on to provide a defense of freedom of expression similar in essentials to the one that follows.

4. John Stuart Mill, *On Liberty*, ed. with an intro. by Currin V. Shields, Library of Liberal Arts (Indianapolis: Bobbs Merrill, 1956). All citations hereafter will be to this edition.

5. Thomas Hobbes, *Leviathan*, Michael Oakeshott, ed. (New York: Macmillan Co., 1962) pp. 137–38. All quotations henceforth will be from this edition.

6. The entire discussion in chapter two addresses the problems that attend subject matter restrictions upon expression. Mill takes up the problems with restrictions based upon mode of presentation and motivation at pp. 64–67 of *On Liberty*.

7. The discussion of the per se violations of the First Amendment that follows at pp. 44–61 will take up this matter.

8. Hobbes, *Leviathan*, p. 136. Hobbes's discussion of the powers of sovereignty for the most part involves a cryptic and uncompromising characterization of them as exceptionless. The following is typical:

Seventhly, is annexed to the sovereignty, the whole power of prescribing rules whereby every man may know what goods he may enjoy and what actions he may do, without being molested by any of his fellow subjects; and this is it men call *propriety*. For before constitution of sovereign power, as hath already been shown, all men had right to all things; which necessarily causeth war; and therefore, this propriety being necessary for peace, and depending upon sovereign power, is the act of that power, in order to the public peace.

The contrast between the foregoing passage and the one immediately following on the subject of freedom of expression should be dramatically evident.

9. Ibid., pp. 137–38.

10. A central feature of Hobbes's political philosophy is the idea that without the existence of government the basic rules of morality, which he terms the "laws of nature," only oblige in conscience but not with respect to our actual dealings with each other. See *Leviathan*, pp. 101–2, 122–23.

11. Hobbes's treatment of this subject in another work, *The Citizen*, provides further textual evidence of the view that he took freedom of expression to be the sole exception to his conception of sovereign power as absolute. The pertinent passage in *The Citizen* (extracted from *Man and Citizen*, Bernard Gert, ed. [Garden City, N.Y.: Doubleday, 1972], pp. 179–80) begins in a manner not unlike the opening sentences of his treatment of freedom of expression in *Leviathan* cited earlier. He then, however, refers the reader to a long footnote in which he says the following:

There is scarce any principle, neither in the worship of God nor human sciences, from whence there may not spring dissensions, discords, reproaches, and by degrees, war itself. Neither doth this happen by reason of the falsehood of the principle, but of the disposition of men, who seeming wise to themselves, will needs appear such to all others. But though such dissensions cannot be hindered from arising, yet may they be restrained by the exercise of the supreme power that they prove no hindrance to the public peace. Of these kinds of opinions therefore, I have not spoken in this place. There are however certain doctrines wherewith subjects being tainted, they verily believe that obedience may be refused to the city, and that by right they may, nay, ought to oppose and fight against chief princes and dignities.

In the above passage Hobbes thus distinguishes controversies in the worship of God and the human sciences generally from doctrines that have an inherent tendency, so to speak, to undermine respect for civil authority. He continues in this passage to cite Catholicism as the worst offender in this respect. Hobbes then asserts that since no one can reasonably deny the sovereign authority to maintain peace by suppressing inherently dangerous ideas such as those he enumerated, it follows that "the examination of those opinions, whether they be such or not, must be referred to the city: that is, to him who hath the supreme authority."

In *The Citizen*, then, sovereign power with respect to the control of expression pertains only to reviewing the dissemination of inherently suspect doctrines, of which Catholicism was the chief example for Hobbes. In sum, the above point of view does not differ substantially from Milton's in *Areopagetica*. This rather extraordinary coincidence of their views on freedom of expression is frequently overlooked.

12. Ibid., p. 71.

13. Ibid., pp. 71–72.

14. Ibid., p. 76.

15. In ordinary speech, people who differ strikingly from others are frequently referred to as "individuals." Thus, one might object that Mill's account of individuality fails to treat an important part of this notion. But although Mill does not equate individuality with uniqueness of character, he regards them as intimately related. In this regard he points out in chapter three that "the differences among human beings in their sources of pleasure and susceptibility of pain and the operation on them of different physical and moral agencies" are so great that if human beings are permitted to develop their individuality [reason] by choosing their own plans of life the inevitable result will be striking differences among people (*On Liberty*, p. 83). This supports Mill's confident statement referred to earlier that wherever strength of character, genius, mental vigor, and moral courage have abounded, so also has eccentricity. Thus, because he accepts the plausible factual premise that there are innumerable sources of pleasure and pain for human beings, Mill holds that the person whose rational abilities and capacities are highly developed will, in all likelihood, be a unique personality.

16. See John Dewey, *Human Nature and Conduct* (New York, Modern Library, 1957), p. 184.

17. Mill, *On Liberty*, p. 67.

18. Ibid., p. 81.

19. Scanlon, "A Theory of Freedom of Expression," *Philosophy and Public Affairs* 1, no. 2 (1972):204–26.

20. See Gerald G. MacCallum, Jr., "Legislative Intent," *The Yale Law Journal* 75, no. 5 (1966):754–87.

21. For a general discussion of the common law of defamation, see William L. Prosser, *Law of Torts*, 4th ed. (St. Paul, Minn.: West Publishing Co., 1971), pp. 736–76. See also the discussion that follows at pp. 78–85.

22. I assume that through some device such as a blind land trust our friend can conceal his status as owner of the pond.

23. *Schenk v. United States*, 249 U.S. 47 (1919). For Scanlon's concession on this point, see Scanlon, "A Theory of Free Expression," p. 213.

24. Scanlon, "A Theory of Free Expression," pp. 220–21.

25. In *Chicago Board of Trade* v. *United States*, 246 U.S. 231 (1918), the Court held that only unreasonable contracts and combinations in restraint of trade violate section one of the Sherman Act. The Court did not, however, enunciate the criteria of unreasonableness applicable in cases of this kind. But by the 1940s the per se approach was firmly entrenched as the primary mode of interpretation of the "rule of reason" standard for section one cases. So, strictly speaking, in antitrust law the

per se approach functions as a rule of construction for purposes of applying the reasonableness standard to section one cases under the Sherman Act. See *United States* v. *Socony Vacuum Oil Co.*, 310 U.S. 150 (1940). Martin Malin reminded me of this point.

26. For examples of the per se approach see *United States* v. *Trenton Potteries*, 273 U.S. 392 (1927)—price fixing; *United States* v. *Topco Associates*, 405 U.S. 596 (1972)—horizontal division of territories; *Northern Pacific R.R. Co.* v. *U.S.*, 356 U.S. 1 (1958)—tying devices; *Klor's, Inc.* v. *Broadway–Hale Stores*, 359 U.S. 207 (1959)—group boycotts. Some recent cases indicate a possible shift on the part of the Supreme Court away from the strict per se approach hitherto employed. For an example, see *Broadcast Music Inc.* v. *CBS, Inc.*, 441 U.S. 1 (1979). At this time, however, the per se approach still predominates overwhelmingly.

27. It should be noted, however, that the per se approach, as it has been applied by the Court in specific cases, has received substantial criticism. One eminent critic, Richard Posner, believes that the Court takes too narrow a view of the fundamental aims of the Sherman Act. According to his view the Act should be thought of not merely as a device for promoting price competition, but more generally as a vehicle for facilitating economic efficiency. For his argument, see Richard Posner, *Antitrust Law: An Economic Perspective* (Chicago: University of Chicago Press, 1976).

Other critics complain that in some cases the Court relies on extremely poor economic analysis in resolving the factual question of whether or not a given kind of economic arrangement tends to undermine price competition. For example, see Robert Bork, *The Antitrust Paradox* (New York: Basic Books, 1978). Such criticism, however, does not really bear upon the use to which I will put the per se approach.

28. See Mill, *Utilitarianism*, chap. 2.

29. See Immanual Kant, *Fundamental Principles of the Metaphysic of Morals*, Thomas K. Abbot, tr. (New York: Liberal Arts Press, 1949), section 2, esp. pp. 37–38.

30. See *The Doctrine of Virtue*, Part II of *The Metaphysic of Morals*, Mary J. Gregor, tr. (New York: Harper & Row, 1964). See especially the translator's introduction, pp. xvii–xxxvi.

31. See Rawls, *A Theory of Justice*, p. 200.

32. Also, I would not rule out that considerations of convenience and economy of which I am unaware at this time may dictate compressing several categories into one.

33. For a comprehensive list of federal and state sedition statutes up to 1940 that also quotes their provisions, see Zechariah Chafee, Jr., *Free Speech in the United States* (New York: Athenaeum, 1969), Appendices II and III.

34. See 18 U.S.C., sec. 2385. The law as originally passed is set forth in 54 State 670 (1940). A comparison of the wording of the Smith Act with that of the Alien and Sedition Acts of 1798, the first federal sedition

legislation in United States history, is instructive. In this regard, see Stat.
596 (1798). Section two of this act reads in part as follows:

That if any person shall write, print, utter, or publish; or shall cause or procure
to be written, printed, uttered, or published, or shall knowingly and willingly assist
or aid in writing, printing, uttering, or publishing any false, scandalous, and
malicious, writing or writings against the government of the United States, or either
house of congress of the United States, or the President of the United States, with
intent to defame the said government, or either house of the said congress, or the
said president, or to bring them into contempt or disrepute; or to excite against
them, or either or any of them, the hatred of the good people of the United States
. . . then such person, being thereof convicted before any court of the United
States having jurisdiction thereof, shall be punished, by a fine not exceeding two
thousand dollars, and by imprisonment not exceeding two years.

35. Sedition must be distinguished from espionage. A law forbidding
espionage seeks to prevent specific information from reaching specific
individuals who will use it for specific undesirable ends. Sedition laws,
by contrast, aim to prevent the dissemination of attitudes and beliefs to
the general public that could possibly have injurious effects upon the
nation's efforts to maintain its security. To be sure, espionage laws could
be drafted in ways that offend the First Amendment. If so, however, such
would be because so drafted they assumed the character of sedition laws.

36. See Chafee, *Free Speech in the United States*, p. 51.
37. *Brandenburg* v. *Ohio*, 395 U.S. 444 (1969); *Whitney* v. *California*,
274 U.S. 357 (1927).
38. *Brandenburg*, p. 447.
39. See *Schenk* v. *U.S.* (cited at chap. 1, note 4); *Frohwerk* v. *U.S.*,
249 U.S. 204 (1919); *Debs* v. *U.S.*, 249 U.S. 211 (1919).
40. 268 U.S. 652, pp. 668–69 (1925).
41. See *Abrams* v. *U.S.*, p. 616; *Gitlow* v. *N.Y.*, pp. 652, 668–69;
Whitney v. *Cal.*, p. 357.
42. For example, *Stromberg* v. *California*, 283 U.S. 359 (1931)—ruled
unconstitutional a version of a widely adopted anti-Red flag law; *Herndon*
v. *Lowry*, 301 U.S. 242 (1937)—Georgia statute outlawing attempt to incite
insurrection held unconstitutionally vauge; *Dejonge* v. *Oregon*, 299 U.S.
353 (1937)—conviction under Oregon's criminal syndicalism law set aside
on the ground that assisting in preparation of a lawful meeting held under
the auspices of the Communist Party is protected activity under the First
Amendment.
43. 341 U.S. 494 (1951).
44. For example, *Yates* v. *U.S.*, 354 U.S. 298 (1957)—Smith Act
construed as having been intended not to forbid the advocacy of violent
overthrow of the United States government as a matter of abstract doctrine;
Scales v. *U.S.*, 367 U.S. 203 (1961)—Smith Act interpreted as only forbidding
membership in an organization dedicated to the violent overthrow of the
United States government if such membership involves knowledge of the

organization's illegal aims and a specific intent to further them (in Scales the conviction under the Smith Act was upheld); *Pennsylvania* v. *Nelson*, 350 U.S. 497 (1956)—held that federal legislation had preempted the field of legislation directed at sedition on a national scale; *Watkins* v. *U.S.*, 354 U.S. 178 (1957)—HUAC contempt citation against witness who refused to name names overturned on due process grounds; *Sweezy* v. *New Hampshire*, 354 U.S. 234 (1957)—held that New Hampshire's attorney general could not ask Professor Paul Sweezy questions about a speech he made at the University of New Hampshire because the law ostensibly delegating him authority to ask such questions was so vague as to violate Sweezy's due process rights.

45. See Thomas Emerson, *The System of Freedom of Expression* (New York: Random House, 1970), p. 260.

46. For example, *Barenblatt* v. *U.S.*, 360 U.S. 109 (1959), and *Wyman* v. *Uphaus*, 360 U.S. 72 (1959).

47. See *Federalist 78* in *Selections from The Federalist*, Henry Steele Commager, ed. (New York: Appleton Century Crofts, 1949), pp. 113–120.

48. Geoffrey Marshall, *Parliamentary Sovereignty and the Commonwealth* (London: Oxford University Press, 1957), contains a valuable extended summary of Harris v. Donges, (1952) 1 T.L.R., a South African case in which petitioners proposed to test the constitutionality of apartheid laws with respect to the suffrage. This politically explosive case provoked a confrontation between the South African Parliament and Supreme Court that resulted in substantial defeat for the latter.

49. See generally, Eugene Gressman and Robert L. Stern, *Supreme Court Practice*, 4th ed. (Washington, D.C.: Bureau of National Affairs, 1969), pp. 26–80.

50. For a parallel account of the general duty of obedience to law, see Yves Simon, *Philosophy of Democratic Government* (Chicago: University of Chicago Press, 1951).

51. See, for example, the cases cited at n. 44.

52. Alexander Bickel's otherwise illuminating account of how the Court may use the devices at its disposal for declining to decide an issue seems to me to overlook this basic conceptual point. See Bickel, *The Least Dangerous Branch*, chap. 4.

53. The leading common law case incorporating this rationale into the legal test for obscenity is *Regina* v. *Hicklin*, (1868) L.R. 3 Q.B. 360. In this case the test for obscenity was declared to be whether the materials in question have a "tendency to deprave and corrupt those whose minds are open to such immoral influences, and into whose hands [the materials] may fall." Among contemporary writers the following advocate restrictions upon obscene literature on the grounds under discussion: Patrick Devlin, "Morals and the Criminal Law," in *The Enforcement of Morals* (London: Oxford University Press, 1965), pp. 1–25; Susan Brownmiller, *Against Our Will: Men, Women and Rape* (New York: Simon & Schuster, 1975), pp.

389–96; Irving Kristol, "Pornography, Obscenity, and the Case of Censorship," *New York Times Magazine*, March 28, 1971.

54. See *Paris Adult Theatres* v. *Slaton*, 413 U.S. 49, 58–60 (1973); Alexander Bickel, *The Morality of Consent* (New Haven: Yale University Press, 1975), pp. 73–76.

55. See *Paris Adult Theatres* v. *Slaton*, pp. 58–60.

56. Mill, *On Liberty*, p. 91.

57. The following quotation from Justice Stevens, writing for the majority in *Young* v. *American Mini Theatres*, 427 U.S. 50 (1975), typifies this approach:

Moreover, even though we recognize that the First Amendment will not tolerate the total suppression of erotic materials that have some arguable artistic value, it is manifest that society's interest in protecting this type of expression is of a wholly different and lesser magnitude than the interest in untrammeled political debate that inspired Voltaire's immortal comment. Whether political oratory or philosophical discussion moves us to applaud or to despise what is said, every schoolchild can understand why our duty to defend this right to speak remains the same. But few of us would march our sons and daughters off to war to preserve the citizen's right to see "specified sexual activities exhibited in the theatres of our choice" [p. 70].

58. Alexander Meiklejohn, *Political Freedom* (New York: Oxford University Press, 1965), pp. 24–27.

59. Ibid., pp. 81, 119.

60. 354 U.S. 476 (1957).

61. For a summary of these vicissitudes see Lawrence Tribe, *American Constitutional Law* (Mineola, N.Y.: The Foundation Press, 1978), pp. 656–70.

62. 378 U.S. 184 (1964).

63. Ibid., p. 197.

64. For example, see Brownmiller *Against Our Will*, and Kristol, "Pornography."

65. 413 U.S. 15 (1973).

66. Ibid., pp. 24–25.

67. Tribe, *American Constitutional Law*, p. 656.

68. The following remark by Hobbes in *Leviathan*, p. 142, about the words "tyranny" and "oligarchy" applies by analogy to "censorship" in the broad sense:

Tyranny and oligarchy (are) but different names of monarchy and aristocracy. There may be other names of government in the histories and books of policy; as *tyranny* and *oligarchy:* but they are not the names of other forms of government but the same forms disliked.

69. In actuality, this definition of censorship is not strictly correct. The problem with it stems from the fact that the phrase "acts of expression" has an extremely broad denotation. That is to say, one may express oneself not only through speaking or writing, but in an infinity of other ways

as well. For example, one can express hostility toward another person not only by insulting him, but also by punching him in the mouth. A definition of censorship simply as the making illegal of precisely identified acts of expression thus has the absurd consequence that laws forbidding assault and battery constitute censorship.

One can avoid this difficulty by introducing a subtle but important change in the definition that makes use of the notion of "action under a description." To explain this idea briefly, any act can be described in a multitude of ways. Quoting philosopher Donald Davidson, "I flip the switch, turn on the light, and illuminate the room. Unbeknownst to me I also alert a prowler to the fact that I am home. Here I do not do four things but only one, of which four descriptions have been given." ("Actions, Reasons, and Causes," *Journal of Philosophy* 60, no. 23 [Nov. 7, 1963]:685–700.)

Now we can characterize censorship as making illegal precisely identified acts of expression *under language describing them as acts of expression.* That is to say, we do not have censorship unless the law forbidding certain precisely identified acts of expression specifically describes the forbidden acts as acts of expression. Accordingly, our definition of censorship should be understood as including this addition.

70. See Anne Lynn Haight, *Banned Books* (New York: R.R. Bowker Co., 1970).

71. *Federal Communications Commission* v. *Pacifica Foundation,* 438 U.S. 726 (1978).

72. According to one usage "prior restraint" is identical with "censorship." In this regard see Thomas Emerson, *The System of Freedom of Expression,* pp. 142–43, 373.

73. Jack Snapper reminded me of the foregoing points.

74. Archibald Cox, *Freedom of Expression* (Cambridge, Mass.: Harvard University Press, 1981), p. 7.

75. I am assuming, of course, that authorities must secure an injunction to enforce prior restraints.

76. For example, one may use deadly force in self-defense only to repel an attack that places one in reasonable apprehension of serious imminent physical injury. This uncomplicated rule has remained more or less unchanged for generations. In the common law one often finds that as a cumulative effect of many cases, each presenting slight complications within a basic fact pattern, over time a given general rule applicable to that pattern becomes increasingly indefinite. Such has not occurred in the case of the deadly force limitation in regard to self-defense.

77. This provision of the Taft Hartley Act was upheld in *American Communications Association* v. *Douds,* 339 U.S. 382 (1950). The provision, however, was deleted with the passing of the Labor Management Reporting and Disclosure Act.

78. See *Borrow* v. *Federal Communications Commission,* 285 F. 2d 66

(D.C. Cir., 1960)—provision denying radio operator's license to Communists upheld; *Kent* v. *Dulles*, 357 U.S. 116 (1958)—passport restrictions against Communists struck down on ground that federal statutes did not authorize the Secretary of State to impose such restrictions; and *Fleming* v. *Nestor*, 363 U.S. 603 (1960)—statutory provision depriving deported Communists of their social security benefits upheld.

79. See *Konigsberg* v. *State Bar of California*, 366 U.S. 36 (1961)—rule barring Communists from the practice of law held not to violate the First Amendment; *Speiser* v. *Randall*, 357 U.S. 513 (1958)—provision excluding those who believe in forcible overthrow of the U.S. Government from receiving veteran's property tax exemption held to violate the First Amendment.

80. See *Dombrowski* v. *Pfister*, 380 U.S. 479 (1965)—court enjoined criminal prosecutions under Louisiana State sedition law where it was determined that the prosecutions were not made with any expectation of securing a valid conviction, but only for the sake of harassment; see also Mike Royko, *Boss: Richard J. Daley of Chicago* (New York: E. P. Dutton, 1971), p. 126. Royko describes how businessmen who displayed campaign photographs of Mayor Daley's Republic rival suddenly found themselves charged with numerous building code violations.

81. See the 1972 AAUP Guidelines.

82. 319 U.S. 624, 642 (1943).

83. The Court has imposed various limitations upon the use of membership or other associated relationships in loyalty oaths. The decision in *U.S.* v. *Brown*, 381 U.S. 437 (1965), strongly suggests that no organization may be listed by name in an oath. In addition, any associational relationships with organizations designated by description must be knowing (see *Keyishian* v. *Board of Regents of the University of the State of New York*, 385 U.S. 589 [1967]); they must be active rather than passive (see *Elfbrandt* v. *Russell*, 384 U.S. 11 [1966] and *U.S.* v. *Robel* 389 U.S. 258 [1967]); and they must involve specific intent to achieve the illegal aims of the organization (see Keyishian). Furthermore, the Court has imposed standards of precision upon loyalty oaths of unparalled exactitude (see *Cramp* v. *Board of Public Instruction*, 368 U.S. 278 [1961]; *Whitehill* v. *Elkins*, 389 U.S. 54 [1967]; *Baggett* v. *Bullet*, 377 U.S. 360 [1964]).

84. 368 U.S. 278 (1961).

85. Ibid., pp. 286–87.

86. See Tribe, *American Constitutional Law*, pp. 682–88.

87. See, e.g., *Cantwell* v. *Connecticut*, 310 U.S. 296, 307, 308 (1940); *Cox* v. *Louisiana*, 379 U.S. 536, 555, 557–58 (1965); *Edwards* v. *South Carolina*, 372 U.S. 229, 236, 237–38 (1963); *Terminello* v. *Chicago*, 337 U.S. 1, 3, 13 (1949); *Saia* v. *New York*, 334 U.S. 558 (1948); *Kovacs* v. *Cooper*, 336 U.S. 77 (1949); *Lovell* v. *Griffin*, 303 U.S. 444, 451 (1938); *Hague* v. *C.I.O.*, 307 U.S. 496 (1939); *Hess* v. *Indiana*, 414 U.S. 105 (1973).

88. The above description of the circumstances surrounding the in-

cident in Skokie is drawn from Judge Decker's opinion in *Collin* v. *Smith*. After having their right to march vindicated, the Nazis declined to do so. See 578 F. 2d 1197 (1978).

89. See Brownmiller, *Against Our Will*, pp. 389–96.

90. See Brownmiller, as well as any of perhaps several thousand public statements of the Palestinian Liberation Organization.

91. Quoted by Chafee, *Free Speech in the United States*, p. 321.

92. Erwin Knoll, "Born Secret," *The Progressive* 43, no. 5 (May 12, 1979):12.

93. "Wrestling with *Leviathan*," *The Progressive* 43, no. 11 (November 1979):26.

94. A student in one of my courses, Wayne Salata, pointed out that the phrase "nuclear energy," as it functions in the Atomic Energy Act, is not very precise either, insofar as it covers virtually all of modern physics.

95. See H. Peter Metzger, *The Atomic Establishment* (New York: Simon & Shuster, 1972).

96. This is not meant to suggest that the rules and procedures for officially classifying information present no problems with respect to freedom of expression. Obviously, these can be, and have been, greatly abused. It would seem, however, that questions about how to safeguard against or remedy such abuses essentially constitute policy rather than constitutional issues. They involve making decisions with respect to such matters as what information a government must disclose and the circumstances under which it must do so. The diversity of possible cases in these regards seems so vast that it could only be dealt with reasonably through comprehensive legislation or administrative orders.

97. See chap. 1, p. 5.

98. See *U.S.* v. *O'Brien*, 391 U.S. 367 (1968).

99. Ibid.

100. Ibid., pp. 378–80.

101. See Tribe, *American Constitutional Law*, pp. 594–98.

102. *Tinker* v. *Des Moines*, 393 U.S. 503 (1969).

103. Ibid.

104. See discussion of penalization at pp. 56–58.

105. 316 U.S. 52 (1942).

106. See *Martin* v. *City of Struthers*, 319 U.S. 141 (1943), and *Breard* v. *Alexandria*, 341 U.S. 622 (1951).

107. See *Pittsburgh Press Co.* v. *Pittsburgh Commission on Human Relations*, 413 U.S. 376 (1973); *Bigelow* v. *Virginia*, 421 U.S. 809 (1975); and 425 U.S. 748 (1976).

108. A finding of unprofessional conduct in Virginia would subject a pharmacist to a monetary penalty or suspension of his license.

109. The Court did not specifically describe the Virginia statute as

overbroad, but the reasoning that controlled strongly suggests overbreadth analysis.

110. See *Virginia Pharmacy Board*, pp. 763–64.

111. Ibid., p. 770.

112. Ibid., pp. 770–73.

113. Ibid., p. 776.

114. Ibid.

115. This remark is not intended to suggest that the NLRB rules limiting expression in Union representation elections present no First Amendment problems whatsoever. To the contrary, I think that such rules merit substantial criticism. Stating the essentials of this criticism requires a few words about the statutory background of union representation elections. Section 7 of the Natural Labor Relations Act (NLRA) gives employees the right to organization. The section goes on to grant employees a number of more specific rights in this regard, e.g., to join labor organizations, to bargain collectively, etc. Section 8a (1) states that "It shall be an unfair labor practice for an employer to interfere with, restrain, or coerce employees in the exercise of the rights guaranteed in section 7." Section 8a(5) declares comparable acts by unions to constitute unfair labor practice as well.

The National Labor Relations Board, which the NLRA authorizes to oversee union representation elections, has interpreted section 8a(1) and 8a(5) as empowering it to set aside such elections where it judges employers or unions to have made statements that were either highly threatening, misleading, or inflammatory (see, e.g., *Dal-Tex Optical Co.*, 137 N.L.R.B. 1782 [1962]; *Lord Baltimore Press*, 144 N.L.R.B. 1376 [1963]; *Celanese Corp. of America*, 121 N.L.R.B. 303 [1958]; *R. L. Polk and Co.*, 123 N.L.R.B. 1171 [1959]; *Shopping Kart Food Market, Inc.*, 228 N.L.R.B. 1311 [1977]; and *Sewell Mfg. Co.*, 138 N.L.R.B. 66 [1962]. The Board has also rendered decisions concerning when union representatives may have access to the employer's premises for the purpose of electioneering, and the circumstances in which an election may be set aside because the employer gained an unfair advantage as a result of a last-minute speech to which the union had no opportunity to respond (*Peyton Packing Co.*, 49 NLRB 828 [1943]; *Republic Aviation Corp.* v. *NLRB*, 324 U.S. 793 [1945]; *NLRB* v. *Babcock & Wilcox Co.*, 351 U.S. 105 [1956]; *Livingston Shirt Corp.*, 107 NLRB 400 [1953]; *NLRB* v. *United Steelworkers*, 357 U.S. 357 [1958]).

From the standpoint of the approach to First Amendment adjudication proposed in this chapter, the crucial question about speech limitations by the NLRB in the context of union representation elections is whether they fall under one or more of the categories of per se violations. It seems that one should focus upon vagueness and overbreadth as the major category in this regard. By setting aside an election because one party or the other made threatening, misleading, or inflammatory statements, the Board hardly acts under sedition or obscenity laws. Nor does its action count as censorship, prior restraint, penalization, or regimentation as I have defined these terms. But the Board's exercise of its authority to set aside elections, unless defined with narrow precision, would appear inherently vague and overbroad. That is, without precise delimitation of its authority, the Board could invoke it in ways that achieved substantially the same ends it could accomplish if it had formal authorization to censor, penalize, and so forth. The same considerations likewise seem to apply with respect to the Board's authority to decree when employers must grant union representatives access to company premises for electioneering purposes, and to set aside elections because of an unfair advantage gained by the employer through a last-minute speech.

Detailed analysis of whether the Board's specific decisions with respect to the above-mentioned issues are vague and overbroad would take up far too much space for present purposes. Quite conclusorily, however, I will say it seems to me that many of these decisions indeed appear highly questionable from this standpoint. For a discussion that, though not employing the concept of per se violations of the First Amendment, nonetheless reaches conclusions that strike me as substantially those one would reach under a per se approach, see Derek Bok, "The Regulation of Campaign Tactics in Representation Elections Under the National Labor Relations Act," *Harvard Law Review* 78, no. 38 (1964): 39–141, esp. 66–106.

116. 393 U.S. 97 (1968).

117. I am using the phrase "theory of evolution" somewhat loosely here to refer to Darwin's theory of natural selection. I do so because this seems to be the theory that most upsets the creationists.

118. See *Bill McClean* v. *Arkansas Board of Education.* 529 F. Supp. 1255 (1982).

119. See the discussion at pp. 35–39.

120. For example, review would be justified where a school board flagrantly violates its own rules, or where school authorities officially incorporate measures that constitute censorship or regimentation into their curricular policies.

121. Section 315 of the Communications Act of 1934, 47 U.S.C. 315, provides in part:

If any licensee shall permit any person who is a legally qualified candidate for any public office to sue a broadcasting station, he shall afford equal opportunities to all other such candidates for that office in the use of such broadcasting station.

122. In this regard see Dorothy Nelkin, *Science Textbook Controversies and the Politics of Equal Time* (Cambridge, Mass.: M.I.T. Press, 1977).

123. Under the Sherman Act, section one, a tying arrangement is unlawful if the seller has market power in the tying product and if the arrangement forecloses a substantial volume of the market for the tied product. See *Times–Picayune* v. *U.S.,* 345 U.S. 594 (1953). Tying arrangements are also unlawful under section three of the Clayton Act, which states, "It shall be unlawful for any person . . . to lease or make a sale

of commodities . . . or fix a price therefore . . . on the condition or agreement . . . in the commodities of a competitor . . . of the seller or lessor, where the effect may be to substantially lesson competition or tend to create a monopoly in any line of commerce."

Chapter Three

1. 283 U.S. 697 (1931) and 297 U.S. 233 (1936).
2. *Near,* p. 703.
3. *Grosjean,* p. 241 (cited in note 1).
4. Ibid., pp. 250–51.
5. For a general discussion of the common law of defamation, see William L. Prosser, *Law of Torts,* 4th ed. (St. Paul, Minn.: West Pubishing Co., 1971), pp. 737–801.
6. Ibid., pp. 774–76.
7. Benno C. Schmidt, Jr., *Freedom of the Press v. Public Access* (New York, Praeger, 1977), p. 71.
8. Zechariah Chafee, *Government and Mass Communication,* vol. 2, (Chicago: University of Chicago Press, 1947), p. 97.
9. Thomas Emerson, *The System of Freedom of Expression* (New York: Random House, 1970), p. 519.
10. At the time the Court considered the *Sullivan* case, several other big libel suits brought by public officials under the same circumstances as in Sullivan were pending. See Schmidt, *Freedom of the Press v. Public Access,* p. 72.
11. 376 U.S. 254 (1964).
12. *Sullivan,* p. 267.
13. Ibid., pp. 279–80.
14. Ibid., pp. 273–77.
15. It is interesting to note that at the time *Sullivan* was decided in 1964, the Court had not yet explicitly passed judgment on the constitutionality of sedition laws, as it did in *Brandenburg v. Ohio.* In this regard, see the discussion at pp. 46–48.
16. 388 U.S. 130 (1967).
17. *Curtis,* p. 154.
18. 403 U.S. 29 (1971).
19. *Rosenbloom,* pp. 45–46.
20. *Rosenbloom,* pp. 57–62.
21. Justice Black simply reiterated his long-held minority view that the First Amendment proscribes any law pertaining to defamation whatsoever. Justice White held that the "actual malice" standard applied in Rosenbloom because the news broadcasts at issue dealt with activities of public officials— namely the police who arrested Rosenbloom for possession of obscene literature. Justices Marshall, joined by Justice Stewart, and Justice Harlan,

in separate dissents, both objected that the notion of "public or general concern" is so broad as to include potentially anything within its scope.

22. 418 U.S. 323 (1974).

23. *Gertz*, pp. 351–52.

24. Ibid., pp. 343–45.

25. In addition to drawing the line at public figures, the Court also made some other pronouncements that have extremely powerful implications for future lawsuits under the common law of defamation. The Court first held that "so long as they do not impose liability without fault, the States may define for themselves the appropriate standard of liability for a publisher or broadcaster of defamatory falsehood which injures a private individual and whose substance makes substantial damage to reputation apparent" (*Gertz*, 347–58). This almost matter-of-fact statement appears to work a very substantial change in the common law rules with regard to defamation. It appears to say that henceforth liability must be conditioned upon fault. That is, the states may frame whatever standards they wish with respect to defamation *provided* they do not impose liability without fault. As mentioned earlier, the traditional approach imposed liability without fault as a matter of course. Consequently, the above statement by the Court calls for a very substantial change. Precisely for this reason Justice White registered a strong dissent (*Gertz*, 369–401).

The Court also held that without a showing of knowledge of falsity or reckless disregard of the truth, the states may not permit recovery of presumed or punitive damages. Instead, recovery should only be limited to "actual damages" (348–50). Since under the common law rules damages in a suit for defamation were *always* presumed, this holding likewise called for substantial changes. As to what the category of actual damages consists in, however, the Court was not entirely clear. But it listed as examples "impairment of reputation and standing in the community, personal humiliation, and mental anguish and suffering" (350). The precise effect of the above pronouncements upon the common law in regard to defamation is still in a state of development.

26. In *Time* v. *Firestone*, 424 U.S. 448 (1976), the Court held that merely by participating in litigation as a plaintiff one does not thereby become a public figure. Three years later the court ruled that neither the fact of having applied for a federal research grant nor of failing to make a court appearance pursuant to a grand jury subpoena make one a public figure (*Hutchinson* v. *Proxmire*, 443 U.S. 111 [1979], and *Wolston* v. *Reader's Digest Association, Inc.*, 443 U.S. 157 [1979]). In *Herbert* v. *Lando*, 441 U.S. 153 (1979), the Court held that a plaintiff who sues for defamation and admits public figure status is entitled to receive in pretrial discovery preparatory material used in putting together the allegedly defamatory publication or broadcast in order to prove knowledge of falsity or reckless disregard of the truth.

27. See *Sullivan*, 293–96; *Curtis*, 170–72; and *Rosenbloom*, 57.

28. 408 U.S. 665 (1972). The other two cases disposed of with the *Branzburg* decision were *In the matter of Pappas*, on *certiorari* to the Supreme Judicial Court of Massachusetts; and *United States* v. *Caldwell*, on *certiorari* from the U.S. Court of Appeals for the Ninth Circuit.

29. *Branzburg*, p. 690.

30. Ibid., pp. 693–95.

31. Ibid., pp. 720–1, 728–26.

32. 436 U.S. 547 (1978).

33. *Zurcher*, p. 566.

34. Ibid., pp. 570–76.

35. *New York Times* v. *Jascalevitch*, 439 U.S. 1301 (1978). In an opinion in chambers Justice White wrote, "There is no present authority in this Court either that newsmen are constitutionally privileged to withhold duly subpoenaed documents material to the prosecution or defense of a criminal case or that a defendant seeking the subpoena must show extraordinary circumstances before enforcement against newsmen will be had" (1322).

36. Noting this particular issue makes it possible to avoid an error of analysis into which evidently one can fall rather easily. In the case of *First National Bank of Boston* v. *Bellotti*, 435 U.S. 765 (1978), Chief Justice Burger in a concurring opinion raised the issue, entirely unrelated to the *Bellotti* case, of whether the press has rights under the First Amendment distinct from those of individuals. Holding that they do not, Chief Justice Burger based his conclusion primarily on the contention that to take the opposing view would open the door to intractable definitional problems. That is to say, the Court would then have to decide how the term "press" should be applied for First Amendment purposes—who should be included and who should be excluded. (In this connection see the *Bellotti* opinion, p. 795.)

To be sure, the above problem is difficult, and, indeed one might well conclude *upon reflection* that it admits of no answer. One cannot, however, reach a conclusion about it without first analyzing the functions of the press and assessing their constitutional significance. That is to say, one can only settle such questions as whether newspapers, but not billboard publishers, have special First Amendment rights by comparing the two in terms of a conception of what is constitutionally important about the role of the press. In other words, the proposition that the term "press" cannot be defined for First Amendment purposes is the conclusion of a constitutional argument. It cannot appear in the premises as it did in Chief Justice Burger's analysis.

37. See *Hearings Before Subcommittee No. 3 of the Committee on the Judiciary of the House of Representatives Ninety-Third Congress on H.R. 717, To Assure the Free Flow of Information to the Public and Related Measures* (1973).

38. Among the reporters who testified were Earl Caldwell of the *New*

York Times, Jack Nelson of the *Los Angeles Times,* and Peter Bridge of the now-defunct *Newark News.* In addition, the Reporter's Committee for Freedom of the Press Legal Defense and Research Fund submitted a case compendium of some thirty-three incidents during 1972 in which newspaper reporters were ordered to divulge confidential material. Virtually all of these incidents involved investigative reporting in connection with local politics.

39. In this regard see the discussion following at pp. 125–29.

40. 412 U.S. 94 (1973).

41. 450 F. 2d 642, 646 (1971).

42. *CBS* v. *DNC,* p. 110.

43. *CBS* v. *DNC,* p. 122.

44. *CBS* v. *DNC,* p. 125.

45. 418 U.S. 241 (1974).

46. *Miami* v. *Tournillo,* pp. 243–54.

47. *Miami* v. *Tournillo,* pp. 254, 257, 258.

48. Jerome Barron, *Freedom of the Press for Whom?: The Right of Access to Media* (Bloomington: Indiana University Press, 1973), p. 321.

49. 250 U.S. 616, 630 (1919).

50. The following summary of the experience in New York is taken from Schmidt, *Freedom of the Press v. Public Access,* pp. 207–09.

51. Price and Morris, *On the Cable* (Sloan Commission Report on Cable Communication, 1971), *Public Access Channels: The New York Experience,* Appendix C, p. 237 (quoted by Schmidt, p. 207).

52. Schmidt, *Freedom of the Press v. Public Access,* p. 209.

53. *CBS* v. *DNC,* p. 120.

54. The following summary again is based on the account of these matters in Schmidt, *Freedom of the Press v. Public Access,* pp. 120–33, 158–66.

55. For those readers even less literate technologically than myself, broadcasting is the transmission of electromagnetic waves over the radio spectrum. When more than one station in a particular geographical area simultaneously attempts to use the same frequency, chaos results.

56. 44 Stat. 1162 (1927).

57. The substance of this provision still remains in force as section 315a of the Communications Act of 1934, the statute under which the Federal Communications Commission operates.

58. The foregoing summary of the Radio Act of 1927 is drawn from Schmidt, *Freedom of the Press v. Public Access,* pp. 128–29.

59. 48 State 1081, as amended, 47 U.S.C. sec. 301.

60. 13 FCC 1246 (1949).

61. Schmidt, *Freedom of the Press v. Public Access,* pp. 160–61.

62. 395 U.S. 367 (1969).

63. *Red Lion,* pp. 388–9.

64. *Red Lion,* p. 379.

65. *CBS* v. *DNC,* p. 117.

66. See Barron, *Freedom of the Press for Whom?* for numerous examples in this regard.

67. For example, the FCC decided that no personal attack was involved when former Philadelphia Mayor Frank Rizzo stated that leaders of a teachers' union were engaging in "blackmail," had "placed a gun to the heads of taxpayers," and were seeking "to extract blood money . . . with the educational welfare of our children as pawns." On the other hand, a reference to a congressman as a "coward" was labeled a personal attack. Along the same line, a statement that a legislator's private interest created an apparent conflict of interent was deemed not a personal attack, but the statement that a professor sought to promote the Soviet form of government was considered one. Similarly, the statement that a person was likely to engage in physical abuse, disruption, and violence was held a personal attack, but an assertion that a school was a breeding ground for revolutionaries, terrorists, and guerilas was not (Schmidt, *Freedom of the Press v. Public Access,* pp. 170–71).

68. *Pell* v. *Procunier,* 417 U.S. 817 (1974); *Saxbe* v. *Washington Post,* 417 U.S. 843 (1974); and *Houchins* v. *KQED,* 438 U.S. 1 (1978).

69. *Richmond Newspapers* v. *Virginia,* 448 U.S. 555 (1980).

70. Ibid., p. 582.

71. Lewis, "A Public Right to Know About Public Institutions: The First Amendment as Sword," *Supreme Court Review* (Chicago: University of Chicago Press, 1980), pp. 1–25.

72. 443 U.S. 367 (1979).

73. Gannett, 379–84.

74. Lewis, "A Public Right to Know About Public Institutions," pp. 13–14.

75. Ibid., p. 14.

76. Ibid., pp. 14–15.

77. *Richmond Newspapers,* p. 581.

78. Ibid., pp. 601–4.

79. Ibid., pp. 577–78, 584–600.

80. To see why this is so one must consider why such a requirement exists. It might seem at first blush to stem from an intrinsic abhorence of the harm suffered by innocent people mistakenly punished. Admittedly, such an attitude seems to provide a natural explanation of the oft-expressed sentiment "Better many guilty go free than a single innocent person be punished." Nonetheless, on reflection it appears that this sentiment has a quite different basis. At least, it must have a different basis insofar as it admits of rationalization. All punishable offenses under the criminal law also constitute civil causes of action. Thus, for example, a person might be both prosecuted for murder and sued for wrongful death, both prosecuted and sued for battery, both prosecuted for theft and sued for conversion, and so forth. In civil cases, however, Courts apply a standard

of preponderance of the evidence rather than proof beyond a reasonable doubt.

One might always regard this difference in standards of proof as an anomaly at odds with the basic rationale for using a beyond-a-reasonable-doubt standard in criminal cases. But such a stance does not seem called for. A plausible account exists of the principal reason for different standards of proof in criminal and civil cases concerning identical kinds of acts. The former kind of case raises fundamental problems about the relation between governors and governed that do not attend the latter. The power necessarily vested in governments to enforce the criminal law is so great that society hedges it with restraints. A requirement that the state prove its case in criminal trials beyond a reasonable doubt constitutes such a restraint insofar as it dramatically affects the ease with which a government may, so to speak, get its hands upon an individual. In contrast to all of this, the civil law, in which private citizens initiate legal proceedings, does not present comparable problems calling for like restraints upon the exercise of governmental power.

81. Lewis, "A Public Right to Know," p. 23.

82. There are far more problems in this regard than the above quotation from Lewis's article suggests. For example, Lewis mentions that when one interprets the idea of a right of access to information as intended to further accountability, it turns out that the right would not sweep Supreme Court conferences within it. This is because "it is not necessary for us as citizens to have access to those conferences in order to scrutinize the Court's work. For the Court acts only by what it does in public . . ." Applying this same approach, could one say that the right of access to information likewise would not require publication of the *Congressional Record* since Congress also only acts by what it does in public? If not, then how does one distinguish the two cases?

83. At the close of his article Lewis advances the following line of argument in further support of the idea of a right of access to information under the First Amendment:

The function of the citizen-critic of government is more important than ever—and harder to perform. If big government is to be effectively criticized and controlled it will take the countervailing force of big newspapers and broadcast networks and public interest groups and lobbying organizations of all kinds. And they cannot succeed without information. In our society information is power. Officials struggle to control it, and in that struggle the citizen-critic needs constitutional support. [p. 25].

Lewis' remarks in the above passage are clearly well taken up to the second conjunct in the last sentence. That is to say, though undoubtedly the kinds of organizations Lewis mentions serve the vital function of criticizing big government, he really does not say why they absolutely need a *constitutional* right of access to information to do their job in this regard. This is not to say by any means, however, that secrecy in government is either generally beneficial on balance or relatively harmless. Indeed, I would agree in characterizing the situation as quite the opposite. I would also concur in a judgment to the effect that as a factual matter, secrecy in government at all levels in the United States extends far beyond reasonable levels. In this regard see *None of Your Business: Government Secrecy in America*, Norman Dorsen and Stephen Gillers, eds. (New York: Viking Press, 1974); Arthur Macy Cox, *The Myth of National Security* (Boston: Beacon Press, 1975), esp. chap. 2; and the dissenting opinion of Justice Douglas in *EPA* v. *Mink*, 410 U.S. 73 (1973). This problem, however, should be addressed through statutory means rather than by way of constitutional adjudication.

Chapter Four

1. Louis V. McIntire and Marion B. McIntire, *Scientists and Engineers: The Professionals Who Are Not* (Lafayette, La.: Arcola Publishing Co., 1971).

2. Nicholas Wade, "Protection Sought for Satirists and Whistle-blowers," *Science* (December 7, 1973):1002–3.

3. See, e.g., David Ewing, *Freedom Inside the Organization* (New York, Dutton, 1977), pp. 11–16.

4. See Gerald Gunther, *Cases and Materials on Constitutional Law*, 9th ed. (Mineola, N.Y.: The Foundation Press, 1975), pp. 906–54.

5. In this regard, see the discussion that follows at pp. 117–24.

6. See earlier discussion at pp. 46–48.

7. Another, and perhaps even more pertinent, example in this regard is the extension of the First Amendment to cover actions of state as well as federal governmental authority. The Court effected such an extension in the case of *Gitlow* v. *New York*, 268 U.S. 652 (1925) wherein it explicitly stated that the Fourteenth Amendment made the guarantees of the First Amendment applicable to the states. This decision reversed what had been considered received constitutional doctrine at least since the Supreme Court's first extensive treatment of the Fourteenth Amendment in the *Slaughterhouse* cases in 1873, 16 Wall 36.

8. The one major exception in this regard, of course, is the unionized segment of the private sector workforce. Typically, collective bargaining agreements contain just cause and arbitration provisions under which employees have the right to grieve any disciplinary action they consider unjust. Grievance procedures typically provide three to five stages, the final one of which is an arbitration hearing presided over by an impartial arbitrator selected jointly by the union and management. In such a hearing, management always carries the burden of proof to establish just cause for discipline or discharge.

As it happens, however, although arbitration under collective bargaining agreements effectively excludes the doctrine of employment at will, by and large, arbitrators have been reluctant to affirm substantial rights of freedom of expression for unionized employees. Section seven of the National Labor Relations Act protects concerted activities of employees. Arbitrators as well as courts interpret the notion of such activities broadly to encompass speech by employees in the capacity of a union official. In sharp contrast, however, little protection exists for individual union employees in situations not covered by section seven. To quote David Palmer, "The issue of free speech in employment whittles down to the question put forth by arbitrator McCoy in a 1972 case, 'Can you bite the hand that feeds you and insist on staying for future banquets?' Arbitrators have usually answered the question with a flat 'no.' " See Palmer, "Free Speech and Arbitration: Implications for the Future," *Labor Law Journal* vol. 27, no. 5 (May 1976):287–300.

    9. 81 Tenn. 507. 519–20 (1884).

    10. 158 Cal. 551, 555; 112 p. 886 (1910).

    11. 456 Pa. 171, 319 A.2d 174 (1974).

    12. The ruling in *Palmateer* v. *International Harvester Corp.*, 85 Ill. 2d 124 (1981), which was decided by the Illinois Supreme Court on March 9, 1981, also has potential for greatly enhancing legal protection of employees against unjust dismissal. Palmateer, an employee of International Harvester, was fired for supplying information to local law enforcement authorities that another employee might be stealing from the company and for agreeing to assist in the investigation and trial of the employee if requested.

    Under the prevailing doctrine of employment at will, Palmateer would have had no cause of action against International Harvester. The Illinois Supreme Court, however, upheld his claim. In *Kelsay* v. *Motorola, Inc.*, 74 Ill. 2d 172 (1978), the court had allowed recovery by an employee discharged for filing a workman's compensation claim. This case, which was the first in Illinois acknowledging a cause of action for retaliatory discharge, left unclear the criteria for determining where recovery would lie. In *Palmateer* the Illinois Supreme Court addressed this matter by saying that the "foundation of the tort of retaliatory discharge lies in the protection of public policy." As to the definition of "public policy" the court said "In general . . . public policy concerns what is right and just and what affects the citizens of the state collectively. . . . Although there is no precise line of demarcation dividing matters that are the subject of public policies from purely personal matters, a survey of cases in other states shows that a matter must strike at the heart of a citizens' rights, duties, and responsibilities before the tort will be allowed." By this standard Palmateer's claim was upheld because "public policy favors the exposure of crime and the cooperation of citizens possessing knowledge thereof is essential to effective implementation of that policy."

    The *Palmateer* case, with its expansive criterion of public policy, contains the potential for substantially extending the legal rights of unjustly discharged employees. In previous cases where courts allowed recovery for retaliatory discharge, the rulings were strictly limited to the respective circumstances with no attempt to go beyond them. (See notes 15–19.) By contrast, *Palmateer* enunciates a general rule that appears on its face to contradict directly the prevailing employment at will doctrine. It remains to be seen what other courts will do with *Palmateer*. In this regard it should be noted that the case contained a vigorous dissent by Justice Ryan, the author of the majority decision in *Kelsay* v. *Motorola, Inc.*, in which he complained about the court's extremely broad definition of public policy. In any event, it seems unlikely that *Palmateer* will be ignored.

13. Horace G. Wood, *A Treatise on the Law of Master and Servant* (Albany, N.Y.: J. D. Parsons, 1877).

14. For a time Wood's Rule enjoyed constitutional sanctity. In *Adair* v. *U.S.*, 208 U.S. 161 (1908), the Supreme Court declared unconstitutional a statute prohibiting the discharge of a railway employee because of his union membership. The Court's rationale was that any statute that disturbed the "equality of right" between employer and employee was an "arbitrary interference with the liberty of contract." Adair was overruled in *NLRB* v. *Jones and Laughlin Steel Corp.*, 301 U.S. 1 (1937); which upheld the Wagner Act. But Wood's Rule stubbornly survives as the general common law approach.

15. *Peterman* v. *Teamsters Local 396*, 174 Cal. App. 2d 184, 344 P. 2d. 25 (Ct. App. 1959).

16. *Frampton* v. *Central Ind. Gas Co.*, 260 Ind. 249, 297 N.E. 2d 425 (1973).

17. *Nees* v. *Hocks*, 272 Ore. 210, 536 P. 2d. 512 (1975).

18. *Bell* v. *Faulkner*, 75 S.W. 2d. 612 (Mo. Ct. App. 1934).

19. *Mallard* v. *Boring*, 182 Cal. App. 2d. 390, 394, 6 Cal. Rptr. 171, 174 (Ct. App. 1960).

20. 391 U.S. 563 (1968).

21. 385 U.S., 589, 605–06 (1967).

22. *Pickering*, p. 568.

23. See discussion of *New York Times* v. *Sullivan* at pp. 78–81.

24. *Where the Law Ends* (New York: Harper & Row, 1975), p. 213. It should be noted here that in this passage Stone himself does not argue specifically for constitutional protection for whistleblowers.

25. For a general discussion of citizens' arrests see William F. Prosser, *Law of Torts* (St. Paul, Minn.: West Publishing Co., 1971) pp. 42–49.

26. In this regard the following study is interesting: James Olson, "Engineers Attitudes toward Professionalism, Employment, and Social Responsibility," *Professional Engineer* 42 (August 1972):30–32.

27. Mill, *On Liberty*, p. 72.

28. Ibid., p. 71.

29. Ibid., p. 76.

30. Ibid., p. 77.

31. Ibid., p. 71.

32. On this point see my paper entitled "Mill's Conception of Individuality," *Social Theory and Practice* 4, no. 2, (1977):167–182, esp. 178–79.

33. Ewing, *Freedom Inside the Organization*, p. 11.

34. John J. O'Connor, "T.V. Sifting Big Business," *New York Times*, Dec. 6, 1973, p. 94.

35. In this regard see, William H. Whyte, *The Organization Man* (New York, Simon & Schuster, 1956). See also R. Blauner, *Alienation and Freedom* (Chicago: University of Chicago Press, 1964) and G. A. Almond and S. Verba, *The Civic Culture* (Boston: Little Brown, 1965). For a general survey of empirical studies in this regard see, Carole Pateman, *Participation and Democratic Theory* (London: Cambridge University Press, 1970), pp. 45–66.

36. See the discussion at pp. 16–17.

37. On this point see my paper "A Theory of Personal Autonomy," *Ethics* 86 (1975):30–48, esp. 47–48.

38. 514 F. 2d. 285 (2nd. Cir., 1975).

39. *Holodnak*, pp. 288–89.

40. Ewing, *Freedom Inside the Organization*, p. 100.

41. Ibid.

42. 326 U.S. 501 (1946).

43. *Marsh* v. *Alabama*, p. 508.

44. The most important public function cases since Marsh, which all involve the question of whether sidewalks and driveways of a large shopping center serve a public function, illustrate how unclear the Court has left matters. In *Amalgamated Food Employees Union Local 590 et al.* v. *Logan Valley Plaza*, 391 U.S. 308 (1968), the Court answered the above question affirmatively. In this regard it maintained that no relevant difference exists between the factual situation in *Marsh* v. *Alabama* and a large suburban shopping center which constitutes the "functional equivalent" of an urban business district. The Court, however, explicitly limited its holding to situations such as labor picketing where the speech involved relates specifically to the operations of the shopping center. It did not explain, however, given its reliance on the analogy with *Marsh* v. *Alabama*, why this should matter.

Three years later in *Lloyd Corp.* v. *Tanner*, 407 U.S. 551 (1972), the Court appealed to the above language of limitation in *Logan Valley* as a basis for distinguishing the facts in that case from a similar situation that involved distributing antiwar leaflets rather than labor pickets. Again, however, the Court failed to explain the relevance of this difference. Four justices dissented in this case.

Finally, in *Hudgens* v. *NLRB*, 424 U.S. 507 (1976), a case that, like *Logan Valley*, involved labor picketing, the Court acknowledged the absence of a pertinent distinguishing feature between *Logan Valley* and *Lloyd* v.

Tanner, and thus overruled the former. In doing so, however, again it failed to provide any analysis in terms of the concept of a public function. Instead, the court simply noted that the ruling in *Lloyd* v. *Tanner* was subsequent in time to the ruling in *Logan Valley.*

45. *Holodnak,* p. 289.

46. 365 U.S. 715 (1961).

47. *Wilmington Parking Authority,* p. 723.

48. Ibid., pp. 723–24.

49. Ibid., p. 728.

50. Ibid., p. 725.

51. Myles Brand instructed me on this point.

52. Gerald Gunther refers to this basis for ascribing state action as the encouragement test. See Gunther, *Constitutional Law,* p. 953. The analysis below should indicate why I prefer the term "facilitation test."

53. 387 U.S. 369 (1967).

54. *Reitman* v. *Mulkey,* p. 377.

55. *Reitman* v. *Mulkey,* p. 387.

56. See the discussion earlier at pp. 114–15.

57. I assume here that the employee's words were neither uttered with knowledge of their falsity or reckless disregard of the truth.

58. The case of trade secrets presents relatively little problem for this approach. In most controversies with respect to the disclosure of trade secrets, an employer sues one of his or her former employees, so the issue of dismissal simply does not arise. The only credible case I can think of where an employee discloses a trade secret and yet remains on the job would involve industrial or corporate espionage, that is, where one company plants a "mole" in another company. Such a spy would not be protected under the Pickering rule as extended to the private sector because knowledge of his or her presence would in all likelihood undermine working relationships to an extent that justified dismissal.

59. Lawrence E. Blades, "Employment at Will vs. Individual Liberty: On Limiting the Abusive Exercise of Employer Power," *Columbia Law Review* 62 (1967):1404–35.

60. Ibid., p. 1422.

61. Ibid., p. 1424.

62. J. Peter Shapiro and James F. Tune, "Implied Contract Rights to Job Security," *Stanford Law Review* 26 (1974):335–69.

63. 408 U.S. 564 (1972) and 408 U.S. 593 (1972).

64. Clyde W. Summers, "Individual Protection Against Unjust Dismissal: Time for a Statute," *Virginia Law Review* 62 (1976):481–532.

65. The phrase "uncharted territory" was used by the majority in *Geary* v. *U.S. Steel,* 456 Pa. 171, 319 A 2d. 174 (1974), to refer to the proposal that courts take the initiative in revising the doctrine of employment at will.

66. Gert, *The Moral Rules.*

67. Robert Nozick, *Anarchy, State, and Utopia* (New York, Basic Books, 1974).

68. Referring to the Lockean state of nature Nozick writes, "[we] focus upon a nonstate situation in which people generally satisfy moral constraints and generally act as they ought. Such an assumption is not wildly optimistic; it does not assume that all people act exactly as they should. Yet this state of nature situation is the best anarchic situation · one reasonably could hope for. Hence investigating its nature and defects is of crucial importance to deciding whether there should be a state rather than anarchy. If one could show that the state would be superior even to this most favored situation of anarchy, the best that realistically can be hoped for, or would arise by a process involving no morally impermissable steps, or would be an improvement if it arose, this would provide a rationale for the state's existence; it would justify the state" (p. 5). Nozick describes his conclusions about the above issue as follows: "Our main conclusions about the state are that a minimal state, limited to the narrow functions of protection against force, theft, fraud, enforcement of contracts and so on, is justified. That any more extensive state will violate people's rights not to be forced to do certain things, and is unjustified" (preface ix).

69. Ibid., pp. 26–28.

70. Ibid., p. 149.

71. Moral rights, as Nozick and others understand them, are infringeable by both governments and individuals. In this respect they differ from constitutionally fundamental rights. Nonetheless, one can hold that a given right is constitutionally fundamental in part precisely because its infringement would violate a basic moral right.

72. Ibid., pref. xiv.

73. For example, Ayn Rand proclaims, "There is only one fundamental right (all the others are its consequences or corollaries): a Man's right to his own life. Life is a process of self-sustaining and self-generated action; the right to life means the right to engage in self-sustaining and self-generated action—which means: the freedom to take all the actions required by the nature of a rational being for the support, the furtherance, the fulfillment and the enjoyment of his own life. (Such is the meaning of the right to life, liberty, and the pursuit of happiness.) The concept of a "right" pertains only to action—specifically, to freedom of action. It means freedom from physical compulsion, coercion or interference by other men" (*The Virtue of Selfishness* [New York: New American Library, 1964], pp. 93–94). A bit more concisely, Tibor R. Machan writes: "The right to liberty implies that, e.g., one's own conduct within the sphere of one's own life—even say taking unreasonable risks or reading pornographic novels— may not be obstructed by others" ("A Reconsideration of Natural Rights Theory," *American Philosophical Quarterly* 19, no. 1 [January 1982]:61). The above principle thus is frequently stated with a sense of deep

conviction by various writers in what one may loosely term the libertarian camp. As far as I can tell, however, very few of them have ever analyzed it with an appropriate degree of care, given the enormous importance they attach to this principle. Indeed, Roger Pilon, whose work will be discussed later, is the only such writer I could find who even begins to reach the most crucial issues.

74. See the discussion of Roger Pilon's views, pp. 136–39.

75. Nozick, *Anarchy, State and Utopia*, pp. 28–35.

76. Rawls summarizes the major problems in this regard succinctly in *A Theory of Justice*, pp. 321–25.

77. 159 F. 2d 169 (1947).

78. Ibid., p. 173.

79. "Strict Liability: A Comment," *Journal of Legal Studies* 2 (1973):205–21.

80. See Calabresi, *The Costs of Accidents* (New Haven: Yale University Press, 1970).

81. Ibid., pp. 26–38.

82. Two leading writers, George Fletcher and Richard Epstein, have each challenged the least cost avoider approach in widely discussed articles (see Fletcher, "Fairness and Utility in Tort Theory," *Harvard Law Review* 85 [1972]: 537–73; and Epstein, "A Theory of Strict Liability," *Journal of Legal Studies* 2 [1973]:151–204, esp. 189–204). I do not, however, regard either of these two challenges as successful. Fletcher proposes an analysis according to which imposition of liability for negligence depends upon whether the defendant subjected the plaintiff to a risk of harm greater than the standard "background risk" associated with the activity in which the plaintiff engaged. Fletcher, however, fails to explicate how one fixes the standard background risk. Sometimes he writes in this regard of the "accepted" risk. But this clearly will not do. If Fletcher means here the degree of risk generally accepted as reasonable by members of the community, then he has enshrined the status quo in a patently unacceptable fashion. If Fletcher has something else in mind, then one wants a further explanation of it.

Epstein proposes a strict liability approach in negligence cases, according to which liability depends primarily upon whether one in fact caused harm. The reasonableness of one's behavior does not enter into the matter. In developing his proposal Epstein enunciates criteria for ascribing causes, which seem reasonably coherent. He fails, however, to make plausible why one should adopt them. He contends that his approach provides a basis for enunciating the limits of liability for negligence that accords more consonantly with our considered moral judgments than does the least cost avoider approach. He believes the latter allows judges far too much discretion in framing standards of liability. Epstein, however, does not present an adequate argument for this conclusion. He simply asserts that if judges regard themselves as bound to apply his approach, they would be less likely to interfere with "individual liberty" than otherwise. But Epstein leaves the notion of "individual liberty" completely unanalyzed. One needs to know how he understands it, and why he considers it important, in order to compare his proposals with the least cost avoider approach. (For parallel criticisms of Fletcher's and Epstein's views, see Richard Posner, "Strict Liabilaity: A Comment," *Journal of Legal Studies* 2 [1973]:205–21.)

83. Roger Pilon, "Corporations and Rights," *Georgia Law Review* 13 (1979): 1245–1370.

84. Pilon conceives of the general rights as ultimately grounded from a philosophical standpoint in what he regards as the most basic standard of morality, the Principle of Generic Consistency. The idea of this principle has been developed by Alan Gewirth in his book *Reason and Morality* (Chicago: University of Chicago Press, 1978). Gewirth's moral theory differs in important respects from the rational contractor approach that underlies my analysis of freedom of expression. Such differences, however, do not bear upon the following discussion of Pilon's views. It should also be noted that while Pilon sees his approach as flowing inexorably from Gewirth's theory, Gewirth, evidently, does not agree. (In this regard see Pilon, p. 1270).

85. Pilon, "Corporations and Rights," p. 1272.

86. Ibid., p. 1290.

87. Ibid., pp. 1352–53.

88. Ibid., p. 1275.

89. Ibid., p. 1272.

90. Hobbes, *De Cive*, p. 175.

91. Pilon also holds that one owns one's body and one's actions. The notion of ownership in these respects, however, does not pertain to this discussion.

92. Pilon, "Corporations and Rights," p. 1278.

93. Ibid., p. 1279.

94. The extreme counterintuitiveness of Pilon's account should also be noted. Assume a five-kilometer square area with two individuals, A and B, originally located in extreme opposite corners. Assume further that the sole water source, an abundant spring, lies one-half kilometer from A. By "claiming" the spring and then forbidding B to use it, even though this would in no way make him worse off, A would insure B's imminent death. According to Pilon, any attempt by B to drink from the spring, and thus assure his bare survival, would violate A's basic *moral* rights!

95. Bernard Siegan, *Economic Liberties and the Constitution* (Chicago: University of Chicago Press, 1980).

96. See discussion at Appendix I.

97. For example, in *Williamson v. Lee Optical Co.*, 348 U.S. 483 (1955), the Court upheld a statutory requirement that opticians not fit old eyeglasses into new frames without a prescription from a licensed opthamologist or

optometrist. Despite uncontradicted evidence that lens fitting is a routine procedure that generally requires no medical expertise, the Court upheld the legislation on the ground that the legislature *might* have believed that the relatively infrequent cases where medical supervision may be necessary justify the general requirement.

98. Siegan, *Economic Liberties*, p. 248.

99. Thomas Emerson, "Toward a General Theory of the First Amendment," *Yale Law Journal* 72 (1963):877–956.

100. Siegan, *Economic Liberties*, p. 262.

101. Emerson, of course, is well aware of these arguments.

102. Siegan, *Economic Liberties*, p. 249.

103. Ibid., p. 252.

104. See discussion at Appendix I.

105. Hayek, *The Constitution of Liberty* (Chicago: University of Chicago Press, 1960), pp. 224–25.

106. See earlier discussion at p. 61–63.

107. See earlier discussion at pp. 63–65.

108. Coase's only evidence for his theory that arrogance of intellectuals primarily accounts for why they disparage economic liberty is an isolated passage from Milton's *Areopagitica*. Coase declares that this sole passage, considered in isolation from others in the same work (not to mention other works by Milton), conclusively establishes Milton's arrogant attitude.

109. In fact, Siegan's ultimate recommendations are considerably more mild than one would have expected given the general thrust of his argument. In this regard see, Siegan, *Economic Liberties*, pp. 322–26.

Appendix I

1. *The Spirit of Liberty, Papers and Addresses of Learned Hand* Irving Dillard, ed. (New York: Alfred A. Knopf, 1959), p. 144.

2. In regard to the last two points see the discussion at pp. 46–50.

3. I am here distinguishing the *power* of the Supreme Court from its *authority*. For immediate purposes the latter notion can be identified with the boundaries of the Court's jurisdiction as conventionally recognized. The *power* of the Court pertains to its capability in regard to securing compliance with its decisions. When characterized in the foregoing manner, obviously power and authority need not coincide.

4. *Lochner* v. *New York*, 198 U.S. 45 (1905).

5. For example, *Adair* v. *United States*, 208 U.S. 161 (1908), in which the Court struck down federal legislation prohibiting yellow-dog contracts on grounds of the fundamentality of the right to freedom of contract (overruled by *NLRB* v. *Jones and Laughlin* Steel, 30 U.S. 2 [1937]); *Coppage* v. *Kansas*, 236 U.S. 1 (1915) (overruled by *Lincoln Federal Labor Union* v. *Northwestern Iron and Metal*, 335 U.S. 525 [1949], in which a state anti-

yellow-dog contract statute was struck down on the same grounds); and *Adkins* v. *Childrens Hospital,* 261 U.S. 525 (1923) (overruled by *West Coast Hotel Co.* v. *Parrish,* 300 U.S. 379 [1937], in which minimum wage legislation in the District of Columbia was struck down). See also Frank Strong, "The Economic Philosophy of Lochner," *Arizona Law Review* 15 (1973):419.

6. *Lochner,* p. 75.

7. Indeed, the general orientation of the Supreme Court during the *Lochner* era can be regarded as one of the approaches to constitutional adjudication under the Bill of Rights represented by the ellipse C in the diagram on p. 27.

8. The arguments that follow were developed in some detail in Felix Frankfurter, "John Marshall and the Judicial Function" pp. 545–65 (cited in chap. 1. note 21).

9. In pondering this issue one must always bear in mind that the McCarthy period cannot be regarded as an event lost in the well of history with only dim reverberations in the present. It is a *recent* phenomenon. Along the same line, after Nixon was forced to resign, some of his apologists complained that such practices as the Ellsberg break-in and the compiling of enemies lists were engaged in to some extent by all of the postwar presidential administrations. This is probably true, and to my mind it consitutes the *real* lesson of Watergate.

10. At times one sees the example of Great Britain put forward to illustrate a society without judicial review whose government respects fundamental rights certainly no less than our's does. The example, however, misses the point somewhat. The question is whether respect for fundamental rights would be substantially less secure in *our* society without judicial review. Britain's culture and historical experience differ significantly from America's in relevant respects; e.g., the British avoided falling into a McCarthy period during the postwar years.

11. 283 U.S. 697 (1931), *New York Times* v. *United States,* 403 U.S. 713 (1971).

12. In this regard see Rawls, *A Theory of Justice,* pp. 363–82.

13. See Marvin Mindes, "Courts, Lawyers, and the Realities of Law," in *Illinois: Political Processes and Governmental Performance,* E. Crane, ed. (Dubuque, Iowa: Kendall Hunt and Illinois Political Science Assn., 1979), pp. 145–54, esp. 150–52.

Appendix II

1. Robert Paul Wolff, *The Poverty of Liberalism* (Boston: Beacon Press, 1968), p. 19.

2. Isaiah Berlin, "John Stuart Mill and the Ends of Life," in *Four Essays on Liberty* (Oxford University Press, 1969), p. 192.

3. Mill, *On Liberty,* p. 14.

4. Ibid., p. 67.

5. Among Mill's earlier critics, James Fitzjames Stephen interprets Mill as does Wolff. See his *Liberty, Equality, and Fraternity* (New York: Henry Holt & Co., 1873), esp. pp. 41–48.

6. Mill, *On Liberty*, p. 71.

7. Ibid., p. 81.

8. All the passages in *On Liberty* that Berlin draws upon to establish his interpretation are from chapter three.

9. Isaiah Berlin, "John Stuart Mill and the Ends of Life," pp. 205–6. When Berlin says it is freedom of choice that distinguishes men from the rest of nature, I take it, in light of other things Berlin says, that he equates *freedom* of choice with the capacity for it.

10. Mill, *On Liberty*, pp. 74–75.

11. This point is explained at pp. 38–39.

12. Mill, *On Liberty*, p. 76.

13. Ibid., p. 77.

14. For an interpretation that parallels Levi's, see Richard Lichtman, "The Surface and Substance of Mill's Defense of Freedom," *Social Research* (1963):469–94.

15. Albert William Levi, "The Value of Liberty: Mill's On Liberty 1859–1959," *Ethics* 69 (1959):37–46.

16. Mill, *On Liberty*, p. 71.

17. Ibid., p. 72.

18. See Mill's remarks about teleology as excerpted in *John Stuart Mill: The Philosophy of Scientific Method*, Ernest Nagel, ed. (New York: Hafner Publishing Co., 1950), pp. 354–55. Also see Mill's essay entitled "Nature" in *The Essential Works of John Stuart Mill*, Max Lerner, ed. (New York: Bantam Books, 1961) pp. 361–402.

Appendix III

1. Thomas Scanlon, "A Theory of Freedom of Expression," *Philosophy and Public Affairs* 1, no. 2 (1972):204–26. The following papers both also emphasize the connection between autonomy and freedom of expression along lines similar to Scanlon's: C. Edwin Baker, "Scope of the First Amendment Freedom of Speech," *UCLA Law Review* 25 (1978):964–1040, esp. 991; Harry H. Wellington, "On Freedom of Expression," *Yale Law Review* 88 (1979):1105–42, esp. 1125.

2. Scanlon, "A Theory of Freedom of Expression," p. 215.

3. Ibid.

4. Ibid., pp. 219–20.

Bibliographic Essay

As I mentioned in the Introduction, this book is intended for three essentially distinct reading audiences: the legal community; people with intense interest and extensive background in political philosophy; and the general literate public with specialized knowledge of neither law nor philosophy. Given these categories of the intended audience, in all likelihood a substantial proportion of readers will be relatively unfamiliar with one or more of the major subjects I have discussed in the previous pages. This bibliographic essay will direct the reader to various sources that will provide further information on the most important broad topics in this book.

This is by no means an exhaustive bibliography. Nonetheless, it should substantially assist the reader who wishes to go beyond my treatment of one or another subject. Some of the sources listed in the following essay have been cited already in the text or notes. In such cases the reader is referred back to the relevant passages. Repetition of a few citations seemed advisable. Given the probable diversity of backgrounds among readers of this book, it seems unlikely that everyone will read each part with a uniformly high degree of attention and interest.

The Justification of Judicial Review
under the United States Constitution

As noted in the text (see chap. 1, pp. 9–11), judicial review under the United States Constitution concerns itself either with issues pertaining to the separation of governmental powers or the violation of fundamental rights. With regard to the former, one finds classic statements of the judicial function in a government with separation of powers by Chief Justice John Marshall in *Marbury* v. *Madison* (1 Cranch 137 [1803]) and by Alexander Hamilton in *Federalist Papers 78*. Marshall's and Hamilton's reasoning was clearly restated one hundred or so years later in an influential essay by James Bradley Thayer entitled "The Origin and Scope of the American Doctrine of Judicial Review," *Harvard Law Review* 7 (1893): 129–56. Thayer's constitutional outlook had a marked influence on Felix Frankfurter's views concerning the proper role of the Supreme Court. Judicial review as a means of giving real effect to the concept of separation of powers is also discussed with great insight by A. V. Dicey in his seminal work, *Introduction to the Study of the Law of the Constitution* (London: Macmillan & Co., 1889), pp. 134–61.

Parliamentary Sovereignty and the Commonwealth by Geoffrey Marshall (London: Oxford University Press, 1957) provides an illuminating study of the experience in South Africa surrounding the case of *Harris* v. *Donges*, in which the petitioners challenged the constitutionality of South African apartheid laws in regard to the suffrage. This case presented the first situation in a country with a parliamentary system of government in which courts were called upon to overturn a parliamentary act on constitutional grounds. Study of the South African experience is enormously valuable, if only to underscore that the practice of judicial review, as it developed in the United States, was hardly inevitable. Indeed, one may think of *Harris* v. *Donges* as a kind of reverse analogue of *Marbury* v. *Madison*.

With regard to the idea that judicial review under the constitution serves to protect the fundamental rights of individuals, one finds the earliest expression of scepticism on the subject in *Federalist Papers 84*, by Alexander Hamilton. In the twentieth century, as noted in the text (chap. 1), Learned Hand and Felix Frankfurter provided the most articulate sceptical arguments (see also chap. 1, notes 20 and 21). Among influential writers who take Hand's and Frankfurter's scepticism as a point of departure, so to speak, for their own views, one finds Herbert Wechsler (see chap. 1, note 15), Alexander Bickel (see discussion in chap. 1), John Hart Ely (see discussion in chap. 1), and Ronald Dworkin, "Constitutional

Cases," in *Taking Rights Seriously* (Cambridge: Harvard University Press, 1977), pp. 131–49.

As for the historical question of whether the framers of the Constitution intended that the courts have the power of judicial review under it, Thayer reviews the evidence dispassionately in his aforementioned essay. A very comprehensive historical analysis, which reaches a negative conclusion in this regard, can be found in W. W. Crosskey's *Politics and the Constitution* (Chicago: University of Chicago Press, 1953). Finally, on a different matter, the following two books may provide a salutary contrast to the unreservedly theoretical orientation of this work. Robert McCloskey's *The American Supreme Court* (Chicago: University of Chicago Press, 1960) provides an excellent account of the brilliantly calculated way, a là Machiavelli, in which John Marshall endeavored to increase the power of the Supreme Court through judiciously stated claims of jurisdiction in his various opinions. Anthony Lewis's excellent book *Gideon's Trumpet* (New York: Alfred A. Knopf, 1964) gives a clear description of the actualities that attend bringing a case to the Supreme Court.

Moral and Political Philosophy

Moral philosophy in the western intellectual tradition seeks to analyze the concept of morality. In this regard it addresses such questions as, "What is morality?" That is, what distinguishes morality from other kinds of norms such as those pertaining to religion, customs, law, personal ideals, and so forth? Most of the great philosophers who addressed this question assumed that morality consists of rules and principles that take precedence over all others. They also assumed that elucidating the nature of morality involves, at least in the first instance, identifying the specific content of those rules and principles.

Answering the "What is _____?" question about morality in a genuinely satisfying way requires that one also consider a number of "Why?" questions. "Why should one attach more significance to morality than to other kinds of norms?" That is, from what does it derive its presumed overriding significance for human conduct? Assuming some reasonable answer to this question, a person can still go on to ask, "Why should I be moral?" "Why should I follow the rules and principles of morality in situations where they conflict with my desires, and no apparent harm will come to me by violating them?"

This last question underscores that, to all appearances, morality at times can conflict with one's inclinations. Some philosophers have maintained that on deeper reflection such conflict turns out to be merely apparent. That is, in the final analysis, morality always pays—for example, in virtue of being an indispensable constituent of personal happiness. Other philosophers have expressed considerable scepticism about such a view. Beside the question "Why should I be moral?" one may also ask about why we are moral. More precisely, how does it come about that human beings develop dispositions to behave morally? Is it through a learning process that essentially involves extinguishing deep-seated natural tendencies? Or, by contrast, does the disposition, in part at least, flow from such natural tendencies? The major philosophical writings on moral philosophy thus all deal with one or more of the above questions.

Political philosophy in the western intellectual tradition, at least since the seventeenth century, begins with the problem of elucidating the basic concept of political authority. To grasp the essential problem here one must focus upon some important respects in which the concepts of political authority, coercion, and moral justification interrelate. First, other things being equal, coercive acts violate the rules of morality and therefore require moral justification. Second, the most essential aspect of the state is that individuals acting in its name routinely exert coercion upon others in a multitude of ways. These two points give rise to the chief philosophical problem about political authority: How, if at all, can one morally justify the existence of an institution, the state, which by its very nature grants some individuals, namely state officials, the right to coerce other individuals systematically and regularly? Explaining the moral basis of political authority inevitably involves taking a stand upon its specific content and scope. What are legitimate governmental functions and what, if any, are the principles that limit the means whereby a government may seek to carry them out? These questions, in turn, lead into the analysis of such concepts as law, liberty, and economic justice. Thus, the discussion of freedom of expression in this book falls squarely within the realm of traditional political philosophy.

The subjects of moral and political philosophy are so vast and multifaceted that any listing of works about them, indeed even any listing of major works, will be highly selective. Nonetheless, general agreement exists, I think, as to a core of books that might be termed classical texts. Any serious study of moral and political philosophy should begin with them. A number of the most important in this regard are, Aristotle, *Nichomachean Ethics* and *Politics;* Plato, *Republic* and *Laws;* Saint Thomas Aquinas, *Summa Theologica,* Questions 90–97; Thomas Hobbes, *Leviathan* and *De Cive;* John Locke, *Second Treatise of Government;* Jeremy Bentham, *An Introduction to the Principles of Morals and Legislation;* David Hume, *An Enquiry Concerning the Principles of Morals* and *A Treatise of Human Nature, Book III;* Immanuel Kant, *Foundations of the Metaphysic of Morals;* G.W.F. Hegel, *Philosophy of Right;* John Stuart Mill, *On Liberty* and *Utilitarianism;* Friedrich Wilhelm Nietzsche, *Genealogy of Morals* and *Beyond Good and Evil;* Henry Sidgwick, *Methods of Ethics;* Jean Jacques Rousseau, *The Social Contract* and *Discourse on the Origins of Inequality.*

An enormous secondary literature exists with respect to each of the above works. The number of extremely good works alone is so large that any listing would be too arbitrary even for my limited purposes here. In any case, however, I believe that one who wants to approach moral and political philosophy in a moderately serious way should begin with the classical texts.

When one reaches the twentieth century, consensus about which works qualify as major texts is much more difficult to achieve. Rather than infuriating or dumbfounding the academic philosophers who read this essay by venturing a list of major twentieth century works, I will demur. Nonetheless, I think one can safely say that all sides highly regard Rawls's *A Theory of Justice,* which plays such a crucial role in my own analysis of freedom of expression. The bibliography of critical articles on Rawls probably now numbers over one thousand. For more background one definitely should peruse *Reading Rawls,* Norman Daniels, ed. (New York: Basic Books). This volume contains valuable critical papers by many leading contemporary, academic, political and legal philosophers. One should also read *The Moral Rules,* by Bernard Gert (New York: Harper & Row, 1970). Gert employs a basic approach very similar to Rawls's in elucidating morality primarily as it applies to interpersonal conduct, rather than to institutions. His book contains extremely valuable analyses of the concepts of rationality and good and evil. I will mention one other author whose works have special pertinence with respect to my efforts in this book.

Since the late 1960s, Ronald Dworkin has written articles on various important contemporary constitutional cases before the Supreme Court, which all appeared in the *New York Review of Books:* "The Right to go to Law School," vol. 23 (February 5, 1976):27; "The Bakke Decision: Did it Decide Anything?" vol. 25 (August 20, 1978):20; "The Rights of Myron Farber," vol. 25 (October 26, 1978):34; "How to Read the Civil Rights Act," vol. 26 (December 20, 1979):37; and "Is the Press Losing the First Amendment?" vol. 27 (December 4, 1980):49. These essays in my opinion have set the standard for philosophically informed constitutional analysis.

The Philosophy of Free Expression

As Chapter Two indicates, I follow many writers in considering John Stuart Mill's *On Liberty* the seminal work on the philosophical bases of free expression. Serious reflection upon this matter best begins with reading Mill. Although *On Liberty* stands on its own, by and large, one's understanding of it as a philosophical essay is enhanced by reading other works of Mill. Perhaps his two most important works, besides *On Liberty*, are *Utilitarianism* and *Considerations on Representative Government*. The former work constitutes Mill's major statement of his general views on moral philosophy. The latter, in addition to applying the utilitarian moral framework in a systematic way to questions about the design of political institutions, amplifies the conception of individuality that Mill develops in chapter three in *On Liberty* (see especially chapters two and three of *Representative Government*).

As for other major defenses of free expression in the tradition of western political thought, one should not fail to read *Areopagetica* by John Milton, written some two hundred years before Mill wrote *On Liberty*. Although in some measure Milton's essay reflects the prejudices of his time (in particular against Catholicism) and I think generally falls short of *On Liberty* in terms of its breadth of philosophical vision, Milton nonetheless anticipated many of Mill's most important arguments. In the twentieth century, Alexander Meiklejohn's *Political Freedom* (New York: Harper & Row, 1960) has exerted considerable influence, especially on the thought of many justices of the Supreme Court. Meiklejohn is by far the most widely cited modern philosophical author in Supreme Court opinions dealing with First Amendment issues. However, the opinions, largely dissenting, of Justices Holmes and Brandeis occupy a no less prominent position (see chap. 2, note 41). Among academic writers, Thomas Scanlon's "A Theory of Freedom of Expression" (see Appendix III) is increasingly cited.

It is not surprising that an enormous secondary literature exists with respect to Mill's *On Liberty*. I personally have found the following works helpful: Isaiah Berlin, "John Stuart Mill and the Ends of Life," in *Four Essays on Liberty* (Oxford: Oxford University Press, 1969), pp. 173–206; Marshall Cohen, Introduction to *The Philosophy of J. S. Mill* (New York: Modern Library, 1961), esp. pp. 41–48; Albert William Levi, "The Value of Liberty: Mill's *On Liberty* 1859–1959," *Ethics* 69 (1959):37–46; Richard Lichtman, "The Surface and Substance of Mill's Defense of Freedom," *Social Research* (1963):469–94; David Spitz, "Freedom and Individuality: Mill's *Liberty* in Retrospect," in *Nomos IV: Liberty*, Carl J. Friedrich, ed. (New York: Atherton, 1964), pp. 176–227; and Dennis Thompson, *Mill's Representative Government* (Princeton: Princeton University Press, 1976).

As is the case with any widely read philosophical work, Mill's *On Liberty* has been extensively and vigorously criticized. Among Mill's contemporary critics, James Fitzjames Stephen is probably the best known (see *Liberty, Equality and Fraternity* [New York: Henry Holt & Co. 1893]). The following contemporary writers all believe that Mill's arguments have serious flaws: Patrick Devlin, "Mill on Liberty in Morals," in *The Enforcement of Morals* (Oxford: Oxford University Press, 1965), pp. 102–23; Gertrude Himmelfarb, *On Liberty and Liberalism* (New York: Alfred A. Knopf, 1974); Robert Paul Wolff, "Liberty," in *The Poverty of Liberalism* (Boston: Beacon Press, 1968), pp. 3–50; and H. J. McCloskey, "Liberty of Expression: Its Grounds and Limits (I)," *Inquiry* 13 (Autumn 1970): 19–37.

Finally, even the briefest of discussions about works that deal with the philosophical bases of free expression must note the existence of an entire tradition of political thinkers who have been either ambivalent about or downright hostile to the ideas of democracy and broad social freedom. The ambivalent thinkers have generally been rather pessimistic about the capability of human beings to shape their own collective destiny as a matter of deliberate social decision. For this reason many have stressed the enormous importance of custom as guide to both individual and social conduct. See, for instance, Edmund Burke, *Reflections on the Civil War in France*, William B. Todd, ed. (New York: Holt Rinehart & Winston, 1959); Michael Oakeshott, *Rationalism in Politics* (New York: Basic Books, 1962); and Patrick Devlin, *The Enforcement of Morals* (Oxford: Oxford University Press, 1964). Freud shared the pessimistic views of the above-mentioned authors but also perceived grave pitfalls in placing substantial reliance upon custom (see *Civilization and its Discontents* [New York: Norton, 1961]). His attitude is even more profoundly ambivalent than those of other writers with pessimistic inclinations.

The writers who appear to reject categorically the very ideas of democracy and social freedom generally couple pessimism about the possibilities for human development on a broad front with the belief that some identifiable individuals are enormously more qualified to govern than others. One finds the most famous expression of these views in Plato's *Republic*. Among contemporary writers B. F. Skinner expresses them in perhaps the most outspoken terms (see *Walden Two* [New York: MacMillan, 1948] and *Beyond Freedom and Dignity* [New York: Alfred A. Knopf, 1972]). As noted in Chapter Two, that most famous (and infamous) advocate of absolutism, Thomas Hobbes, seems to have made an exception for freedom of expression (see chap. 2, pp. 34–35 and n. 8 and 11).

First Amendment

Literature dealing with the First Amendment, like that pertaining to the other major topics covered in this short essay, is so extensive that one cannot hope to present even a broad overview of it. Two works stand out, however, as virtually indispensable for the reader who wishes to pursue the subject. The first of these books, Zechariah Chafee's *Free Speech in the United States* (New York: Atheneum, 1969, originally published by Harvard University Press, 1941), covers in depth the period from 1920, when the Court rendered its First Amendment decision in *Schenk* v. *U.S.*, to 1941, one year after the passage by Congress of the Alien Registration Act. This book so magnificently combines detailed analysis, breadth of vision, and common sense that the attentive reader can scarcely avoid having his or her thoughts about the First Amendment shaped by it in very large measure. The other work, Thomas Emerson's *The System of Freedom of Expression* (New York: Random House, 1970), provides a comprehensive overview of every aspect of First Amendment case law up to 1970. I would restate my praise of Chafee with equal force about Emerson. These two works stand out as preeminent in First Amendment scholarship.

Among the recent contributions of value, Emerson has written an extensive review article discussing both new theoretical contributions to First Amendment jurisprudence as well as the First Amendment decisions of the Burger Court (see "First Amendment Doctrine and the Burger Court," *California Law Review* 68 [1980]:127–81. The latter are also discussed with insight and good sense by Archibald Cox in *Freedom of Expression*, (Cambridge, Mass.: Harvard University Press, 1981). Lawrence Tribe covers the subject of freedom of expression very intelligently in his *American Constitutional Law* (Mineola, N.Y.: The Foundation Press, 1978), pp. 576–737.

As for articles dealing with specific First Amendment issues or leading cases, an utterly massive literature exists, much of it in the more than five hundred scholarly legal periodicals published in the United States. Predictably, with such a large body of literature an enormous qualitative range exists, and one really has no reliable way to separate the gold from the dross in advance. One helpful feature of many law review articles is worth mentioning, however. Such articles frequently begin with an introductory section that summarizes, as background, case law and statutes pertinent to the matter under discussion. Thus in many instances an otherwise undistinguished article can provide the reader with valuable information to orient him or her to a given subject.

These points for the most part also apply to the subjects of freedom of the press and freedom of expression in the workplace, which I treated in separate chapters of this book. With regard to these topics I will note a few works that have been especially helpful to me. On freedom of the press, in the late 1940s the Commission on Freedom of the Press sponsored a report that dealt with various problems under the general heading of government and mass communication (see Zechariah Chafee, Jr., *Government and Mass Communication*. vols. 1 and 2 [Chicago: University of Chicago Press, 1947]). These volumes contain valuable discussions of constitutional and policy issues with regard to the press. More recently, Benno C. Schmidt's *Freedom of the Press v. Public Access* (New York: Praeger, 1977) provides an excellent discussion of the right to a media forum. For a discussion of the confidentiality privilege issue closely paralleling my own, see Ronald Dworkin,

"The Rights of Myron Farber," *New York Review of Books* 25 (October 26, 1978): 34. On the topic of freedom of expression in the workplace, David Ewing stands out as by far the leading advocate of employee rights. Over the past ten years he has written and spoken tirelessly about diverse aspects of the subject. His eminently readable book *Freedom Inside the Organization* (New York: Dutton, 1977), provides a good overview of the issue. One especially valuable resource on freedom of expression in the workplace is the *First National Seminar on Individual Rights in the Corporation: Individual Rights Sourcebook,* vols. 1 and 2, Alan Westin and Stephen Salisbury, eds. (prepared by the Civil Liberties Review), which contain numerous exerpts from various publications, all of them quite useful.

Although my own approach to First Amendment jurisprudence minimizes the importance of historical questions about the framers' intent, I certainly would not deny that exploring this issue can provide one with a useful perspective on First Amendment questions, even if it does not constitute a dispositive basis for resolving them. To this historiographically untutored reader, Leonard Levy's *Freedom of Speech and Press in Early America: Legacy of Suppression* (New York: Harper & Row, 1963) seems to come as close as one can to establishing how those who approved the First Amendment at the Constitutional Convention intended that it be understood.

Table of Cases

Index

Smith Act: summary of cases involving, 167–68; text of, 44–45
Snapper, John, 173
Snyder, Aaron, 163
Spitz, David, 198
State action, 107, 108, 112, 117, 118; facilitation criterion of, 122–24; public function criterion of, 119; significant state involvement criterion of, 119–22
The States, 9, 144, 145
Stephen, Sir James Fitzjames, 198
Stern, Robert L., 168
Stevens, Justice John Paul, 101, 169
Stewart, Justice Potter, 52, 59, 70, 71, 86, 103
Stone, Christopher, 113
Strong, Frank, 190
Summers, Clyde V., 128, 129, 130
Supreme Court: attempts in Congress to limit its jurisdiction, 48; *certiorari* jurisdiction of, 49; duty of justices in politically explosive cases, 46–50; role in cases under Bill of Rights, *see* Judicial review, as means of protecting fundamental rights
Sutherland, Justice George, 77
Symbolic speech, 65–69

Thayer, James Bradley, 158, 193
A Theory of Justice, 13, 196; *see also* Rational Contractor Theory; Rawls, John
Thompson, Dennis, 198
Thought control. *See* Freedom of expression, connection with truth
Time, place and manner restrictions.

See Vagueness and overbreadth
Trade secrets, 185
Tribe, Lawrence, 53, 171, 200
Truth, connection with free expression. *See* Freedom of expression, connection with truth
Tune, James F., 127, 128, 129

Ullian, Joseph, 161
Unions. *See* Labor unions, free speech issues concerning
United States Constitution: Article III, secs. 1 and 2, 8; Article VI, 9; Amendment I, *see* First Amendment; Amendment XIV, *see* Due process
Unjust dismissal, proposals for legal protection from. *See* Employee rights, proposals for legal protection of
Utilitarianism, 37

Vagueness and overbreadth: defined, 59; as per se violation of the First Amendment, 59–60
Van Alstyne, William, 162
Verba, S., 184

Wade, Nicholas, 181
Wechsler, Herbert, 158, 161, 193
Westin Alan, 201
White, Justice Byron, 82, 86, 98, 99, 102
Whyte, William, 184
Wolff, Robert Paul, 149–50, 198
Wood, Horace G., 183
Wood's Rule. *See* Employee rights, in private sector